The Politics of Elite Culture

The Politics of
Elite Culture

EXPLORATIONS IN THE
DRAMATURGY OF POWER IN A
MODERN AFRICAN SOCIETY

Abner Cohen

University of California Press

Berkeley • Los Angeles • London

University of California Press
Berkeley and Los Angeles, California
University of California Press, Ltd.
London, England
© 1981 by
The Regents of the University of California
Printed in the United States of America
1 2 3 4 5 6 7 8 9

Library of Congress Cataloging in Publication Data

Cohen, Abner.
  The politics of elite culture.

  Bibliography: p.
  Includes indexes.
  1. Elite (Social sciences). 2. Power (Social sciences). 3. Profes-
sions. 4. Bureaucracy. 5. Elite (Social sciences)—Sierra Leone—
Case studies. I. Title.
HM141.C67   305.5'2   80-15568
ISBN 0-520-04120-8 (cloth)
    0-520-04275-1 (paper)

For Tammy

In the inner circles of the upper classes, the most impersonal problems of the largest and most important institutions are fused with the sentiments and worries of small, closed, intimate groups.

C. WRIGHT MILLS (1956:69)

Contents

Preface

This book is an attempt to analyze the dramatic process underlying the development of a mystique in the articulation of elite organization. The body of symbolic beliefs and dramaturgical practices involved forms a normative culture which through various processes of mystification resolves a major contradiction in the formation and functioning of an elite group.

To carry out its universalistic functions, i.e., its services to the public, an elite is forced to organize itself particularistically, to keep itself in existence, and enhance its image. Conversely, an initially particularistic elite is forced to seek legitimacy for its high status by assuming universalistic functions. The same organization is thus evolved to serve both universalistic and particularistic ends, and elites can therefore be located on a continuum from the most particularistic, least universalistic, at one end, to the most universalistic, least particularistic, at the other. In time, an elite may move from one end of the continuum to the other, and history repeatedly records the rise and fall of elites.

These processes operate in all countries, developed or developing, liberal or autocratic, communist or capitalist.

They can be clearly seen in recent developments in some African societies.

In the summer of 1977 the world witnessed an astonishing political confrontation in Ghana. The country's professionals—doctors, lawyers, engineers, surveyors, accountants, teachers—staged a strike which lasted for weeks in order to force the military government to relinquish power and hand it over to civilians. Their challenge was: "You have the guns, but you cannot govern without us" (Mackenzis, *The Times*, 21 July 1977; and Duodu, *The Times*, 24 July and 7 August 1977). Mackenzis remarked: "There has been nothing quite like it since the Europe of 1848." What was surprising was that the military, rather than using their guns, listened, negotiated, and gave way. The Ghanaian professionals had come to maturity. Since independence they had grown into a unified elite who shared corporate interests. They coordinated their actions partly on a formal basis, in professional associations, and partly on an informal basis, in communal relations governed by exclusive cultural norms, beliefs, and practices—their style of life. (For some background information see Kilson, 1975.)

A decade earlier, the professionals of Sierra Leone, having risen long before their Ghanaian counterparts, being more concentrated territorially and more culturally homogenous, had staged a comparable confrontation with the government of the day. They succeeded in helping the opposition force it from office, thus making history by effecting the first change of government by democratic elections in sub-saharan Africa (Cartwright, 1970).

Elsewhere in Africa, though no such dramatic confrontations have, as yet, been reported, professional elites have been steadily organizing to promote their sectional interests along with public interests, developing in the process their own ideology and culture. Nearly everywhere in sub-saharan Africa (Kasfir, 1977) the executive—in many cases the military—does hold the gun and formal authority. But the regular affairs of state are conducted by the new "state elite," the professionals in the bureaucracy and in occupations related to state services. They have steadily and unobtrusively come into their own as wielders of effective power.

Everywhere in the world today, the state regulates complex public services and activities which are difficult for any formal rulers to comprehend or supervise, and are therefore delegated to the experts. Indeed, even in his day, when state activities were less complex, Marx foresaw the development of an autonomous, secretive, "conspiratorial" bureaucracy. In many countries the executive, rather than controlling the professionals, are themselves informally controlled by them.

The cohesion and autonomy of the professionals are articulated mainly in a covert manner, in a few cases under official secrecy acts, but more often through the existence and operation of a special culture, the analysis of which is the subject of this book.

This analysis further develops my attempts in previous works to formulate the instrumental functions of the symbols of normative culture in the organization of power groups. The heuristic model of society with which I then operated was that of a bounded nation-state, consisting of a plurality of interest groups of various types, competing for power and privilege for themselves on equal footing. The present study extends the model to cover the universalistic functions that many of these groups perform, their hierarchical relations to one another, and the variations in both complexity and size among them. More significantly, it attempts to probe the nature of sociocultural causation by analyzing an extensive series of cultural performances in terms of symbolic functions, forms, and techniques.

The problem concerns not just elites but social groups generally. As Durkheim (1933) shows in his analysis of the division of labor, nearly all social groups have both universalistic and particularistic functions. Thus the medical profession is strictly organized to ensure standards of knowledge, training, skill, and ethics among its members in the interest of the public; at the same time, it is organized to develop and maintain its own sectional interests by establishing itself as a monopoly, and maximizing its own material rewards and privileges. With insufficient attention to its particularistic interests, the profession would weaken, and its universalistic functions would suffer, to the detriment of the public. This contradiction at the heart of group organization is most clearly evident at the higher levels of social hierarchy—notably among elite groups.

An elite is a collectivity of persons who occupy commanding positions in some important sphere of social life, and who share a variety of interests arising from similarities of training, experience, public duties, and way of life. To promote these interests, they seek to cooperate and coordinate their actions by means of a corporate organization. Some of these interests can be articulated in a formal association, as in the medical profession. But there are functions and interests, both universalistic and particularistic, that the elite cannot organize formally. Indeed, in the liberal societies of the West, elites are not recognized as such, i.e., as part of the formal social structure. The members of such an elite are not recognized *as a group*, but only as a category of persons who have achieved their status by merit, within a highly competitive system. However, even when this *is* actually the case, those who earn their way into elite status soon begin to coordinate their actions in an increasingly systematic and consistent way. They also seek to perpetuate their status and privileges by socializing and training their children to succeed them. Thus, the category evolves in time into a group with corporate interests. These particularistic interests are incompatible with the principle of equality of opportunity usually upheld by the formal constitution of society, and therefore cannot be advanced by a formal association. There are also universalistic functions that are not best served by formal organization. Senior civil servants, for example, must often coordinate their actions through personal contacts, dealings, understandings, and compromises, without the exchange of formal documents. These "undercover" dealings may well be in the public interest, but they cannot be formally articulated. Some of them can be effected under the protection of official secrecy acts; but many others are carried out by private contacts between persons who share the same culture and who can trust one another.

Interests and functions that cannot be advanced by formal association are usually articulated in what Weber (1947:

136–9) called "communal relationships," i.e., kinship, friendship, godparenthood, and a host of other primary relationships. If such relationships do not already exist, they are soon developed, on the basis of common interests, duties, and sentiments, in the course of intensive interaction within series of overlapping, intimate, exclusive gatherings. A common culture will thus develop both to express and to uphold the group's corporate interests. In the words of Meisel (1962 : 4), the elite will develop three C's: consciousness, cohesion, and conspiracy. In some cases its members may be recruited from one culture group, with a ready-made symbolic system easily adapted to serve the interests of the new elite. There is a dialectical relation between power and culture, the one acting on the other.

This book is thus concerned with the analysis of elite culture in its articulation of particularistic and universalistic functions within a pluralistic, hierarchical system. My ultimate aim is to explore the causal relation between the normative symbols underlying that culture and the power relationships in which members of an elite are involved. I seek to demonstrate further the view that communal relationships and communal organization form a dimension of power, the analysis of which is essential to understanding the power structure of any state. "Class groups" are abstract sociological constructs that cannot be comprehended apart from the symbolic mechanisms that knit their members and families together, and thus transform them from mere categories of people into concrete, cohesive, cooperating, and relatively enduring corporate groups. In his historical, more scientific writings, Marx conceived of classes not as monolithic unidimensional entities, but as conglomerations of a multiplicity of groups, where members share similar work functions, values, interests, and way of life. Marx was writing about nineteenth-century societies; the case for the pluralistic nature of classes in today's highly differentiated capitalist societies is far more pronounced.

The relatively small-scale, concrete, corporate sociocultural groups into which the more abstract, overarching "classes" break down are not discrete systems that can be studied on their own. They have to be seen in relation to the wider class system; but that system cannot be studied apart from its concrete manifestations. Clearly, the study of class society will have to proceed dialectically, from the parts to the whole, and from the whole back to the parts. It remains a matter of practical expedience whether a scholar should attempt original research on both the whole and the parts, or concentrate on one level and rely "naively," as Devons and Gluckman (1964) would put it, on the latest findings by other scholars for the other level.

The present analysis is based on the study of one elite, recruited from a group of people loosely referred to as the Creoles of Sierra Leone. Although the ethnographic present tense is used throughout, the account refers to conditions prevailing in 1970. It is important to bear this in mind, as we are dealing here with an essentially changing and developing social system. Indeed, for reasons that will become evident, the publication of this monograph has been intentionally delayed so that changing conditions in Sierra Leone would render misunderstanding or misinterpretation harmless. At the time the fieldwork was done, the state was monarchical, with the queen of England at its head, and the political system was remarkably liberal, allowing the existence of opposition parties. Today, the state is a republic, and the whole structure of the polity is changed. Many of the persons covered by the study are now either dead or retired from public office.

In 1970 the Creoles formed a part of what Miliband (1969:46–62) calls a "state elite," which he regards as a distinct and separate entity in its own right (ibid.:51). Not all members of the Sierra Leone elite were Creoles. Nearly all the executive, most of the legislature, and the whole of the police and the army were controlled by men from other ethnic groups. But a substantial number of senior civil servants and members of the professions that were directly related to state institutions, such as medicine, law, and teaching, were Creoles. Under normal circumstances, the distinctions between the Creole and non-Creole elite would have disappeared soon after independence, and it would be sociologically misleading to consider the Creoles as a distinct category within the state elite of the country. But a number of circumstances, which will be discussed in detail in this book, led to the maintenance of Creole cultural distinctiveness within the state elite. This is only partly because of historical continuities resulting from the Creole lead in such status, their concentration in Freetown, the dense network of amity relationships that link and cross-link their various families, and the distinct culture that governs this network. During the colonial period, Creole society and culture were flexible enough to allow the incorporation, indeed the Creolization, of the rising elite from other ethnic groups in the country. However, as a result of the major confrontation between the Creoles and the provincials during most of the 1947–67 period, the elite from the provinces were inhibited from identifying themselves with the Creoles; in fact, those of them who had been Creolized in the past opted out of Creoledom when they saw formal political power pass from the British to provincial politicians, deciding that they would gain more from reasserting their provincial origins. Another factor was the developing cleavage between the Mendes and the Temnes during the second half of the 1960s, which prevented either of these numerically dominant ethnic groups from establishing hegemony in the country. Indeed the cleavage that developed between them over the years led—almost forced— the Creoles to assume the role of the neutral, mediating stranger, and this developed their social and cultural distinctiveness even more than before. As a result of these processes, the Creole role in maintaining and running the Sierra Leone state system was crucial. As will be shown later, not all Creoles were in elite positions; but Creole society generally was so integrated and structured that the non-elite among them played a significant part in making it possible for the other members to assume and maintain elite positions.

Sierra Leone was chosen for the study because it is a relatively small nation-state, with a population of about two-and-a-half million (Government of Sierra Leone, 1965: 13–16). The Creoles number only 41,783, and thus comprise less than 2 percent of the population. Even so, they would normally be too large a group to be studied "holistically" in the methodological tradition of social anthropology, particularly in view of the complexity of their society and the occupational differentiation among its men and women. A number of special circumstances, however, have made such a study practicable. The Creoles are said to be the descendants of slaves who were emancipated by the British between 1787 and the mid-nineteenth century and settled in the "Province of Freedom" in Sierra Leone. Within the small area of Freetown peninsula, their society and culture have developed in the full light of recorded history. Being predominantly literate and highly educated, they themselves have produced a great deal of informative literature about their lives. They have probably been the most intensively studied group in sub-saharan Africa. Their history has been studied by Fyfe (1962), Porter (1963), Peterson (1969), Kreutzinger (1968), and others. Banton (1957) gives a detailed picture of their social and cultural life in Freetown in the early 1950s. Great detail about their role in the modern political life of the country is given by Kilson (1967), Cartwright (1968), and Clapham (1976). Spitzer (1974) provides a penetrating analysis of their encounters with Western civilization and colonialism over a number of decades. In a comprehensive study of the professionals in the country, two-thirds of whom are Creoles, Harrell-Bond (1975) provides interesting data about their marriages and family life.

Apart from these studies, a colossal amount of information is available in various reports, findings of commissions of inquiry, and other government records. Of even greater importance for any sociological study is the carefully and expertly conducted household survey of a 10 percent sample of the population undertaken by the Statistics Department of the Government of Sierra Leone in 1966–67. Some of the findings of that survey have been published (see Government of Sierra Leone, 1967, 1968). With the kind permission of the Statistics Department, some of the unpublished data were duly processed and used in the present study. Without these various studies and sources of information, the present analysis could not have been undertaken.

I was fortunate in having my wife, Gaynor, with me. She carried out a project of her own, investigating the socialization of children in middle-class families in Freetown and their recruitment into the professional class. Inevitably, a great deal of her work was concerned with Creole families. She conducted extensive surveys of the social background of school children and visited the families of many of them. In addition, she took down and systematically recorded the biography and extensive social network of an old, serious, experienced, shrewd Creole woman, who had lived through a number of interesting phases of Creole history in Freetown (E. G. Cohen, 1973).

Miss (now Dr.) La Ray Denzer assisted me by conducting an extensive analysis of some Sierra Leonean newspapers since the end of World War II in accordance with criteria formulated especially for this study.

My own work also included collecting the biographies of men and women, and intensive observation and recording of a large number of ceremonies of different sorts, in different spheres of social life.

The field study lasted for a year and was financed by the School of Oriental and African Studies, University of London. In Sierra Leone, I was given the status of visiting research fellow at the Institute of African Studies, Fourah Bay College, University of Sierra Leone. I would like to thank both institutions for their generous help. I have a debt of gratitude to many Sierra Leoneans—officials, professionals, clergymen, and many ordinary men and women— for their hospitality, courtesy, open-mindedness and generous help. In particular, I would like to record my deep gratitude to Mr. J. G. Edowu Hyde, Professor Harry Sawyerr, Professor E. W. Blyden III, Professor M. Carter, Professor J. Peterson, Professor E. D. Jones, Canon G. L. O. Palmer, Mr. A. Thompson, Ms. Zara Johnson, Ms. Nimata Madhi, Ms. Miranda Burny Nicole, and Professor M. E. K. Thomas.

I am indebted to those who have read the text and commented on it: Dr. Richard Tapper, Dr. Geoffrey Richards, Dr. E. G. Cohen, and Ms. Muriel Bell. The final draft was prepared while I was a fellow at the Center for Advanced Study in the Behavioral Sciences at Stanford, California, and I would like to express my thanks to its staff, Mrs. Dorothy Brothers in particular, for valuable assistance and encouragement, and to the National Science Foundation for financial support (Grant No. BNS 76–33943 A02).

I would like to thank the honorary editor of *Man*, the journal of the Royal Anthropological Institute, for permission to reproduce parts of my article "The Politics of Ritual Secrecy" (*Man* 6 [1971]: 427–48).

In 1970, the Sierra Leone currency unit was the Leone (Le) and was worth £0.50 (or $1.20). The net national income per capita (Clapham, 1976:132) was equal to £65.70 (or $157.70).

Many of the arguments made in this book were presented in classes and lectures in universities in Britain and the United States. I am grateful to the students and faculty of these universities for their criticism, comment, and suggestions.

A. C.
Stanford, 1979

Introduction: 1
The Power Mystique

Cults of Eliteness
Between Conflict and Consensus
The Problem
Power Cults in Western Societies
The Dramaturgy of Power

In stratified societies, power groups seek to validate and sustain their elite status by claiming to possess rare and exclusive qualities essential to the society at large. In some cases these claims are rejected by the rest of the society; in others they are accepted in varying degrees; and in yet others they are developed and bestowed by the society. In closed and formally institutionalized systems of stratification, these qualities are explicitly specified and organized. In more liberal, formally egalitarian systems, on the other hand, the qualities tend to be defined in vague and ambiguous terms and objectified in mysterious, non-utilitarian symbols and dramatic performances, making up what amounts to a mystique of excellence.

Cults of Eliteness

In a letter to *The Times* (16 January 1941; in Guttsman, 1969:289) early in World War II, Colonel Bingham complained that with the rapid expansion of the British army at the time, men from the middle and working classes had been receiving the king's commission, but failing dismally to provide effective leadership. He claimed in explanation that leadership requires certain specialized abilities, that these abilities cannot be learned from books, and that only upper-class men, educated in special, exclusive schools, can cultivate them.

Writing some decades earlier, under less egalitarian circumstances, Cardinal Newman made the same kind of claim in more elaborate terms:

> All that goes to constitute a gentleman,—the carriage gait, address, gestures, voice; the ease, the self-possession, the courtesy, the power of conversing, the talent of not offending; the lofty principle, the delicacy of thought, the happiness of expression, the taste and propriety, the generosity and forbearance, the candour and consideration, the openness of hand;—these qualities, some of them come by nature, some of them may be found in any rank, some of them are a direct precept of Christianity; but the full assemblage of them, bound up in the unity of an individual character, do we expect they can be learned from books? Are they not necessarily acquired, where they are to be found, in high society. (J. H. Newman, 1876; in Guttsman, 1969:210–11.)

What was implicit in Colonel Bingham's formulation is here made clear and explicit. The mystique of eliteness, the full assemblage of the qualities of excellence the cardinal cites, can be learned only informally, in "high society."

It is obvious from Newman's list that the mystique is not just an ideological formula, but is also a way of life, manifesting itself in patterns of symbolic behavior that can be observed and verified. The ideology is objectified, devel-

2

oped, and maintained by an elaborate body of symbols and dramatic performances: manners, etiquette, styles of dress, accent, patterns of recreational activity, marriage rules, and a host of other traits that make up the group's life style. These patterns of symbolic activity arise from different private motives and serve a variety of purposes, and cannot therefore be dismissed as mere strategies adopted to legitimize an ideology of eliteness. They are nevertheless invariably intimately related to such an ideology, and their consequences, though often unintended by the actors, are crucial in maintaining power groups. Ideological content and explicit dramatic performance continuously act and react on one another in forming the cult of eliteness. This is a highly elaborate cult and is acquired only through long periods of esoteric socialization and training, largely within informal social contexts—the family, the peer group, the club, and the extracurricular activities of exclusive schools.

Inevitably, the symbols and dramatic performances of the cult are mysterious and highly ambiguous. This is partly because they are addressed to different audiences, and are motivated by different individual and group purposes at one and the same time. Their import is partly revealed and partly concealed, partly conscious and partly unconscious on the part of its bearers. Parts of it are staged for the exclusive benefit of members of the group and are thus hidden from outsiders. Sometimes this secrecy is formally organized and strictly observed, as in Freemasonry. But even when it is not, it is nevertheless created by the very exclusiveness of the elite. As Simmel (1950:345–76) points out, what is unknown eventually appears to be fearsome and mighty.

The forms and processes of mystification implicit in the cult of eliteness vary from system to system, depending on the culture, the rigidity of hierarchical structure, and the scale of the society. If the cult were just "expressive" in its nature, or if it were a mere epiphenomenon of power and privilege, its study would have little sociological significance. Some features of the cult can indeed be described as "expressive," falling into the usual pattern of the ongoing

3

life of power groups. People dress, eat, behave, and think, and these activities are conditioned by their wealth and status, and are in that sense expressive. But the cult is nevertheless essentially instrumental, in that it validates the status of the elite in the eyes of the public, and gives the elite the conviction that they are naturally qualified for their position. It also enables them in a variety of ways to coordinate their efforts to develop and maintain their power and to train themselves and their children in its exercise.

The cult would have equally little sociological significance if it were simply a brazenly manufactured claim on the part of particularistic sectional groups pursuing their own private interests. If the claims to exclusive qualities of excellence and to the importance of these qualities for the general benefit of the society, are rejected, or if the mystifications employed are unmasked, then the cult becomes hollow, and its study pointless. And, indeed, the history of ruling elites shows clearly that when the symbols of their cult lose their potency, when outside audiences cease to defer to them, such elites lose their legitimacy and are likely to lose power.

It *is* a fact, however, that in ongoing hierarchical systems, most elite positions are given to members of groups who claim a monopoly on qualities of excellence. Thus, in Britain and the United States, graduates of prestigious, exclusive universities are recruited to such positions quite out of proportion to their numbers in the population as a whole. In many systems, ordinary subjects genuinely believe that their rulers are "born" to rule, that they are most qualified for organizing the lives of their countrymen.

The qualities under consideration here are not specific, specialized technical skills in which people can be trained. Such skills can be acquired by any ordinary person who has the intelligence and the opportunity for training. We are concerned here with vague, mysterious qualities that elude precise definition and, as Bingham, Newman, and many others have maintained, cannot be learned formally from books or from courses. This is the mystique sometimes referred to as "civilization," "culture," "nobility," "excellence," or "refinement."

4

Between Conflict and Consensus

The question that immediately arises is whether the power mystique is the particularistic, sectional creation of the group that assumes it to enhance its own interests, or essentially the universalistic creation of the social system as a whole in the general interest.

This question, in fact, poses the whole problem of the distribution of power in society. Its analysis has been dominated by two major theories developed by opposing schools of thought among sociologists, historians, political scientists, and philosophers. The first is essentially that of the Marxists, the second that of the elitists.

According to Marxist or conflict theory, the power mystique is a subtle, particularistic ideology developed by a privileged elite to validate and perpetuate their domination and thereby to support their own material interests. The cult consists of various techniques of mystification, implicit in philosophy, religion, art, drama, and life style, to persuade the masses that it is only natural for this power elite to rule and that this is in the best interests of the society as a whole. As Marx and Engels put it (1970:64):

> The ideas of the ruling classes are, in every epoch, the ruling ideas: i.e., the class which is the dominant *material* force in society is at the same time its dominant *intellectual* force. . . . The dominant ideas are nothing more than the ideal expression of the dominant material relationships, grasped as ideas, and thus of the relationships which make one class the ruling one; they are consequently the ideas of its dominance.

The elitist, or consensus, theory of stratification, by contrast, maintains that all social order is necessarily hierarchical, and that leadership is a specialization necessitated by the division of labor in all societies. The theory has a long and varied ancestry; it appears in one of its crudest forms in the contract theory of Hobbes, who argued that to escape from the "solitary, poor, nasty, brutish and short" life in the state of nature, men entered into a contract agreeing to surrender their freedom to a sovereign, who represents their general will and who maintains social order in their own interest, if necessary against their individual wills. In other words, the power mystique of the rulers is created and invested in them by society as a corporate body.

Another version of the theory refers to the perennial conflict between the individual and society, or the group to which the individual belongs, in respect of rights and obligations. As Fortes and Evans-Pritchard have pointed out (1940:19), in its pragmatic and utilitarian aspects, the autonomy of the group is a source of immediate private interest and satisfaction to the individual members. But as a common interest it is non-utilitarian and non-pragmatic, a matter of moral value and ideological significance. Hence the necessity of an authority that would exert pressure on the individual to honor his obligations. In the process, the rulers are endowed with mystical powers which enhance their status, and raise them to a higher level than that of ordinary individuals. Indeed, in many tribal societies the chief is endowed by the society with such mystical powers as magic, rainmaking, healing, witchcraft, and sorcery. He is thus not only respected and admired, but also feared.

A classic example that the consensus theorists cite is the caste system in India, where, many scholars maintain, men are so content with the status assigned them by the ideology that a low-caste individual would not want to change to a higher caste. The society is so programmed by the blueprint of the *varna* that peace, tranquillity, and order are the blessing of all. The Brahmins are the guardians of the *varna*, and their status is clearly defined in symbols of purity and pollution.

The view has had a long ancestry in the history of political thought. Plato in his *Republic* argued that the ideal society would be regulated and ruled by philosophers, who achieved their status by merit in a lengthy program of socialization and education.

But by far the most influential school in modern times in this field is that of the elitists who, often in opposition to Marx, maintain that modern society is ruled not by a ruling class but by a plurality of elites arising independently within separate institutional spheres, achieving their status by merit. Thus, the consensus theorists would argue, the mystique of eliteness is created and sustained by society as a whole for its own benefit. Society, while differentiating the elite from other groups, enhances and upholds their power and authority to enable them to perform universalistic functions.

These two schools of thought, though opposed in many respects and still the source of hot debates in sociology and political science, are in fact focusing on the two extremes of one continuum. In all societies, power groups assume mystiques, i.e., ideologies and techniques of mystification, that are both particularistic and universalistic.

The conflict theory does, in effect, subscribe to the consensus theory up to a point. Thus Marx and Engels write (1970:65–66):

> For each new class which puts itself in the place of one ruling before it, is compelled, merely in order to carry through its aim, to represent its interest as the common interest of all the members of society, that is expressed in ideal form: it has to give its ideas the form of universality, and represent them as the only rational, universally valid ones.

What this means is that, for at least some time, the universal interest of the society as a whole will coincide or substantially overlap with the particular interest of the dominant group. In other words, the dominant group will embody the universal interest of the society. The mystique of that group, its ideology and symbolic patterns of behavior, will thus function during that phase, for the benefit of society as well as for the benefit of the group.

The elitists for their part would accept the view that the power mystique is not merely an instrument for the perpetuation of the elite's power and status. Thus Mosca (1939) and Michels (1958) maintain that elites develop and maintain their status by means of their organization, which is largely articulated covertly, in terms of communal relationships. As Parry (1969:118) puts it, it is essential for any theory of elites to establish the extent to which any leading group is successful in developing such an organization.

Thus, the elitists would concede that, while serving the general interests of society, elites develop organizational mechanisms to advance their sectional interests. The conflict theorists, on the other hand, would concede that, while serving their own sectional interests, dominant groups develop ideologies purporting to articulate the general interests of society.

This means that both schools would agree that the mystique of the elite is partly universalistic and partly particularistic. As Marx and Engels point out, the mystique of the same group can contain more, or less, of either of these elements at different times. At any one time, particularist and universalist elements interact, sometimes conflicting with and sometimes supporting one another, in a continuing sociocultural dialectic. Both theories acknowledge the reality of the mystique, and one of the major tasks of the student of society is identifying and separating between the two elements.

The two theories seem to be in opposition mainly because their subscribers tend to be unidimensional in their approach, concentrating their attention on power relations, with little attention given to the instrumental functions of the body of symbolic beliefs and practices among the groups involved. Many sociologists do mention the importance of lifestyle in the analysis of stratification, but a survey of the relevant literature shows scant analysis of this dimension. This applies to the Marxists as well, who, though every now and then stressing the importance of "ideology" or of the "superstructure," tend to focus solely on the power dimension.

Making the cult of power the subject of analysis throws new light on the nature of stratification. The more orthodox Marxists may object that the power mystique exists only because of the existence of the state, that the state exists only because there is an exploiting dominant class behind it, and that after the socialist revolution, class domination will disappear, the state will wither away, and, along with it, the mystique of authority. The mystification of the masses will give way to a disenchanted, rationally organized society. This may or may not be a utopia for the unforeseen future. At present, however, the power mystique is at least as dominant in communist societies as elsewhere. The important point is that today all societies are regulated by elite minorities, who employ ideologies and techniques of mystification to maintain themselves in power, as well as serve the public. Indeed, sociologists from the communist countries of eastern Europe appear to be showing increasing interest in functionalism, the consensus theory of society. Alvin Gouldner (1970) suggests in explanation that these countries have now achieved a state of "equilibrium" to which the orthodox Marxian conflict theory of society is no longer applicable; otherwise, such a theory would create counter-revolutionary movements (see also Binns, 1978; Lane, 1979).

The Problem

The power cult is everywhere embedded in the total culture of elite groups, and the first task in analyzing it is to identify its major symbolic forms in order to discover their organizational functions, and hence their political significance. The analysis will eventually face the question of the nature of mediation, of the causal interconnection between the symbolism of culture and the power structure. *How* do the various elements of the cult achieve their different functions? In due course, this will lead to the study of the various techniques of symbolization, or mystification, of achieving what Gramsci (1971) called hegemony. It will also lead to examining the problem of doubt and belief among the actors, both as individuals and as a collective.

The synchronic examination of the structure and functioning of the power cult will have to be combined with the analysis of historical development: How have the different parts of the cult been created? Was this creation a conscious, rational, intended endeavor? Or was it unconscious, non-rational, unintended? Or was it a combination of the two in different proportions at different stages in time?

Finally, there is the question of scale, both in complexity and in size. The potentialities of the different techniques of mystification for organizing power groups of different sizes, within societies with different degrees of institutional differentiation, need to be assessed.

The problem that is posed here is not confined to the na-

9

ture of elite organization or to the nature of hierarchy. Ultimately it is the wider problem of the nature of power articulation and institutionalization in society. Power cannot be seen as an entity. It is rooted in the relations of production, exchange, and distribution, and in the ultimate control of physical coercion. But, in the current day-to-day organization and functioning of the social system, its reality is couched in symbolic terms. It is everywhere embedded in interpersonal and intergroup relationships and is therefore always mystified in the process. It is like money, a token extensively used in transactions, saving, exchange and so on, but of little value in itself, its real value being the capital, goods, services, and the relations of domination and subordination that it represents. It is nevertheless a system in its own right and its nature and functioning require analysis. The analogy with money should not be pushed far, but the lesson is that power should be studied in its various symbolic manifestations. By their very nature, symbols are highly mystifying, in that they connote different shades of meaning to different people, or to the same people at different times. Power is everywhere mystified. This is true of communist as well as capitalist societies. Its study ultimately leads to the study of the nature of authority, which MacIver (1947) described as the Central Myth, which is continuously created and recreated in society, and of the processes of leadership, both routine and charismatic.

Power Cults in Western Societies

An investigation of this problem can be carried out only through the comparative study of actual cases, not through a semantic analysis or armchair theorizing alone. And indeed, the great theoreticians who have concerned themselves with the study of the distribution of power developed their formulations after examining specific societies at different stages of their history. Marx's analyses were based on the detailed examination of the structure and history of the industrial societies of Europe. Weber's sociological generalizations were discussed and extensively documented in terms of detailed studies of contemporary European countries as well as ancient societies, including those of India and China. The elitists (Mosca, Michels, Pareto, and others) have similarly developed and often documented their hypotheses in terms of the rise and fall of specific elites in different societies, at different periods.

More recently, sociologists and political scientists who have been trained in the systematic handling of empirical data have applied themselves more systematically to studying the structure and functioning of elite groupings in contemporary societies.

One of the most ambitious, comprehensive, stimulating, and influential of these works is C. Wright Mills's (1956) study of the "power elite" in the United States, in which he attempts to reconcile Marxian and elitist theories of power. Mills rejects the "romantic pluralism" of the elitists who maintain that society is a universe of competing groups, with separate elites, and that the unintended consequences of their interaction result in the best interests of order and happiness. During the previous thirty years, he maintained, the formerly discriminating public had been converted into an uncritical mass; the middle level groupings had lost their influence and had become politically insignificant. Power thus came to be concentrated in the hands of three dominant elites: economic, political, and military. Formally, these three elites are separate and autonomous, their members coming from different parts of the country. Informally, however, they are intimately interconnected through multiple directorships, the continuous exchange and circulation of personnel, and the liaison function of law firms. Most important of all, they are knit together into what practically amounts to one ruling class through the mediation of their culture, their style of life.

Their members are brought up in similar ways, in the same or similar neighborhoods, the same types of houses, in the same religious tradition. They are educated at nationally selective, exclusive schools and the Ivy League universities. The relationships of comradeship which they develop in school and university are continued in adulthood in clubs, and through sports and other leisure activities, thus developing into a network of overlapping cliques of friends.

11

Through patterns of selective dating and annual gatherings, their boys and girls are thrown together for chaperoned occasions. Their marriage pattern is, as a result, highly endogamous, and is the basis for the development and maintenance of overlapping cousinhoods. "In the course of time, each meets each or knows somebody who knows somebody who knows that one. Nowhere in America is there as great a 'class consciousness' as among the elite; nowhere is it organized as effectively as among the power elite" (ibid:283). Status and snobbishness secure privacy for them, so that their activities are often hidden under the cover of secrecy, partly official and partly unofficial.

Mills's work inspired a whole generation of sociologists and political scientists. But it has also been severely attacked by many writers. Its arguments will be discussed further in parts of the text. One of its most crucial limitations is that it attempted to deal with the structure of power in the whole of the United States, a vast, highly complex and differentiated society, with no homogenous culture and no traditional ruling class.

This methodological difficulty is partly overcome by studies of the structure of power in Britain. Britain has about a quarter of the population of the United States, is much smaller in territory, less complex, and with much greater homogeneity of culture and historical continuity. In the United States the central controversy is whether there is or ever has been a ruling elite at all, with some social scientists denying its existence while others, following Mills, proclaim it. In Britain, on the other hand, there is no doubt that a ruling class has existed historically, and the controversy among social scientists today is whether the old ruling class had "decomposed," or whether it continues to exist, though less visibly.

Although empirical sociology and political science in Britain developed much later than in the United States, there have been a number of studies which, using some of the insights of American writers, and working under more favorable conditions for empirical enquiry, throw further light on the cult of power.

One of the most important of these studies is a short paper

by Lupton and Wilson (1959) on the social and cultural background of nearly 500 top "decision makers" from political, administrative, finance, and business hierarchies. The particular significance of this paper is the meticulous documentation of links of kinship and affinity, friendship, membership in clubs, and of old school and university ties between many of these decisionmakers.

This work was followed by a more comprehensive and systematic sociological study by Guttsman (1963), *The British Political Elite*, which traces the various processes involved in the development of the main British political groupings from the mid-nineteenth century to the end of the 1950s. It is an extensively documented piece of research, which Guttsman later supplemented with *The English Ruling Class* (1969), containing excerpts from over a hundred source texts of different kinds. Along the lines set up by Mills, Guttsman stresses and documents (see diagrams in *The British Political Elite*, pp. 363–67) the mobility of personnel between the different elites. Like Mills, he also dwells on the significance of kinship and marriage, club membership, and, most important, on similar educational background within a limited number of select public schools and Cambridge and Oxford. He concludes (1963:356) that, "There exists today in Britain a 'ruling class,' if we mean by it a group which provides the majority of those who occupy positions of power and who, in their turn, can materially assist *their* sons to reach similar positions." Although Guttsman dismisses any "facile application of Mills's model of the American power elite," he nevertheless confirms Mills's observation about increasing mobility between the different power hierarchies, an increase in the number of what he calls (p. 359) the pluralists of power, i.e., "men who over a number of years or occasionally, even simultaneously, exert influence through a number of advising or decision-making bodies. Power attracts such men and power breeds more power and influence."

There have been many other studies of these issues by sociologists and political scientists, represented in such collections of papers as Richard Rose, ed., *Studies in British Politics* (1966), Urry and Wakeford, eds., *Power in Britain* (1973), and Stanworth and Giddens, eds., *Elites and Power in British Society* (1974). A more comprehensive, but less empirical study encompassing Britain, the United States and other Western systems is Ralph Miliband's *The State in Capitalist Society* (1969). These, and many other studies of this type, provide valuable information and insights, but between them inevitably give a fragmentary account of the culture of the power elite and of the crucial role which culture plays in linking the different elites into a power group. This is because they have had to grapple with formidable methodological, theoretical, and epistemological problems arising from the colossal scale and complexity of the societies with which they are concerned, from the inaccessibility of the inner circles of the elite to the researcher, and sometimes also from the assumption that the culture, or lifestyle, of the elite is only an epiphenomenon, an idiom expressive of the "down-to-earth realities" of economic and political power, and therefore of little value.

These problems have been to some extent avoided by social anthropologists who have studied small-scale, culturally homogeneous, institutionally undifferentiated, preindustrial societies. Most of the studies carried out in this way have been concerned with unfolding the political functions of institutions that are formally non-political, like those of kinship and religion, and with the demystification of hierarchy. But for a variety of circumstances they have dealt mainly with local polities that were part of the colonial system, and after independence became part of the structure of the new nation-state. It is only in recent years that anthropologists have begun to tackle the problem of the relation between sectional groups and the wider social system into which they are incorporated.

The Dramaturgy of Power

One way of meeting these methodological problems is to study elite cultures within relatively small-scale, developing nation-states. In the present monograph, an attempt is made to isolate, define, and analyze the culture of a small state elite, that of the Creoles of modern Sierra Leone.

The following two chapters delineate Creole identity in terms of two distinct variables: culture and power. The cultural variable is expressed in terms of a number of *symbolic forms*, or cults: those of "origin"—the church, the family, the dead, secret rituals—and decorum. The power variable is manifested in command of high positions in the state bureaucracy, and the strategic professions of law, education, and medicine. The same men and women who command these public positions are those who develop and maintain the symbolic forms of Creole culture.

Subsequent chapters deal with the dialectical relations between the two variables in the lives of these men and women. Chapter four discusses the ways in which frequent and extensive private "family" ceremonials lead to the creation and recreation of a close-knit network of amity, a grand cousinhood, linking and cross-linking the members of this elite in moral relationships characterized by cooperation in the politico-economic field. Chapter five highlights the crucial role played by women in the development and maintenance of that network.

Chapter six discusses the articulation of an informal, invisible, corporate organization among the elite to enable them, first, to protect and enhance their particularistic interests. This is achieved principally in the course of organizing and observing secret rituals which are formally non-political. Chapter seven shows how the elite use the same informal organization to coordinate their activities in their public roles in the performance of state-level universalistic functions. In other words, the same organization is made to serve both universalistic and particularistic interests. In the process, the contradiction between the two types of interests is mystified.

Chapter eight, the longest and most important, attempts to probe the processes by which culture and power continuously affect one another in the course of different series of frequent dramatic performances involving different actors and audiences. Culture is analyzed in terms of symbolic functions, symbolic forms, and dramatic techniques. Politico-cultural causation operates in continual series of dramatic performances on different levels of social organization.

These performances objectify norms, values and beliefs, interpret the private in terms of the collective, the abstract in terms of the concrete, confirming or modifying relationships, temporarily resolving contradictions, and always recreating the belief, the conviction, of the actors in the validity of their roles in society. Familiar, everyday symbolic events are taken out of their ordinary ideological sequences and, as Brecht would put it, thrown into crisis by showing their involvement in major power struggles in society. Thus I take such familiar performances as a ball, a university graduation ceremony, a funeral, and a thanksgiving service to show how they repetitively reproduce or modify power relationships, and how they combine in a culture which functions instrumentally in transforming civil servants and professionals into an interacting and cooperating elite.

In the Conclusion, the analysis is placed within a broad comparative perspective in an attempt to delineate a paradigm for the cross-cultural study of elites and other power groups. Some of the implications for the development of social anthropology generally are also examined in the final section.

Mystified Identity

Power is often an elusive phenomenon. It is articulated in terms of different patterns of symbols and of symbolic activities. These are highly ambiguous forms, which help to conceal power as well as to publicize it. In liberal societies that are officially egalitarian, an elite may deny its own existence as an organized collectivity by adopting different techniques of mystification, assuming a low profile, and attempting to fade into the wider sociocultural landscape. "Class awareness," writes Giddens (1973:111), "may take the form of *a denial of the existence or reality of classes.*" When under some circumstances it becomes necessary for the elite to define their identity they do so in terms of ambiguous formulations. These strategies may sometimes be consciously formulated by leaders, but are often unconscious on the part of the rest of the group.

The Mythology of Origin

To study such an elite, the student can proceed by adopting a combination of two lines of enquiry. The first is the observation of visible patterns of symbolic formations and action. The assumption here is that if symbols are live and significant, it is because they are adopted by a group of people for whom they are "collective representations." The search will thus proceed by identifying the members of the group and unraveling the interests they share. The second approach is to start from the other end and try to identify interest groups, such as a professional group, or groups of senior civil servants or businessmen. The assumption here is that if the interests of such a group are significant, then the group will have some basic organizational mechanism to coordinate the members' activities to promote those interests. In this way the group will be defined in terms of two dimensions: culture and power.

A good deal of light can be thrown on these methodological and theoretical issues through the study of such groups developmentally, as they "go invisible" in some respects and "public" in others, in a series of sociocultural metamorphoses, displaying both continuity and change.

Like most elites in "open" societies, the Creoles of Sierra Leone are hard to delineate or define. Indeed, it has recently even been claimed that they have never existed, at least not as a unified and self-conscious community. Thus, in one short article, Skinner and Harrell-Bond (1977) castigate almost every historian, sociologist, anthropologist, and political scientist who has written about the Creoles. They argue that some kind of Creole identity developed when the elite of the colony came under pressure, particularly during the 1950s, and that historians, notably Fyfe (1962) and Porter (1963), simply projected such identity into the past; social scientists, usually limited by methodological and theoretical parameters, relied on the historians' interpretations, and thus helped in the perpetuation of the myth of the existence of the Creoles.

In contrast with this extreme view, there are some writers, such as Banton (1957) and Porter (1963), who argue that it was in the past that the Creoles were self-conscious and coherent as a group, but that since World War II they have rapidly become integrated or assimilated within the wider Sierra Leonean population. And indeed, it *is* the case that in the last two decades the Creoles have themselves been vociferous in rejecting Creole distinctiveness and a few of them have even begun to change their names to African ones. They are supported in this by the official ban since 1968 on all reference to tribal or ethnic identification in official documents. But all this does not mean that these ethnic entities have ceased to exist, or did not exist. And it is, of course, highly plausible to argue that Skinner and Harrell-Bond (1977) are themselves projecting into the past contemporary government-sponsored, and also Creole-backed, ideology.

But the issue of Creole identity cannot be clarified by a polemic about the etymology of the term, or by relying on the labels used by informants in answer to superficial questionnaires or on declarations made in public. As I show elsewhere (Cohen, 1971*a*), the Creoles began to play down their distinctiveness as a community at the very time when they united, in the face of serious pressure during the 1950s and the 1960s. Overt statements by informants should not be taken at face value. Their validity or ideological nature can be examined only in the light of the detailed observation and recording of social action, of behavior patterns, in different situations and under different circumstances, principally within the two realms of power and culture. A collectivity of men and women who share politico-economic interests, and who sustain a specific life style, is a distinct corporate group, irrespective of their publicly declared label, or even of whether they are conscious of their identity and exclusiveness.

Some Creoles still see themselves, and are seen by the majority of the rest of the population, as descendants of different groups of slaves who were emancipated by the Brit-

19

ish and were settled in the Freetown peninsula between 1787 and about 1850. Until recent years this belief was perpetuated and celebrated by "settlers' descendant associations" like those of the Nova Scotians and of the Maroons. There are many Creole families who trace their origin to other parts of West Africa, particularly Nigeria, and a number of men who were interviewed stated that they had visited their communities of origin to seek information about their ancestors and to establish firmer links with the past. Moreover, the Creoles are officially defined in law as "non-native," meaning that they are not members of any of the country's sixteen native ethnic groups.

These beliefs about origin implicitly assume that recruitment to Creoledom is ascribed by descent, and that the Creoles observe a rigid principle of descent and practice absolute endogamy. But the Creoles are bilateral in their kinship organization, and within what he regards as his family a man will often include patrilateral, matrilateral, and affinal relatives, as well as friends. Throughout the history of the Creoles, men and women of native descent were Creolized through various processes (see Banton, 1957; Porter, 1963). By acquiring the symbols and lifestyle of Creoledom and being incorporated in the Creole social network, such natives became Creoles. On the other hand, there is evidence of simultaneous movement in the other direction, whereby Creoles came to identify with one or another of the country's native ethnic groups, and became natives. But the incidence of this movement should not be exaggerated. Most of those who have recently opted out of Creoledom by changing their names are known, and know themselves, as being originally provincials who turned Creole after being brought up and educated by Creole families. For others, the process has been slow and problematic. The Creoles have lived mainly in Freetown and known one another well, and it is difficult for people to announce suddenly and brazenly that they are not Creole. Moreover, as will become clear in the following chapters, the Creoles are deeply involved with one another in a network of multiplex relationships that are in many ways essential for the maintenance of their economic and political interests, both individually and collectively. Under these circumstances a man who publicly abandons his identity as a Creole is likely to alienate himself from the rest of the Creoles, and thereby lose their support.

This process whereby *individuals* opt out of Creoledom may be accelerated to some extent in the next generation, partly because many Creoles today give their children African names. The stand publicly adopted by most Creoles is, however, to oppose "tribalism" and play down the significance of ethnic identity within contemporary Sierra Leone society.

Creoledom in modern Sierra Leone is essentially a status grouping marked off from other social groups in the country by a special lifestyle and by a dense network of social relationships. The Creoles are Christians and are organized in almost exclusively Creole churches. Some writers (see Peterson, 1968; 1969) have argued that the Aku, who number about 5,000 and are Muslims, are in fact Creoles because they are non-natives and share a similar tradition of origin and the same history in the Freetown peninsula. The argument is largely a question of naming and categorizing. A writer who wishes to call both groups "Creoles" can certainly do so without difficulty.

Sociologically, however, such categorization can be very misleading. There are fundamental economic, social, and cultural differences between the two groups. The Aku have for a long time been involved in indigenous trade and are thus part of a traditional trading network organized under Islam (see Cohen, 1971b), while the Christian Creoles are essentially professionals and civil servants. The Aku are formally polygynous and, being mostly wealthy traders, practice polygyny extensively, while the Christian Creoles are formally monogamous. Aku women go through Bundu initiation, which includes clitoridectomy, while Creole women not only do not do this but are appalled by it. The Aku send their children to special schools that give Islamic instruction, and their households are fundamentally different in structure from Creole households. It is also important to note that Christian Creoles do not identify the Aku as Creoles. The

Aku, for their part, call themselves Aku and maintain they have more affinity with the predominantly Muslim native ethnic groups than with the Christian Creoles. At a time when even Christian Creoles are trying to shed their traditional identity, the Aku have not been at all keen on being identified with their Christian compatriots. Throughout this monograph, the term Creoles will be consistently used to denote Christian Creoles only.

A 1962 census (Olson, 1969:72–74) puts the number of Creoles registered in churches as 33,500. Non-Creole Christians in the country numbered 45,700, but these had separate congregations. Of the ten Creole Anglican churches in Freetown, only one had a small minority of non-Creoles, and of the 13 Creole Methodist churches, only one had some non-Creoles.

Christianity has played a crucial role in the development of Creole society and culture. For over a century and a half, the churches have provided the framework of Creole communal life, including highly sophisticated schools that have given modern education and training to generations of men and women. Even today, by far the best schools in the whole country are the Christian mission schools. Both Anglican and Methodist churches are now independent of foreign ties, with the Anglican church known as the Sierra Leone Church. The clergy in all the churches are predominantly Creoles; most of them were trained at Fourah Bay College, which was until a few years ago affiliated with Durham University in Britain.

Church activities still punctuate a good deal of the social life of the Creoles. Attendance at church services and activities is regular, though as a result of involvement in masonic lodges, the men are now somewhat less punctilious in their attendance at weekly services.

Almost every Creole man or woman, child or adult, is registered in a church and regularly pays class dues. No Creole who is not so registered can expect to receive the final death service, a terrifying prospect. Apart from ritual services, membership in a church involves participation in various committees and in social functions. Not only are individual rites of passage enacted in the church but also those celebrating important dates in the history of associations such as schools, which have regular thanksgiving services in Freetown's principal churches.

An Exclusive Ball: From Ethnicity to the Refinements of Decorum

As they throw doubts about the validity of their ethnic distinctiveness, the Creoles now emphasize the crucial significance of the refinements of "culture" and decorum in making the man.

At an early stage of the Freetown field study, I attended a mysteriously organized ball, staged by a social club I shall call the Moonlight Club at the Paramount Hotel, the most luxurious in the country. The tickets for the ball had been distributed informally through personal contacts, and it was emphasized that formal dress was required.

About 130 men and women came. The atmosphere was sombre, the music played softly, and the participants talked in polite, low voices. All the men wore black suits, and the women appeared in exquisitely and individually designed evening dresses, many of which—I understood later—had been specifically ordered for the occasion. To contemporary Westerners, the whole affair would have seemed unreal, perhaps a replay of a Victorian upper-class event. Men bowed politely as they asked the ladies to dance, with the other men around the tables standing up as courtesy required. Many men dutifully asked their friends' wives to dance with them, displaying a great deal of deference throughout.

All the dances were European ballroom dances, with slow waltzes and tangos predominating. After dinner, people left their tables in the garden to resume dancing in the adjoining air-conditioned hall. At one stage, a large group formed a circle to make room for a number of couples dancing the lancers, with one gray-haired, dignified-looking gentleman (a high court judge, I learned later) standing on a side platform, calling out the steps in a clear voice. Most of the dancers were middle-aged, but they danced beautifully

23

and skillfully. Large women danced nimbly and gracefully, with their long dresses flowing elegantly around them. People were drinking throughout the ball, but in moderation.

All this was in sharp contrast to many of the balls I later witnessed, some of them in the same hotel. Most of these were attended by hundreds of people—in one case by over a thousand. Men and women were dressed variously, many of them informally; the dancing was wild, with deafening rock-and-roll and highlife music filling the air. Both men and women drank heavily, and no particular respect was shown the women. And, as it emerged later, whereas men at the first ball brought only their legal wives, some men at the other balls were accompanied by their mistresses.

The ball seemed in many ways a mystery, which I pursued through numerous enquiries during the following months. Who were the Moonlight Club? Why had they not advertised the ball on the radio and in the papers, as was the case with most of the other balls? Why were the tickets not sold publicly by the usual agents? Who were the participants?

After a few weeks, I discovered the identity of one member who then arranged for me to interview the club secretary, a professional woman with a senior position in one of the ministries. She was a middle-aged spinster, a graduate of a British university.

The secretary said the club had been founded by women whose aim was to inculcate "comportment" in the public, particularly among the men. She patiently explained that the club had come into being when some ladies had noticed with alarm that manners had been deteriorating in Freetown society, that men no longer knew how to approach women respectfully, and that civilized living generally was being threatened by the "masses." In their own small way, the ladies of the club were seeking to rectify the situation, to keep "decorum" and "civilized manners" alive.

The core membership of the club was limited to twelve women, who met once a month to discuss current problems in social behavior. Each member also discussed such problems frequently with many other women they knew. The club staged a few meticulously prepared balls every year.

They did not advertise or sell tickets to the public. Instead, many weeks before the ball, each member would approach people through personal contacts to invite them to come to the ball "if tickets were still available." In a meeting a few weeks later, the members would examine the lists of the people who wanted to come. The names were carefully scrutinized and those of persons with a "bad reputation" or known to be bad-mannered were struck out. The club member who had approached them would later tell them regretfully that all the tickets had been sold. I obtained a list of all the men and women who attended the ball and during the following months I met most of these in a variety of situations, interviewed some of them at length, and also talked to most of the core members of the club.

One striking feature of the list of participants in the ball was that, apart from four Britons and one man from the provinces who was a government minister, every person on it, like all the members of the club, was Creole. The clubwomen insisted that this was sheer accident. The secretary strongly emphasized that in matters relating to manners and "culture" generally, there could be no distinction between Creoles and non-Creoles. Manners, not tribe or religion, made the man or woman; talk about tribes was passé. The club sought to cultivate civilized manners in all people, irrespective of sectional affiliations.

There is no doubt that these were genuinely held views. The sociocultural exclusiveness of the gathering can certainly be explained away on many grounds. The twelve members of the club had probably known one another since childhood, and their networks of friends and acquaintances had been developed within narrow circles in school, church, kin gatherings, and other social clubs. Since the tickets to the ball were sold informally through personal contacts, it was almost inevitable that most of the people attending would be Creoles. Moreover, some provincials may have been approached but have declined. Provincials generally do not feel at home in predominantly Creole gatherings. Also, the price of a ticket was relatively high, and few people were prepared to pay it; club members themselves were probably reluctant to ask anyone they were not certain could

25

afford the expense. Furthermore, many provincial men do not want to be seen as too intimate with Creoles, and this is particularly the case with members of the provincial elite who at one time or another have had strong Creole attachments.

Creoles have always put strong emphasis on the refinements of culture, but in the last twenty-five years their views have become progressively more emphatic and the ideology behind them more elaborate. Beginning in the early 1950's, provincials increasingly came to challenge the Creoles on their own grounds—namely, their claims to superior education. The number of provincials achieving secondary and university education has been steadily increasing. Competition for jobs and for promotion within the bureaucracy has become very intense. Increasingly, Creole candidates find themselves competing with provincials who are academically as qualified as they are.

One of the first arguments Creoles advanced in reaction to this development was that many provincials were educated in "low-status" institutions. Secondary schools in Sierra Leone are as much ranked in prestige and reputation as they are in Britain and the United States. Until recently the Creoles tended to predominate in well-established schools like the CMS Grammar School for Boys and the CMS Annie Walsh Memorial School for Girls. Provincial children, on the other hand, being latecomers to the educational scene, tended to predominate in relatively newly opened schools in Freetown and in the provinces.

Within a short time, however, the situation began to change. More provincial children now study along with Creole children in the same schools, though the proportion of Creole children in the secondary schools of Freetown is still much higher than their proportion of the population. In the two most prestigious schools, those just mentioned, Creole children still outnumber provincial children. It is nevertheless recognized that claims to superior formal education can no longer be maintained in principle.

Instead, the Creoles refined an ideology that emphasized and enhanced their distinctiveness in terms of "cultural" excellence. Talk to any Creole on the issue of formal education and qualifications for jobs, scholarships, or promotions, and you will almost invariably be told that education alone is an inadequate qualification. No matter how highly educated a provincial may be, "die-hard" Creoles maintain, he will never attain the same kind of "mentality" or "culture" as the Creoles. These qualities, the argument continues, are the outcome of centuries of "civilization" and can never be bought by money or achieved by formal education. This claim is made over and over again in different contexts.

In numerous conversations with Creoles, I tried to elicit the precise criteria they had in mind when advancing such claims to superiority. On one occasion I spent nearly two hours conversing with a mature, well-educated man on the subject. He had told me that education and clothes did not make the man, and that he could immediately spot a provincial even when he was wearing European clothes. I persistently inquired how an educated provincial wearing European clothes would be different from a Creole. He kept replying with phrases such as "From the way the man carries himself." "What do you mean?" I asked. "I mean his comportment, the way he talks," was the response. And again, with movements of the hand indicating posture, "The way he carries himself." When I pressed the point, he became angry at my obtuseness. In desperation and as a final statement, he said that everyone knew that the Creoles had distinct "decorum."

I had a similarly long conversation with a Western-trained, self-employed professional woman, who said that no matter how poor a Creole was, she could instantly identify him from among a crowd of similarly dressed provincials. "How?" I asked. "The Creole has 'culture' about him, distinguishing him from provincials of the same material level," was the reply.

These words and phrases—"culture," "decorum," "comportment," "air," "civilization," "deportment," "demeanor," "propriety," "the way you carry yourself"—were almost household words in Creole circles, an integral part of the Creole ideology and world view. They were tossed around in an offhand way, as if their meaning were self-evident. Yet when one looks them up in dictionaries, one is struck by their flexibility and ambiguity, and by their tendency to be used in defining one another. Demeanor is, to quote the dictionaries, one's "manner of comporting oneself toward others"; decorum is "propriety and demeanor"; comportment is "personal bearing or carriage"; deportment is "manner of conducting oneself"; and so on. The words are vague, and are given to many shades of interpretation. This is why they form part of a *mystique*, a body of symbols of obscure nature and hidden meanings.

It is in this context that we should consider an event such as the ball. The message of the occasion was this: tribalism is bad; there is no longer a distinct, particularistic group called "Creoles," but there is a group of cultured men and women who distinguish themselves in refinement, correct manner, and etiquette; they acquire these characteristics not from books or formal education but by informal processes of socialization from early childhood. The criteria are universalistic principles of social excellence that are expressed and cultivated in exclusive, legitimate gatherings of this type. The Moonlight Club ball articulated this form of distinctiveness. Through the esoteric manners which are manifest in their procedure, participants at such events convince themselves of the reality and validity of their identity.

Many other aspects of this ball and of similar performances will be discussed later. What I want to highlight at this stage is that the Creoles are in the throes of what may be described as a crisis of identity, or of the need for the redefinition of identity, amidst fundamental changes in Sierra Leone. Many of them genuinely doubt the validity of their traditional ethnic distinctiveness in Sierra Leone, and realize that there has been a great deal of "mixed blood."

During the past twenty-five years or so Creole culture has changed in many respects. Some patterns of behavior have disappeared; new patterns have emerged. Some distinctively Creole cultural patterns have been adopted by other Sierra Leoneans, and have thus ceased to be exclusively Creole or to articulate Creole distinctiveness. On the other hand, some specifically provincial patterns have been

adopted by the Creoles. On the face of it, the Creoles seem
to have become integrated with the rest of the population,
and their existence as a distinct cultural group seems to
have been lost within the sociocultural landscape of the
country. Their traditional particularism has given way to
national universalism.

Yet one need not probe very deep before discovering
that this trend towards universalism is countered by a continued trend towards a *new* particularism. The Creoles
seem to be even more exclusive than in the past. They are
now one of the most heavily and intensively ceremonialized
groups to be found anywhere. Their ceremonials are massive in scale, costly in time and resources, and highly constraining in their obligatory nature. All this despite the serious doubts expressed by many of the Creoles themselves
about the validity of the beliefs underlying these cultural
performances.

Culture as Symbolic Form

"Culture," writes Raymond Williams (1976:76), "is one of
two or three most complicated words in the English language." It is a highly ambiguous term, extensively used in
many different senses, and thus too broad in its various connotations to be useful in sociological analysis. It is indeed
astonishing that anthropologists should continue to use this
term in the global, ragbag definition of nineteenth-century
writers. In its current usage, the word often covers both
utilitarian and normative traits; both objective and subjective phenomena.

Marxist writers use the term "ideology" as a substitute.
Indeed as Anderson (1976) points out, most Western Marxists have been preoccupied principally with the definition
of ideology, mostly by interpreting and reinterpreting statements made by Marx and his followers in different contexts.
Hundreds of publications on the subject have appeared in
recent years. The most systematic and comprehensive analysis is that of Althusser (1969: 1970; 1971). What makes the
literature more confusing is that both Marx and Althusser
changed their views about ideology in the course of their

29

careers. The result is that the concept is now as confused as that of culture. Ideology has been conceived of as an epistemological concept, the process by which men know their world; as a systematic body of values, norms, and beliefs; as synonymous with all culture, including ritual and ceremonial beliefs and practices. It has been described as "false consciousness," inspired by the ruling classes to mystify people and prevent them from uncovering exploitation (and, as such, existing only in class societies). Althusser (1969:231–35), on the other hand, has emphasized that ideology is an organic part of every social identity, that it is indispensable in any society, communist or capitalist. Some writers conceive ideology as expressive of, or determined by, the relations of production; others, including Althusser, regard it as relatively autonomous, and instrumental in recreating the relations of production.

One way of avoiding some of the difficulties and ambiguities involved is to apprehend culture or ideology in their manifestations in symbolic performances that are objective and collective, and hence observable and verifiable, indicating normative patterns of action in sharp contrast to utilitarian and technical patterns.

Creole culture can thus be expressed in terms of different patterns of symbolic activity, of dramatic performances, referred to as ceremonials. Creole ceremonials differ in *form*, depending on the kind of symbols they employ, the sentiments they evoke, the social situations in which they are staged, the type of obligation they involve, and the techniques they use to ensure the potency and efficacy of their symbols. A major symbolic form is often represented as a "cult," in the sense of a body of beliefs and ceremonials devoted to persons or things.

The Creoles thus observe a church cult, a cult of the dead, the cult of Freemasonry, a cult of "family," and a cult of decorum. These cults derive from different traditional cultures but are continuously integrated with one another, to create one culture. Thus, the history of the formation of Creole society out of diverse ethnic and social groupings is also the history of the homogenization of Creole culture through the accretion of different traditions and innovations.

As will become clear later, there is "class" differentiation among the Creoles themselves. Nevertheless, their cultural traits are similar, and their important gatherings, particularly those of "family," contain both the relatively wealthy and the relatively poor, all of whom tend to display the same patterns of symbolic behavior.

Until the end of World War II, there was some differentiation within Creoledom between liberated Africans, the descendants of those rescued from slavery en route to America, and settlers, i.e., the descendants of the slaves who had been exposed to Western civilization and who were the first settlers in Freetown. The settlers regarded themselves as an "aristocracy," having lived for a long time in "civilized" countries in the West. Already during the second half of the nineteenth century, the liberated Africans had improved their status greatly by success in trade, and had begun to emulate the settlers in their lifestyle. (For details see Peterson, 1969.) After World War II, a great deal of integration between the two groups was achieved through increasing intermarriage. A high degree of cultural homogenization also occurred in their religious organization. In the past, there tended to be differentiation of status on a denominational basis. This was mainly the case between Anglicans and Methodists. However, one of the most dramatic changes in Creole culture in the last twenty-five years has been what may be described as "the anglicanization of the Methodist Church" in Freetown. The Methodist cult has been heavily ritualized. Apart from the prominence given to the sermon, the Methodists have adopted the high ritualism of the Anglican church, and there is now little difference between the two denominations in church symbolism.

The distinction made so far between the various symbolic forms in Creole culture is in many ways arbitrary. This is because these forms are highly interdependent, and often tend to combine together on the same occasion. Thus, a wedding will call for a feast for the dead in the morning, a formal church ceremony in the early afternoon, followed by a Western-type reception with speeches and toasts, and culminate in noisy African music and dancing in the evening. Communion is taken at christenings, confirmations, marriages, and deaths. The celebration of death and the dead involves beliefs and practices derived from Christianity, from traditional African rituals, and, in some cases, from Freemasonry.

Thus different symbolic forms combine to mark the same occasion, and produce the same effect on social relationships. On the other hand the same symbolic forms may mark different occasions and produce different changes in social relationships. Indeed, it will become necessary at some stages of our analysis to abandon the distinction between forms, and to analyze culture in terms of symbolic functions and dramaturgical techniques.

This interdependence between the various symbolic forms can be most clearly analyzed if it is studied developmentally. During the past twenty-five years, most Creole cultural traits have undergone change, and detailed analysis will show how change in one form has affected change in other forms. For example, many informants emphasize that during this period, Creole men have become more secular in their thinking and less observant of the traditional Christian services, and indeed Creole churches today are maintained predominantly by women. During this same period a large proportion of Creole men have become active in the rituals and organization of Freemasonry. It is easy to see the relation between the two developments. Men who are involved in this order have less time and less need for church worship.

Some change may be caused by factors and developments outside the culture, yet may produce change in the *relations* between the symbolic forms, even when these forms do not themselves change. Other changes may be produced by sheer technological development. For example, the introduction of refrigeration for corpses has turned Creole funerals into highly elaborate, extended ceremonials, by making it possible for the bereaved family network to provide food and drinks for a lavish, large-scale wake, to prepare special clothes for mourning, and to assemble a wider funeral congregation.

On the face of it, the major cultural forms of a group may

continue to survive without any apparent change for a considerable period. Yet substantial change may be brought about by subtle changes in these forms' internal structure, and in the relations between them. Culture generally has a limited repertoire. It is mainly the "a little more here and a little less there" type of development that produces change.

The Burden of Elite Culture

The ceremonials mentioned so far are non-utilitarian activities, in the sense that they are not directly the means of achieving material ends. Yet their cost in terms of time and resources is colossal.

Apart from the weekly services, many Creoles also attend classes and meetings of various sorts in the churches. From interviews with numerous men and women, it is evident that in the course of a year an average adult Creole attends several funerals, weddings, meals for the dead, parties, balls, and other ceremonial occasions. Many of the Masons, who comprise over a quarter of all adult Creole males, spend several full evenings a month in lodge activities. Until recently, absence from work to attend these ceremonials was high, even though serious attempts had been made to curtail it. Most of the funerals are now held on Sundays to avoid time lost from work (and also to avoid tying up traffic in the city). Some professional couples with a large number of relatives on both sides can hardly find time for their own children or for themselves, since they are almost daily hurrying to attend one family celebration or another, often with presents in hand. Informants complain bitterly of the burden these obligations entail, and many of them look forward to stints abroad that will free them from the constraints, tensions, and expenditure involved.

The cost in cash and other resources spent on clothing, alcoholic drinks, fees for halls, food, and services is considerable. As the community is small, one meets the same people over and over again in these ceremonials. Women do not appear on two major occasions in the same outfit, but endeavor to have a new one for each event. For weddings, many women have to have two different new outfits, the one formal, complete with wig, matching hat, handbag, shoes, and gloves, worn at the Church service and to the reception that follows it, and the other a uniform dress worn at night by all the women celebrating the wedding in one house. A wedding can involve many such parties, given simultaneously by several sponsors on either side. In the case of one wedding I attended in 1970, there were fourteen parties in fourteen different houses scattered all about the city. At the same wedding I counted about 350 women at the church service dressed in elegant outfits. With few exceptions, all wore wigs which then cost at least £15 each. Excluding the wigs, I would estimate that on the average each woman's outfit cost a minimum of £25. For funerals and mourning, the cost of the outfit is lower, but can still reach large sums. The mourning color is decided by the immediate bereaved family if no specific wishes have been expressed by the deceased. The color can be either black, navy blue, or white. White is the most expensive, as each woman in mourning must have six dresses to allow for frequent changes during the day—sweating in the heat soils dresses very quickly—and also to allow for Sunday best. The cost of clothing for men is lower than for women, though Masons have to spend a substantial amount of money on their regalia, one set for each grade.

The cost of alcoholic drinks served on these occasions is perhaps many times higher per person than the cost of clothes. In 1970 prices were generally much higher than those in Britain. Beer, whiskey, gin, and brandy particularly, are served on most occasions. During a "wake," held the night before the funeral, drinks are served throughout the night as relatives and friends come to keep the bereaved company, to sing hymns, and, particularly when the deceased is an old person, to dance. Apart from parties connected with the standard family celebrations, drinks are also served during the special ad hoc feast when persons in affliction "cook for their dead."

The food provided on these occasions is also a symbol of status and prestige. Chicken, costing two to three times what it does in Britain, is frequently served. There are many other items of expense. Invitation cards, for instance, are the most elaborate and expensive to be found anywhere. All invitations to a wedding service and reception contain a small booklet that lists the families of the couple, the bridesmaids and best men, the officiating clergymen, the organist, the chairman presiding over the reception, and the proposers and respondents of the different toasts, together with the entire service (prayers, hymns, etc.). Similar booklets are printed and distributed at funerals.

Not all the cost of these ceremonials is borne by the persons directly involved in them. All relatives and friends contribute. Contributions vary from a sum of money to a bottle of brandy or a number of chickens. On some of the occasions I attended, the family giving the ceremony did not themselves spend very much. They had saved some alcoholic drinks from previous occasions and with the help of contributions they were able to stage the ceremony with relatively little expense. But in most cases the family concerned pays the greater part of the cost, depending, of course, on their status. A feast for the dead in 1970 cost £80 on the average, exclusive of contributions received by the family staging it.

More resources are expended on other ceremonials. Balls, dinners, and celebrations of all kinds are given throughout the year by societies, clubs, and associations. The annual ball of the Medical Association, attended in 1970 by over 2,000 people, most of them Creole, cost £4 a ticket.

Inevitably expenditure on ceremonial depends on social status. Patronage is one of the most basic principles of social organization, and prominent and wealthy men are under constant pressure to sponsor or patronize this or that wedding or cause. The higher the status, the stronger the pressure. And every patron has to face the problem of deciding at what point to say no. Some are too anxious about their status to refuse, and a number of eminent men have in consequence ended up in financial difficulties.

Why do the Creoles spend so much of their resources, energies, and time in these non-utilitarian pursuits? The ceremonials certainly include pleasurable activities. Many people enjoy good food, alcoholic drink, dancing, singing, talking in company. This element of pleasure is limited, however, and is not always present. The ball described earlier in this chapter did give pleasure to many of the participants, but there was a somber air about the occasion and many participants were rather subdued. I was later told by informants that if one missed many of these balls, cocktail parties, and similar events, one would be out of circulation, and lose contact with friends and acquaintances. People would either forget one or think that one had sunk into insignificance. I attended many church services that lasted for hours, with packed congregations sitting in 90° heat. Men, women, and children seemed stifled by the conventional European clothes they wore. Children are subjected to severe discipline to teach them the rules of decorum. The cult of the dead is accompanied by a great deal of apprehension. Family ceremonials are often attended as a matter of duty, and are not always free from tension.

Thus, pleasure and recreation are not always elements in these symbolic activities. An alternative may be that we are dealing here with values and norms that have their explanation in belief and ideology. There is certainly an appreciable element of this present, but again, its significance must be qualified in many respects. Many informants complained bitterly of the heavy burden of these ceremonies and claimed they did not believe in the norms and ideologies underlying them. Whether they were describing what they actually experienced, or were only saying what they thought would be the correct thing for educated men to tell a foreigner, is not always very clear. However, there is no doubt that even the most devout, dutiful, and conforming people entertain doubts at one time or another about the validity of the beliefs and norms that are associated with these ceremonial activities. Indeed, people often begin to believe only as a result of the performance of ceremonials and not the other way round.

When pushed for a more definite answer, individual Creoles would say they conform only in deference to, or under pressure from their parents, uncles, aunts, and friends. But why do these exert such pressure? What is the nature of the impelling "ought" of the collectivity?

Identity and Closure

This constraint will be analyzed in detail in the following chapters. At this stage, it is relevant to point out briefly the effect of these ceremonials on Creole identity and exclusiveness within Sierra Leone society.

The symbolic forms discussed here are by no means uniquely Creole. Some of the elaborate ceremonials connected with the family and with the dead can be found among the other main cultural groups in the country. Similarly, Freemasonry has some non-Creole members, and is formally "universalistic" in that it is officially open to all. Moreover, the Temne and the Mende have their own cults of secrecy, the Poro for men and the Sande for women. Again, Christian worship is not a Creole monopoly, for there are almost as many non-Creole Christians as there are Creoles. In accent, clothing, housing, manners, and etiquette the Creole have no complete monopoly. Moreover, the Creoles have acquired many cultural traits from the provincials. When the formal wedding ceremony and reception end, the women hurry to their homes to change into African-style dress, and "unwind" from the burdens of decorum by dancing to the wild beat of *Gumbe* music.

Creole culture is indeed "syncretic," a blend of African and European traits, and is far from being a hollow reproduction of English culture. The symbolic forms of Creole culture are not, therefore, specifically Creole, and cannot be taken by themselves as indices of Creole identity.

However, what is sociologically significant is not the tabulation of cultural traits and the marking of their absence or presence in a collectivity of people, but the ways in which these traits affect and are affected by social relationships. Creole family ceremonials and rituals for the dead are private gatherings, and are exclusively Creole. There is a similar Creole exclusiveness in the organization and activities of the Masonic rituals. And with one or two exceptions, the scores of Creole churches are exclusively Creole too. Indeed, this tendency to organize in exclusive associations has become particularly strong in the last two decades. This is especially noticeable in associations that are not formally Creole but have a "universalistic" character, in the sense that they are not exclusive to any predefined group. For example, of the two sororities at Fourah Bay College in 1970, one was almost purely Creole. When interviewed, its secretary was emphatic that this exclusiveness was absolutely accidental. The same statement was made in relation to the membership of other associations. Again, the associations of old boys and old girls of well-known secondary schools are predominantly Creole. Creoles on the whole tend to have Creoles as intimate friends.

This exclusiveness is in many ways only natural and to be expected. The Creoles, after all, are the natives of the Freetown peninsula. From early on, they are grouped together in age sets in the churches. Their relationships in school and college are continued through other exclusive gatherings, including the Masonic lodges. In addition, they share the same lifestyle and come from similar social backgrounds, so that it is natural that they should seek one another's company. Indeed, as I show later, they are in effect related to one another as "cousins" through the ramifying kinship network.

This involvement in multiple primary relationships leaves Creole men and women little opportunity to develop similar relations with non-Creoles. Thus, even if exclusiveness is not intended, it is "in the nature of things." But whether intended or unintended, it effectively demarcates the group, and to a large extent closes its boundaries to outsiders.

These boundaries closely overlap with the boundaries of a specialized elite who command crucial positions in the state administration and exercise a great deal of power. As is the case in all systems, the members of this elite interact intensively, formally and informally, to coordinate state and public affairs. A measure of closure to outsiders becomes a political necessity. Ultimately, Creole culture is systematized, not by any kind of logic inherent in its symbols, but by the power structure of the society generally.

The Power Behind the Symbols   3

Officialdom
Professionalism
Retreat from Business
Security in Property
Recruitment through Esoteric Socialization
State Functionaries

The symbolic process involved in the formation, objectification, and definition of an elite group and of its lifestyle is intimately related to the mobilization, exercise, and maintenance of power by that group. Power is embedded in social relationships, and these are objectified and maintained by symbolic formations and activities. The two variables go together, and neither can be understood without the other, although they are not reducible one to the other. The symbolic order of the group consists of different forms that are rooted in different psychic processes and derived from different cultural traditions. The parts are brought together to form a structure, or system, in continuous interdependence with the power order.

Thus among the Creoles, the family ceremonials, church communion, decorum, Masonic rituals, and other symbolic forms do not by themselves constitute a system, but are continually systematized in the course of changing political involvements. The same men who subscribe to these forms are the men who are engaged in the struggle for power within the national polity, and the two orders are interlinked in their psyches. Their most intimate, intrinsic, spiritual beliefs are thus causally interrelated with, and conditioned by the power order. Men do not generally face the ultimate problems of human existence on their own, but are aided by the beliefs and values of the power groups to which they belong.

The Creoles, who are identified as a group of people who share an homogenous and socially enclosing culture, can also be identified as a group of people who enjoy and exercise a great deal of power in Sierra Leone. This power stems essentially from the senior positions they occupy in the civil service and the professions. Their ascendancy is also secured and perpetuated by the extensive property in land and in buildings in Freetown and the rest of the Freetown peninsula which they control. Formally, they are "individualists," achieving their elite positions by personal merit and endeavour, and their fortunes by individual inheritance and savings. However, like all other elites everywhere, they cooperate informally as a group through their culture to develop and maintain their interests, and endeavour to pass them on to their own children, so that these may succeed them and thus perpetuate their high status and privileges. Culture and power thus interact dynamically in the formation, definition, and continuity of the group in response to changing circumstances. During the past twenty-five years, the Creoles have evolved into a "state elite" specializing in the objectification, maintenance, and coordination of state institutions and functions.

Officialdom

The 1963 census of Sierra Leone gives the number of Creoles in the whole country as 41,783, only 1.9 percent of the total population of 2,180,355 (Government of Sierra Leone, 1965). They are essentially metropolitan, with 37,560 of them concentrated in the small Freetown peninsula, known during the colonial period as the Colony and since independence as the Western Area. Of these, 27,730 live in the city of Freetown and the remaining 9,830 in nearby villages, referred to in official documents as the Western Rural Area. Most of these Creole villagers commute regularly to Freetown, as the villages are just a few miles away. Indeed, many of the villages are practically suburbs of the city. Nearly all the village Creoles have kin in the city, and many of them look after land belonging to city Creoles. The 4,223 Creoles who live in the hinterland are not permanent residents, most of them being mobile government officials or teachers, many of whom leave their families and households in Freetown and travel regularly to visit them. As all land in the provinces is tribal land, they do not own land or houses at their places of work, and any property they own is in the Freetown area, to which most of them eventually return.

The 1963 census gives no detailed breakdowns for the various ethnic groups in the country. For such details, one has to rely on the 1966–67 Household Survey, which was carried out on a 10 percent sample of the population. From this survey, it can be seen that among the Creoles nearly 60 percent of the men and 50 percent of the women are employed in government institutions.

Some detailed information on the Creoles working in the civil service of Sierra Leone can be obtained from an analysis of the annual *Government Staff List*, which gives all government employees by name, sex, date of first appointment, date of present appointment, incremental date, and grade. It gives no direct information about the ethnic identity of the civil servants, as this is now prohibited by law. But if one takes the simple, though crude, criterion of identifying Creoles by European names and goes over the list with two or three good informants, one will easily be able to distinguish the Creoles from the provincials on the one hand and from the expatriates on the other. The final number may be an underestimate, because, as mentioned before, some Creoles now have African names.

Whatever method is adopted to ascertain the number of Creoles in the civil service, the proportion is colossal, probably amounting in 1970 to about 35 times their ratio of 1.9 percent of the population. In an exhaustive study, Harrell-Bond (1975:35) found the Creoles constituting 64 percent of all professionals in Sierra Leone, with the Mende and Temne, who together amount to about 60 percent of the total population, accounting for only 21 percent.

There is nothing surprising about this. The Creoles have grown up in a tradition dominated by two centuries of contact with Western education. Already during the nineteenth century, many Creoles had worked in the colonial administration, not only in Sierra Leone but all along the coast of West Africa. Their early conversion to Christianity secured for them steady education in missionary schools, and the fact that they lived in Freetown meant that they always had easy access to the best schools in the country. The income from their property, and in earlier decades from business, have enabled them to pay the expenses of long educational careers for their children.

The proportion of Creoles in the civil service has slowly declined. In 1953, it was 92 percent, but today it is much lower, although because of the steady increase in the number of posts, this does not necessarily mean a decline in absolute number. What is politically significant, however, is not the ratio of Creoles in the civil service generally, but their command of the most powerful posts in the bureaucracy. The *Report of the Commission of Inquiry into the Civil Service of Sierra Leone, 1970* (Government of Sierra Leone) shows that in 1970 there were 12,260 established posts in the civil service. Of these, 68 percent were in the Freetown area, with less than 10 percent of population of the country. The provinces, with more than 90 percent of the population, had only 32 percent of the posts. The 1,465 senior posts, of which 1,176 (over 80 percent) are in Freetown (*ibid*: 31–32), are predominantly Creole. Again, in 1970, of nineteen permanent secretaries in the various ministries, seventeen were Creoles. All provincial secretariats, and directorships of three out of four major government corporations, were held by Creoles (Jordan, 1971).

It should be emphasized that, while it is true that the Creoles have uninterruptedly worked in the state bureaucracy for a very long time, their predominance in the senior posts of the service is relatively recent. During the nineteenth century, a number of Creoles were appointed to senior positions in the colonial administration, but by the end of the century the British had changed their policy, and as those Creoles died or retired, they were replaced by Britons. In 1949, only 54 (11 percent) of 490 senior civil servants were Africans.

When decolonization began in 1950, however, in preparation for independence a decade later, the British rapidly Africanized the civil service. As most of the junior civil service positions were already held by natives, this meant the rapid replacement of senior British civil servants by Africans. At the time, very few provincials had sufficient education or experience to qualify for these posts, and it was inevitable that most of the new recruits would be Creoles. The British did their best to train Africans, particularly from the provinces, for the newly vacated jobs by giving them scholarships for further study overseas. Even so, 60 percent of the holders of those scholarships between 1951 and 1956 were Creoles (Cartwright, 1970:24). By 1962, 785 (70 percent) out of a total of 1,111 senior civil service positions were held by Creoles, and in the mid-1960s, 51 out of 74 administrative officers were Creoles (Jordan, 1971).

During the Mende-dominated SLPP (Sierra Leone People's Party) regime, most of these Creoles remained in their positions. But, as the bureaucracy expanded, new positions were created, and were given to Mendes whenever possible. After the 1967 coup, however, many of these new positions fell vacant as their holders either left the country or went to prison, and many of them were eventually given to Creoles.

The rapid ascendancy of the Creoles in the civil service has created a situation that has, in effect, informally modified the country's formal political system. When the British left in 1961, executive power was handed over to provincial politicians, while the senior administrative power was virtually handed over to the Creoles. During the colonial period, both forms of power had been held by the British, but now they were informally divided between two groups that had bitterly opposed each other for a long time. During the 1950s the major political cleavage was between the Creoles on the one hand and the provincials on the other. The SLPP, which ruled the country until 1967, was initially formed as an alliance of provincial groupings aimed at thwarting attempts by the Creoles to dominate the country, or to achieve independence in the colony. But the 1960s saw accommodation between the two sides. The overwhelming majority of the Creoles came to terms with provincial hegemony, and in their turn provincial politicians realized that they could not rule without the full cooperation of the Creoles.

Creole ascendency in the civil service has been of immense significance for the political system in the country as a whole. The SLPP was a loose coalition of diverse groups and factions, and was completely lacking in any kind of overall party organization. Its elite, who ruled from Freetown, relied for the mobilization of power and support from the country on the paramount chiefs in the provinces. As the threat of Creole domination, which had rallied the party initially, receded, the coalition began to disintegrate and to give rise to new conflicts and cleavages within its ranks. Under these circumstances, it was the Creole senior civil servants who, from behind the scenes and often in opposition to their ministers, initiated policies and regulated the functioning of the state.

As I show in later chapters, Creole civil servants in the various ministries and in different grades, both senior and junior, are related to one another by a multiplicity of primary interpersonal relationships. They are all Freetonians, were educated in a few prestigious schools, attended the same churches from childhood on, and are linked and cross-linked by bilateral and affinal relationships, as well as by relationships of friendship and comradeship. Many of them are also Masonic "brothers." These relationships are of immense significance for the functioning of the administrative system. Issues that would officially require prolonged and complicated correspondence and discussions are settled between friends and "cousins" quickly and efficiently. Inevitably, these relationships are brought to bear on the formal relationships between the same men in the bureaucratic system. Personal and bureaucratic issues become involved and interdependent.

The lines of this informal cooperation are both horizontal and vertical, across departments and ministries as well as within them. A senior official from one department deals with his counterpart in another; senior and junior officials within the same department communicate with one another informally, exchanging information and cooperating. This has inevitably given rise to suspicions among provincial civil servants and politicians, and accusations of nepotism in recruitment and in promotions have been made. However, all appointments and promotions are determined by the qualifications of the candidates involved, and all that the Creoles have needed to do to ensure their ascendency has been to uphold the rules and stick to them, and generally to try to maintain a liberal, open regime in the country, with free competition.

Professionalism

Many of the jobs in the civil service require professional training, and the Creoles have had more than a century's lead over the provincials in this respect. Early in the nineteenth century, the colonial administration sent a number of Creoles to be trained in medicine and in law. Later, as the Creoles prospered in business, a steady number of young Creoles were sent to Britain to study in the universities (for details, see Fyfe, 1962). This tradition was con-

45

tinued even when towards the end of the century the colonial administration stopped appointing Creoles to senior professional and administrative positions. During that period many of the trained Creoles went to work elsewhere in West Africa. Then, when Africanization of the civil service began in the early 1950s, a large number of Creoles were sent on scholarships for university training, and many of those who had worked outside Sierra Leone came back and were appointed to senior positions in government.

Few of the professionals begin their careers in self-employment. Most of them take up government jobs for a while, continuing their training by refresher courses abroad and by gaining experience, and then retire early, or leave before retirement, in order to work privately in their own professions. But even when they work privately, these professionals are associated with state institutions in a variety of ways. Indeed it is in the very essence of the professions that they attend to modern public interests and not to private advantage alone.

Of great political significance has been the Creole role in the judicial process. In many ways the State is but a body of laws that are legislated, kept alive, and applied by a body of professionally trained people working as public functionaries in the service of the State or practising privately. In 1969, three of the four members of the Court of Appeal were Creoles; the fourth was a Ceylonese. Of the nine members of the Supreme Court, six were Creoles, one was Mende, one Aku, and one Gambian. Of the twenty-seven lawyers employed by the government in the country, fourteen were Creoles. And of the forty-four barristers and solicitors practising privately in the whole country, twenty-six were Creoles. The Creoles are also predominant in the various senior administrative positions in the Ministry of Justice.

A second profession dominated by the Creoles has been medicine, which has figured even more prominently in the Creole tradition of professionalism. As law is related to politics and to the State, the Creoles had not been particularly encouraged by the British to take it up. But the case of medicine was different. Early in the nineteenth century already, the British sent Creoles to be trained as doctors. It had been costly for the government to keep British doctors in Sierra Leone, and those who had been so employed were decimated by disease (see Easmon, 1956).

Another kind of medical "practitioner" has been the licenced druggist, many of whom had been mobile, administering drugs for minor, and sometimes major, ailments. In a population with poor and inadequate medical services, the boundaries between druggists and doctors are not always maintained. In 1969, there were eighteen government-licensed druggists, of whom fifteen were Creoles, two Mende, and one Sherbro (the Sierra Leone *Daily Mail Year Book*, 1969). Both doctors and druggists who work for the government tend to go on to private practice after early retirement from government service. The druggists tend to combine curing and dispensing with business as general chemists, selling a variety of hygiene and cosmetic articles.

Creole predominance in teaching can be easily understood if one remembers that for many decades all schools were concentrated in Freetown, and that it was the Christian missions who introduced, developed, and organized modern education in the country. Creoles dominate the profession from nursery school to university. At Fourah Bay College, most of the African teaching and administrative staff are Creoles.

Closely related to education in Sierra Leone are the clergy. Fourah Bay College was originally founded as a missionary college for the training of African clergymen who would spread and consolidate Christianity in the hinterland as well as in the rest of West Africa. Until the 1950s, clergymen enjoyed a status of prestige and respect reflected in both relatively high income and in deference. They used to give reference for good behaviour. Families used to endeavour to have one or more of their sons trained as clergymen. But during the last two decades, the income of the clergy has fallen behind, and new opportunities were opened in other white collar professions. Recently, some men from other professions or from business have sought prestigious status by being ordained.

Other professional pursuits dominated by the Creoles include journalism, literature, and engineering (with thirty-one out of forty government-licensed surveyors in 1970 being Creoles).

Retreat from Business

Viewed retrospectively, this developing specialization in "state eliteness" among the Creoles has been associated with the dramatic loss of their niche in business. During the second half of the nineteenth century, the Creoles dominated trade in European goods and foodstuffs, and large numbers of Creole traders were actively operating in various parts of the mainland. But by the early decades of the present century, they were rapidly losing their hold on business. The reasons for this decline have been the subject of speculation by a number of writers.

The decline was linked to various developments, involving a number of factors operating contemporaneously, and it cannot therefore be attributed to one single factor. The Hut Tax War waged by people from the protectorate in 1898 was directed against the Creoles as much as it was against the British, and a large number of Creole businessmen, officials, and missionaries were killed.

At about the same time, and certainly during the following years, there was a sharp change in British policy in the administration of the country. The British sought consistently to reduce Creole power in the administration, and to prevent the Creoles from establishing political dominance over the provincials. Many Creoles believe that, as part of this change in policy, the British intentionally encouraged Lebanese, Indian, and European businessmen to replace the Creoles in trade.

These developments coincided with the depression of the 1920s and 1930s, when businesses everywhere became risky and insecure. Creole business organization had until then been on a small scale. In the best of times, the businessman had had to maintain a precarious balance between lavish spending in response to heavy kinship obligations and saving to maintain and develop business. As the years rolled on, the scale of business generally had to expand, and organization on a large scale became necessary. As this called for the employment of people from outside the immediate family, problems of trust and responsibility led to the collapse of many businesses.

At about the same time, considerations of prestige and job security led Creole businessmen to spend fortunes on the education of their children both at home and abroad. Education became the major form of investment, since it was the channel leading to secure, well-paid jobs in the civil service and the professions.

The Creole tradition of building the family house and, generally, of investment in real estate, i.e., in land and housing, now began to yield significant dividends. Since the end of World War II there had been a growing demand for land and housing in the Freetown area, and many Creoles became small-scale rentiers, getting a steady income from letting their houses, shops, and lands to people from the protectorate and to foreign businesses, particularly the Lebanese.

As a result of these different processes, Creole businesses dwindled significantly, with most Creole men concentrating their resources and energies on education, the civil service, and the professions, and with real estate serving as a basis of security and financial consolidation.

This does not mean that the Creoles are today completely uninvolved in business and trading activities, but only that their role in these is no longer significant. There are a fair number of Creole women engaged in small-scale petty trading in the market place, selling mainly farm products, principally vegetables, supplied by farmers from the villages of the peninsula. Most of the land in those villages belongs to Creoles who live and work in Freetown, but is managed by poorer relatives. The Creole villagers do not engage in farming themselves, but usually lease the land to migrant farmers from the provinces. The products are transported daily to Freetown markets, where Creole village women sell them.

Another category of business is conducted by retired Creole men. Retirement age in the civil service is between

45 and 55. This is a "hangover" from the colonial period, when expatriate civil servants were retired early to compensate them for working overseas under harsh conditions, often away from their families and homes. This early retirement age was retained in many African states after independence in order to ensure a relatively rapid turnover of personnel. In slowly developing economies, the number of educated and trained personnel is growing without a corresponding growth in the number of suitable positions in public administration. A quick turnover of personnel will, therefore, prevent the growth of bitterness and resentment among the newly educated who seek appointment and promotion.

With some cash that he receives on retirement, a man may start a small business, such as a petrol station, running a hall to let for weddings and other ceremonies, or a small retail shop. Very few of these enterprises succeed, however, because of the lack of expertise and business sense.

At the 1970 Creole Convention (see chapter 6, below), there was strong agitation for the development of Creole business to absorb educated young Creoles, who according to the gathering were being discriminated against in employment in the public sector. There was also a movement among some professionals and public employees, who had saved money from letting houses and from their own high incomes, to invest their money in business.

On the whole, however, this was all in the realm of expressing intentions, and nothing practical resulted. Creole culture, ideology, family structure, the socialization of the young, all are essentially geared to the training and organization of an educated meritocracy, principally for state employment. Graduation ceremonies, ceremonies for going to or returning from training abroad, or for appointments or promotions, are as significant as initiation or marriage ceremonies. The Creole "extended family" and the Creole cousinhood created by it are particularly structured for cooperation in the educational sphere and in mobility in the job. And the values inculcated in Creole children throughout socialization have nothing to do with a business ideology or ethos. From very early in life, the Creole is trained both formally and informally in the ways of state officialdom and professionalism.

Security in Property

More significant than business as a source of power and privilege, is the Creoles' control over a large tract of freehold land and houses in the city of Freetown and the adjacent villages. This is a recognized fact well-known to both Creoles and non-Creoles, though very difficult to document and quantify, except by circumstantial evidence.

It must be remembered that the Creoles founded and developed the city and the villages of the peninsula, where they have maintained unbroken residence for nearly two centuries. Throughout all this time, the Creoles have continually increased their land and housing estates. Land has always been the principal form of secure investment and hedge against inflation in a highly uncertain and fluctuating economy. During the nineteenth century Creole businessmen invested much of their profits in the purchase of land, which became the criterion of social status in Freetown (see Peterson, 1969:271–78; Fyfe, 1962; 1968).

As Fyfe (1968:6) states: "Wealth in Freetown was (and to a large extent still is) literally grounded in the city. From the earliest days house property was the principal investment outlet. Those who saved put their capital into building or buying houses. . . . Urban wealth reinforced urban growth. . . . Corporate wealth too was invested in Freetown property. Church members formed trusts to manage church property giving the trustees the experience of corporate ownership. Similarly, private trusts were formed to control family land."

Thus, while the Creoles have been urban landlords for a long time, the provincial immigrants coming to the capital or to the peninsula were for decades mainly unskilled labourers or tenant farmers, and without capital. It is only lately that some provincials have been coming with money from diamond digging to buy houses.

Most of the Creoles I interviewed lived in their own houses, and many reported having rights in other houses in Freetown as well as landholdings in the villages. There are whole streets in Freetown whose houses are owned by Creole families who live on the first floor and let the ground floor as shops. The houses of other streets are known to be owned by Creoles but are let to others, provincials or foreigners. Many of the villas in and around Freetown have been built in recent years by Creoles, and are let to foreign embassies and business organizations. A significant number of civil servants, university teachers, and others live in government-owned houses at nominal cost, and let their own houses in town to tenants at high rents. The bulk of the lands in the villages in the peninsula are Creole-owned, and are leased to provincials for cultivation. The rate payers' associations in Freetown, which have played a significant role in the city and in the Creole political movement for achieving autonomy in the peninsula, are overwhelmingly Creole in membership. A number of Creole families are known to have vast estates in the area.

Land and houses have greatly appreciated in value since the end of World War II, more particularly so since independence, because of an increasing demand by foreign diplomatic and trade missions, by wealthy provincials, and by the rapidly expanding government administration. It should be remembered that throughout the Freetown peninsula land is freehold, while everywhere else in the country it is still considered tribal property and cannot be sold, only leased. Thus a provincial can invest money in property only in the peninsula. And indeed, many of the provincials who have accumulated money in one way or another have been pressing to buy property in Freetown. They want not only a secure investment, but also a base in the capital, where economic and political power is concentrated, and where the bulk of government administration and all the important schools are located.

One of the dramatic developments occurring in this respect has been the increasing centralization of the administration of the country in the wake of independence. During the colonial period, the British tended to decentralize the administration under the policy of indirect rule. They had developed Bo as the protectorate capital, in which they had a whole administrative setup. After independence, this policy was reversed and most of the administrative establishment at Bo was transferred to Freetown. This concentration of administrative and of political and economic institutions in Freetown has inevitably increased the attraction of the city to different categories of provincials, and has led to an ever-increasing influx of the wealthy and the elite from the provinces, which has created an even greater demand for land and housing.

In 1962, the Land Development Act No. 61 was passed, prohibiting the sale of land to foreigners, but the demand for real estate continued to rise, and Creole owners have been under strong pressure to sell. A few of them, thinking the future insecure for Creoles in the country, were said to have sold some of their property and sent the money abroad. On the whole, however, very few Creoles have succumbed to such temptations, and the majority continue to hold on to their property.

Although most of the Creoles who formerly lived in the villages of the peninsula have long since moved to Freetown, they have kept their village land-holdings, sometimes without even letting them to tenant cultivators. There is a belief, or an ideology, that sooner or later minerals, or even oil, will be discovered in these rural areas. Thus, despite political threats, alluringly high prices, and the dwindling ratio of Creoles in relation to the population of the country, the tendency has been for them not only to continue to hold the estates they own, but when possible to add to them. Associated with this tendency of the Creoles to accumulate and maintain estate holdings are two major cultural mechanisms: the institution of the "family house" and the cult of the dead (see chapter 4, below).

In Creole ideology, a man does not fulfill his mission in this life and make a success of it if he does not bequeath a house to his descendants. It is therefore one of the principal aims in the life of a man to build his own family house.

When he dies, he will certainly ask in his will that the house be kept as a family house, which means that his children will not be able to sell or divide it. It has been estimated that 10 percent of Freetown houses are undivided property of this sort. In recent years, even women have been building their own family houses. This trend has been particularly intensified by the instability of Creole conjugal relations, and by the rapidly increasing entry of Creole women into the labour market.

At the same time, the Creoles are severely inhibited from selling their property by their reverence for, and fear of, the dead. As the dead are believed to continue to live in their houses and to be associated with the land they held during their lifetime, the alienation of these holdings to strangers is a betrayal of the trust of the dead and is fraught with serious mystical dangers. For if the dead are angered, they can inflict a great deal of harm. Men *can* sell houses and land that they themselves have acquired during their own lifetimes, but cannot do so with the estate they have inherited.

Thus a large number of Creole houses are not sold, even when their owners do not need them, and even when their market value is temptingly high. In 1970 one could frequently find old, tottering houses interspersed with some of the most modern and expensive high-rise buildings in the centre of Freetown on plots that are worth a good deal of money. The owners of these old houses were often subjected to a great deal of pressure by developers to induce them to sell, without much success.

This freehold property is of immense, though indirect, economic and political significance for the Creoles. In the first place, it is the basis of security for both individuals and the group. The steady income that accrues from it gives the Creoles the privilege of commanding goods and services. More fundamentally, it contributes significantly in the battle for education, and hence for the continual recruitment of young Creoles to the professions and to administrative positions. Education in Sierra Leone, in all of its stages, is very expensive. Furthermore, the concentration of Creole property in Freetown and its surroundings places the Creoles conveniently near the best schools in the country, and in the centre of jobs and opportunities.

More important, this property is also politically significant. Many Creoles believe that as long as they continue to control much of the land and houses of the peninsula, they will be able to maintain their privileged position in the country. They will continue to be truly "the owners of the land" in this area, and will thus be the hosts to the provincials and the government.

The relation between property and politics is not a new development in Freetown. As early as 1909, three ratepayers' associations were established in the city, one for the East Ward, one for the West Ward, and a third for the Central Ward. They were formed for purposes of election to the Freetown Council, their three thousand members being the only residents who had the right to vote in a total population of 34,000 (see Kilson, 1966:221). Each association had a president, vice-president, financial secretary, treasurer, general secretary, and executive council. They collected membership fees and held regular monthly meetings. The overwhelming majority of the members were Creoles.

Within a short time, the associations assumed responsibility for social services in matters of health, sanitation, and welfare, and became active socially and culturally. More significantly, they played an active part in the political events of the five decades following their foundation. It is significant that they came into being at about the time when the British had changed their policy and stopped appointing Creoles to senior administrative positions. After an unbroken succession of Creole mayors in Freetown, moreover, the office was consistently given to Europeans from 1930 to 1954.

Thus the combined ratepayers' associations assumed political functions in the course of time. In 1948 they forced the colonial government to include their representatives on the committee which had been set up to amend the Freetown Municipality Ordinance. The associations were among

55

the most active Creole groupings in opposing the 1947 constitutional proposals. In 1950 they became part of the alliance behind the National Council of Sierra Leone (NCSL), an almost all-Creole party which was formed to oppose the coming to power of the provincials and to demand independence for the Colony (i.e., the Freetown peninsula). A party of die-hard Creoles, the NCSL served as the opposition until it was defeated in the 1957 election. In that year, the franchise for election to the council was widened; the holding of property as a qualification was abolished, and the basic requirement for eligibility to vote became simply residence on the date of registration. From that time on the associations lost a great deal of their political significance, and national party politics began to penetrate the city council (for details see Sierra Leone Government, 1969; Pratt, 1968:154–65).

This did not mean that the Creoles completely lost power in the government of the city. Many of the officials remain Creoles; among the offices they hold are the all-important position of town clerk and several other positions that require technical training. There is no doubt that Creole landlords exercise a good deal of influence in local politics. On the whole, however, Creole ownership of land and building properties do not play a *direct* crucial role in the politics of the country.

Recruitment through Esoteric Socialization

Creole positions in the bureaucracy and in the professions are achieved mainly by personal merit in an essentially liberal and competitive system, and the single most important key to them is educational attainment. The educational system, from nursery school through primary, secondary, and college education to overseas training, is an open one, and in principle offers all sections of the population equal opportunity. But a number of factors have combined to enable the Creoles to make the most out of it, with the result that up to the present a far greater proportion of their children have achieved educational success than have those of the provincials. Among these factors are Christianity, a long history of educational experience, accessibility, steady and secure income, and the support of poorer Creole children by wealthier relatives. School admission is generally decided on the basis of merit, but priority is given in well-established secondary schools to children whose parents have attended them. As these schools have existed for many decades, and as generations of Creole men and women had been through them, this inevitably favours Creole children.

But access to formal education is only half the battle, and is not by itself sufficient to secure ultimate success. As E. G. Cohen (1971) shows, there are informal cultural factors that significantly affect Creole success. The major factors are language, religion, and sustained socialization for achievement. The formal language of education is English, which almost every Creole can communicate in. This is the language of the church and the language of the bureaucracy. Many of the children come to school with the ability to speak and understand English. In predominantly Creole schools, children are punished when they do not speak in English, and in many professional Creole homes parents insist that their children speak English. Thus most Creole children come to school already conversing in the language of the school and their success in acquiring the skills of reading, writing, and thinking in this language is almost assured.

The second factor is religion. Most of the leading status schools are still Christian, as are the Creoles. The ideology and culture in these schools is thus familiar to the Creole child.

A third reason, perhaps related to religious ideology, is socialization for achievement. The Creole family is achievement-oriented, with the growing child seeing all round him the success story of professionalism, with its privileges, security, and esteem. This is accompanied by systematic attempts by both the family and the school to train the child to work systematically. Discipline is often harsh and the pressure on the children to succeed is unrelenting.

Added to all this is the importance of the dominant role that the Creoles play in running all stages of the educational system in both teaching and administration. This means that Creole children are often taught by relatives and friends of their families with the same culture and value system.

State Functionaries

The Creoles have little or no executive power in Sierra Leone. From the early 1950s government passed gradually—and on independence in 1961 completely—into the hands of provincial politicians, most of whom were at the time hostile to the Creoles. The Creoles also lack any source of potential physical force. There are few Creoles in the police or the army, and they have neither the ability, the tradition, nor the organization to mobilize physical force from among their ranks.

Their role in the economy as producers of tangible goods is negligible. They are, of course, economically privileged in the sense that their income per capita is higher than that of the rest of the population. Nearly 60 percent of gainfully employed Creoles work for the government in secure jobs, with steady incomes, and sometimes fringe benefits. They also have steady income from the leasing of their land and houses. With income from both sources, they can command a good deal of goods and services. But because of their small numbers, their weight as consumers is not great. They do derive some kind of power as landlords in possession of the relatively scarce supply of housing and land. But their most valuable properties—modern houses in Freetown—are let mainly to foreigners. As ratepayers in Freetown, they have in the past played a significant role in municipal politics, but with the extension of the franchise and the entry of the national parties into local politics, that role has become less important. In business, the Creoles' role is very small indeed, and the few enterprises they command are small in scale and have perennially hovered on the margins of bankruptcy.

Privilege tends, however, to breed more privilege. Creole success in business during the latter half of the nineteenth century helped in the education and training of the next generation, who were thus recruited to professionalism. It also led to the amassing of more property, which in its turn yielded income that was invested in the education of yet more Creole children. The conversion of one resource into another can be seen in the biographies of individuals, not just over generations. A man may start off with a university education paid for by his father, become a civil servant, acquire property by inheritance or from savings, and retire early enough to establish some kind of business. This is a fairly frequent pattern.

The Creoles, however, exercise power derived from their command of the higher posts in state bureaucracy and from the professions. In almost all political systems, the senior bureaucrats not only advise ministers but also initiate and carry out a great deal of public policy. They are part of the "state elite," wielding state power as a distinct and separate entity. "The fact that the government does speak in the name of the state and is formally *invested* with state power, does not mean that it effectively *controls* that power. . . . Everywhere and inevitably the administrative process is also part of the political process; administration is always political as well as executive, at least at the levels where policy-making is relevant, that is to say in the upper layers of administrative life" (Miliband, 1973:47). Thus the hundreds of senior Creole civil servants wield a great deal of power in running the Sierra Leone state.

It can, of course, be argued, as Marxists often do, that the State is an instrument working in the interests of the ruling class—in the case of Sierra Leone, the traditional chiefs together with business interests—or in the interests of the capitalist system generally, or of neocolonialism, and that Creole power is, therefore, ultimately derived from the economic interests which they serve. This may be the case, but I am concerned here only with discussing the part played by the Creoles in state organization as it was in 1970.

The Network of Amity
and Its Ceremonials

The Web of "Family" Connections
Links through Property
Collaboration in the Battle for Education
The Grand Cousinhood and Its Ceremonials
Cult of the Dead

The elite collaborate informally through their exclusive network of amity—a web of primary relationships which are governed by moral rights and obligations, and objectified and kept alive in the course of frequent, elaborate, and costly ceremonials.

A man aspiring to identify with the elite may succeed in acquiring such external markers as accent, housing, clothing and other items of conspicuous consumption. But he will not thereby become automatically affiliated within the power elite and partake in their privileges. To do so, he must achieve the much more difficult task of "grafting" himself onto the inner network of primary relationships which link the members of the group together. It is this inner, highly exclusive, network which provides the real basis of identity and serves as a system of channels for collaboration in developing and maintaining the interests of its members.

In large-scale industrial societies, such networks of privilege are highly extensive and complex. They consist of different types of primary relationships: kinship, affinity, friendship of different sorts, comradeship within different clubs, professional gatherings, old-boy groupings, fraternities, and so on. Imagine the men and women of such a power group as being represented in a diagram by dots, and the relationships between them by lines of different colours, each type of relationship being represented by one colour. The diagram would then present different sectional networks, each in a different colour, partly overlapping and partly cross-cutting one another. Each sectional network would tend to be developed and maintained by a different body of symbolic forms and activities. To comprehend how the total network functions, we need to discover ways in which the different sectional networks are interrelated, and to construct the total "culture," or the body of symbolic forms and ceremonials that sustain it. The differently coloured sectional networks need to be "translated" in terms of one unified colour standing for the total network which is supported by one unified body of symbols. The relationships making up this total network are not contractual, but essentially moral and normative, relying on categorical imperatives that make demands on the totality of the person. They therefore need to be repetitively created and recreated through different types of ceremonials, exploiting different kinds of psychic resources. It is this complexity of the network and of its culture that make the study of power elites in a large-scale society so difficult. And it is here that the Creole case can shed some light, by showing closely the nature of the interconnections between network and ceremonial in the development of an elite.

The Creole network is also complex, consisting of relationships of friendship, of ritual brotherhood and parenthood, of old school links, and so on. But because of their small number, their concentration in one locality, and their tendency to marry within their group, the Creoles have tended to articulate their total network in the idiom of one institution, the cousinhood, which is maintained by frequent, extensive, and expensive "family" ceremonials.

The Web of "Family" Connections

When you ask a Creole what he means by "family," he is likely to smile patronizingly and say: You foreigners cannot understand this; the family with us is an extended family; it is an African family. But as you press further in your enquiry about the composition of this "family," the complexity of the problem becomes clear.

In the first place, the Creoles do not put any special emphasis on either patrilineal or matrilineal descent. Relations are traced in both lines, and property is inherited according to British civil law, without favoring one line over the other. Men freely decide on whether to adopt the family name of their father or of their mother, usually depending on which of the two is associated with the higher prestige. In some cases they adopt both names, linking them with a hyphen. On marriage, a woman may adopt her husband's family name, or retain her father's or mother's name, or hyphenate one of her parents' names with that of her husband.

There are many other deviations from Western family norms. The nuclear family consisting of husband, wife, and children, as we know it, is among the Creoles the exception rather than the rule. A survey conducted in primary schools in Freetown revealed that only about a third of the children were living with their father and mother (Toth, 1969:25–30). Another third were living with only one of the two parents, and the remaining third were living with other adults, to whom they might or might not be related. There was no significant difference between Creole and non-Creole children in these respects.

Some Creole girls begin their sexual careers when they are still in high school by taking as lovers men who are almost always much older than themselves, and of a higher social status than their parents or guardians. Some of these girls eventually become pregnant and have children. Informants say that in the past there was a good deal of stigma attached to such children or to their mothers. Men were reluctant to acknowledge their paternity, and the children used to bear the family name of the mother. Whether or not this was actually the case in the past, today these children, whom the Creoles call "outside children," are given the name of the genitor at christening. In the party following, he puts in a brief appearance. The father finances the celebrations and contributes to the upkeep of the child. Most high-status Creole men, including respectable clergymen (see Fashole-Luke, 1968 : 136) have "outside children" who publicly bear their names.

One of the peculiarities of Creole social organization is the numerical preponderance of females over males. This sexual imbalance is made more serious by the fact that men, who generally struggle hard to achieve status, marry at a late age, while women start their sexual lives at about fourteen. And as the Creoles are Christian and pride themselves on being monogamous, many of the women are without husbands. While a few of them remain unattached to any one man, many develop permanent or semi-permanent extramarital relations. Some of these will, intentionally or unintentionally, have children; others will not. Some of the men involved will be already married, while others may not. In some cases the men who are not already married will eventually marry their "sweethearts" (as they call them in Krio) and take over normal custody of the children; but many men will not. When single men eventually marry, they often succeed in persuading their future brides to adopt their outside children. Those who are already married may even persuade their legal wives to take their outside children into their household. These wives often agree, particularly if they themselves happen to be barren, but on condition that the husband sever his relationship with the mother of such children. The "outside mothers" accept this condition, and give away their children to be fostered in their lovers' houses, because the father is likely to give them a much better education and a higher standard of living than the mothers themselves could give. Also, relief from the burden of caring for illegitimate children will leave these mothers free to pursue an occupational career or to marry and have a new family. In Creole society, as in some other West African societies, families do not experience the intense relationships between parents and children which are characteristic of many families in a Western society. Even in unbroken families, it is not unusual for one or both of the parents to leave their children in the care of relatives, sometimes for years, so that they can travel abroad to study or work.

Further complexity is introduced into the Creole family by two other institutions. One is fostering; the other is the ward system. Children from poor families may be fostered and brought up by the family of one of their well-to-do relatives. Through the ward system, provincial families from the hinterland give one or more of their children to be brought up in the household of a Creole family. Some Creole households have one or more wards, but for a variety of reasons this institution is declining. In some cases the ward is assigned domestic tasks and in return is given some kind of education, but equally often the ward is treated as one of the family. In the past, many of these wards eventually achieved a high degree of education, became Christian, and adopted the name of the fostering family. Indeed there are some prominent men in Sierra Leone who were brought up in this manner.

It is evident from all this that under these circumstances it is almost impossible to establish any clear boundary for the group a man will call "my family." Almost invariably he will include within it some remote parental cousins, together with people who are related to him by affinity. He will also include friends as members of the "family," and in response to protest will argue: "They are of course members of my family. When I am ill they help me, when I go abroad they cook for me."

One point that stands out immediately in this situation is that even if only two generations in the genealogy of a man are traced and followed through the ramifications of both lines, the number of relatives will be very great. If all the other links are added, those who are potential members of a "family" will be so numerous that they may include the whole of Creoledom, particularly if one remembers that this is a small, localized, highly exclusive community, concentrated in a relatively small town. It is indeed no exaggeration to say that any Creole can trace some kind of kinship relationship to every other Creole. No sooner do two Creoles develop a friendship than they "discover" a link that shows that they are cousins. And there are always "knowledgeable men," respected for their vast "knowledge" of all family links, just as there are professional genealogists in some other societies.

But it is, of course, highly impractical for any person to have a family of this magnitude. A man will have neither the time, nor the energy, nor the resources to maintain close relationships with so many people. He will therefore be forced to limit the size of his family. That size will be finally determined by the reciprocity of obligations that he develops and maintains with a selection of relatives.

For the Creoles, as for people generally, obligation towards kin is a categorical moral imperative which has value in its own right. A Creole will be genuinely offended if any suggestion is made to the effect that his relationships with his kin are partly utilitarian. It is nevertheless a fact that Creole kinship relationships are instrumental in the regulation of cooperation in housing, in holding property, in education, in getting jobs, and in fixing matters with the bureaucracy.

Links through Property

Almost invariably, a man will ask his family not to divide or sell his family house after his death. Often this is done in a written will, and is thus given legal support. Much greater support, however, is provided by the beliefs and practices which form part of the cult of the dead, which is one of the most important institutions of Creoledom. As the spirit of the deceased will continue to live in the house he or she has bequeathed, it can be calamitous to sell the property to strangers. Indeed, when under some circumstances a family is forced to sell such a house, they have to go through a good deal of explanation and argument with the dead. They hold feasts for them and beseech them to move with them to a different house.

As the number of descendants of the founder of a family house increases, and as all the men among these and a few of the women will eventually manage to build their own family houses, it becomes impracticable for all the descendants to live in that house. In some cases, one descendant will live there and take care of the repairs and maintenance, while the others retain the right to seek accommodation in the house whenever they need to do so. In other cases, the house is let by the descendants to a tenant, and after deducting maintenance costs they distribute the proceeds among themselves. There are many other ways in which the family house may be used. In any case, it remains an important factor—economically, sentimentally, and ritually—binding a number of kin together. And in the hour of need everyone can make use of his "right," whether legal or moral, to have free accommodation in such a house. Usually a man will have such rights in more than one house, through patrilateral, matrilateral and, sometimes, affinal links.

Collaboration in the Battle for Education

Another fundamental link between kin is that of cooperation in the field of education and professional training. As the Creoles are essentially civil servants and professionals, their only method of recruiting their children to these statuses is through education. There is no free education in Sierra Leone, whether on the primary or the higher school levels. All children must pay fees and the main struggle for education is first and foremost the struggle for fees. As there are some relatively poor Creoles, as well as wealthy ones, it might be expected that the wealthy would always produce the successful professionals while the poor would fail to do so. But the Creole system is such that any child who has the intelligence and the ability, whether he or she is from poor or wealthy parents, has the opportunity for full development. All Creole children go to school. When parents are not able to pay the fees, it becomes the obligation of one of their kin to do so. Sometimes kinsmen not only pay the fees but are forced by moral pressure to take the child into their homes and to bring him/her up together with their own children.

Furthermore, kin often make it possible for married students to leave their wives and children, or only their children, behind in the care of relatives so they can spend a period of further education and training abroad, sometimes lasting for many years. Many Creoles pursue higher education and training in "hops," with periods of training alternating with periods of work. A woman whose child is being or has been educated and brought up by a wealthy relative may reciprocate by looking after the relatives' small children, thus making it possible for both husband and wife to pursue a professional career. Some poor relatives are employed as nannies, or baby-sitters in the homes of their wealthier kin. Again, Creole professionals and civil servants working in the provinces or abroad in other African countries often leave their children in the custody of relatives to be educated in Freetown. It is no exaggeration to state that the organization of the Creole family and household and the Creole style of life are geared to the full mobilization of capacities and resources for the production of professionals and civil servants.

The Grand Cousinhood and Its Ceremonials

On a higher level of organization, when the whole of the Creole community is considered corporately, these "family" relationships emerge as a dense network of kinship relationships, consisting of overlapping "families" and forming one Grand Cousinhood. This cousinhood provides channels for cooperation in more general economic and career matters. The civil bureaucracy in any country is slow, and its work is beset by procedural formalities and complications. For a group like the Creoles, who own property, demand education, and seek appointments, promotions, and social and cultural associations, claims on the bureaucracy are great. As is the case in many other countries, both developed and developing, the most effective way of operating under these circumstances is through informal personal contacts. Indeed, as I show in detail later, no bureaucratic establishment can operate effectively without such informal links, even in matters of government. Among the Creoles such contacts are made through "cousins," and the network of cousinhood is literally coextensive with the whole of Creoledom in Sierra Leone.

But before elaborating on this point, I must return to the discussion of "family" ceremonials. Two major points stand out from the analysis so far. The first is that family relationships are fundamental for a Creole in education and training, in holding property, in the smooth running of his affairs, in finding a job, in promotion, in fixing matters with the bureaucracy and in the maintenance of mutual cooperation in a wide variety of domestic matters. The second is that there are no clear prescribed principles for defining the extent and limit of family relationships, and hence of obligations, with the result that there is a good deal of selectivity from among a large number of potential kinsmen.

It is essentially in this last respect that the extensive and intensive Creole family ceremonials should be understood. To put it bluntly, your "family" consists of the persons who come, with presents and contributions in hand, to eat, drink, and dance or grieve in your ceremonials. If a relative fails to come to a succession of your ceremonials without an acceptable excuse, then to all intents and purposes that person ceases to be a member of your family. If, on the other hand, a mere "friend" were to participate frequently in your ceremonials, he would in due course become a "cousin," as it is not too difficult within such a kinship system to discover an appropriate link.

The situation is far more dynamic than the Creoles are conscious of, or would like to admit. In almost every family ceremony that is staged there are new "relatives" joining in and other "relatives" opting out. A person's potential kinship network changes and ramifies all the time, forever creating new possibilities of having more relatives. Every new marriage within the family network gives access to new "families." Close friends are eventually "hooked" onto the family network. Generally speaking, the wealthier and the more influential the person, the larger the number of people who will be keen on joining his or her ceremonials.

But, as it is impossible for any man to activate, keep alive, and exhaust all of his potential kinship relationships, some relatives gradually lose touch with him, and fade out of his ceremonials. Others may pick a quarrel over one or another of the many issues that bedevil family relationships, and cease to participate.

Creole professionals and other successful men and women usually attempt to interact socially more with those relatives who are of equal status than with relatives who are of a lower status. Although the Creoles generally are a privileged status group in Sierra Leone, there are inequalities among them. Until the outbreak of World War II, there was a sharp cleavage between a small Creole "aristocracy," based on much inherited wealth and on achieved high professional statuses, and a larger number of Creoles who were relatively poor. The higher status families tended to be not only Anglican but also affiliated with prestige churches, more particularly with St. George's Cathedral. They also tended to identify themselves as "settlers" in origin, i.e., as the descendants of slaves who had actually lived in the United States, and thus been exposed to Western civilization, before coming to the country.

But the situation changed drastically after World War II. During the war years, the British had established army workshops, particularly at Hastings and Juba, where a large number of Creoles were employed at fairly high wage rates. Many of these saved enough money to finance higher education for themselves or for their children, and also to buy property. When the British began to Africanize the civil service during the 1970s, many of these were employed by the government.

In this way a new large Creole "middle class" developed, practically bridging the gap between the higher and the lower sections of Creole society. Today, the most significant "class" differentiation within Creoledom is related to educational attainment, with the qualified professionals at the top and the less qualified below them. Property is still important in determining status, but tends to be intimately related to educational attainment, on the ideological assumption by the Creoles that the one affects the other. The picture that emerges is of an upper class of professionals who are also property holders and control high positions in the state bureaucracy. These are followed by school teachers, junior civil servants, clerks in private organizations, and salesmen. Below these are some petty traders, and skilled and semiskilled workers.

Many Creoles complain that when a man rises in status, he tries to sever his relationships with his poorer relatives. Successful men, on the other hand, complain of the incessant demands made on their resources and time by needy relatives. They will tend to invite men of equal status to some of their parties, and to neglect to invite their poorer relatives. They will also tend to ignore some of the invitations of these relatives to the latter's own parties and festivities. If these tendencies were allowed to operate fully, the consequences would be the development of a deep division on "class" lines within Creoledom, which would be disintegrative of Creole unity in their confrontation with other groups.

Cult of the Dead

The threat of the development of a class cleavage within Creoledom is thus always present, but it is counterbalanced by one major force—the mystical powers of the dead. It is principally the cult of the dead which brings the upwardly moving status-seeker into the fold of the "family." Family ceremonials are occasions for communicating with the dead. In the traditional ideology of Creoledom, death is only a phase in the career of man or woman. After death, people continue to live as spirits, frequenting the same family house, or houses, along with their descendants and other relatives. The Creoles do not see any incompatibility between these beliefs and Christianity. They invariably point out that the spirits of the dead partake in the Communion of Saints, in which many Christians believe. An eminent Creole clergyman, a canon of the Anglican Church, explained to me that in Christian theology, every person who has been baptized is a saint, and thus by definition part of the Communion of Saints.

The dead are everywhere around us, continue to be concerned with the lives of the living, and demand to be kept informed about events involving them. They also want to be consulted about every major step taken by their surviving relatives. They can help, either through their own mystical powers or through intercession with the higher mystical domains. But they can also act vindictively, inflicting harm on those who do not respect them. They must therefore be appeased and, as the Creoles often put it, kept happy. The Creoles regularly communicate with their dead by visiting their graves, through dreams, or through ordinary conversation. Questions are put to them, and the dead answer back, usually by the manipulation of the four halves of two kola nuts. On the occasions of the major rites of passage of their surviving relatives, or in times of personal crises for these relatives, a special "cook," or meal, is arranged which is offered the dead in the presence of relatives and friends, usually by the more articulate and experienced among the eldest relatives, who "understand their language" best.

There are set occasions on which graves are visited: Christmas Eve, New Year's Day, and Easter. Before the formal visit, members of the family weed the grass around the graves, whitewash them, and decorate them with flowers. Then a number of men and women gather around the grave and offer libations of water, "to cool the heart of the dead," and of alcoholic drink (the kind depending on what the deceased liked when alive) "to make the dead happy." Speeches addressed to the occupant of the grave are made. After some of the alcohol is poured on the grave, the bottle is passed around. All those present drink in turn, and the empty bottle is then left at the graveside. After the libation and the speeches, two kola nuts are split and the four halves are cast to see whether the dead have accepted the offering. No food is offered the dead at the grave. Such visits and libations are also performed when unscheduled contingencies, such as a trip abroad, arise.

Meals for the dead (*awujoh*) are also prepared on such

family occasions as weddings, christenings, graduation, or the building of a new house; in cases of affliction such as illness; and when surviving relatives wish to consult the dead over crucial issues in their lives.

Apart from the large-scale *awujoh*, a "small cook" is held on minor occasions. Often drink is simply left on the table overnight, so that the dead can help themselves. During weddings and other celebrations, it is common to see a man murmuring some words and pouring a few drops of alcohol on the ground to make the dead happy.

These beliefs and practices in relation to the dead are highly constraining. Thus a wealthy man invited by a poorer relative to a party or a wedding may offer excuses for not attending. But if his relative were to say: "I am having a 'cook' for my [deceased] mother, on such and such a day," he would most certainly turn up for the occasion with contributions in hand.

When a man hears that a poor relation, whom he may not have seen for some time, has died, he will rally to the bereaved family without hesitation, offer money, and see to it that his deceased relative has a proper "send-off." Indeed, as Fashole-Luke (1968:138) points out, if two sections of a family quarrel beyond any possibility of reconciliation, they will hold two separate feasts for the dead.

Thus, every Creole "family" has both wealthy and relatively "poor" members. Its structure tends to be determined essentially by two organizational principles: genealogical links and patronage. These two principles are dramatically reflected in the death announcements on the radio. Such an announcement will usually give a whole list of "survivors," who are mentioned by name, address, profession, position, and nearness of kinship to the deceased.

Of great significance is not just who the list includes, but in what order they are ranked. Often, high-status relatives are mentioned first, particularly when the bereaved family is relatively poor. Informants say that families often spend hours on end discussing the composition and order of such lists.

What we must realize here is that if a wealthy man is mentioned in the list of "survivors," he will thereby become publicly associated with the bereaved family. His general apprehension of the dead, combined with the concern for the prestige and status of his family, will force him into becoming deeply involved in the bereavement, and into rallying to the aid of his relatives.

What emerges from the discussion so far is that the poor among the Creoles are "distributed" among patrons, and that the latter are constrained into taking care of their poorer relatives by beliefs in the mystical powers of the dead, among other things. The wealthy are thus under continuous pressure to assist in fostering one child, pay the school fees of another, help a junior clerk to be promoted, look after an impoverished or sick relative. This is why, for example, the poorest Creole child has almost as great a chance of becoming a professional as a child from a relatively wealthy family.

The dead are everywhere, scrutinizing and judging behavior, and their anger can cause terrible afflictions to those who offend them. Serious illness and cases of misfortune are always suspected as being the sanctions of the dead for disrespect or neglect. Elderly kinsmen, "who have finished with this world," though still alive, and who "understand the language of the dead best," are consulted, irrespective of whether they are poor or wealthy. They help in diagnosing the cause of the affliction and in identifying the particular dead who brought it about. They also help in putting the matter right by mediating with the dead.

The question as to which of the dead can afflict, or help, which of the living is as complex as the system of kinship relationships among the Creoles. The cult has wrongly been called "ancestor worship" by some writers. It is indeed neither worship nor necessarily concerned with the ancestors in any one genealogical line. A man may invoke his deceased father, mother, siblings, aunts, uncles, wife, or others. In offering libations he may say: "You, father. . . . You, mother. . . . You . . . auntie. . . . etc.," but will always follow the names of these relatives by an appeal: "and you all, all of you, over there." As he always does this in the company of other relatives, these will in turn add more invocations to other deceased members of the "family." The related dead who are mentioned specifically by name are thus in effect the links, or the agents of intercession, with the much wider and less differentiated realm of the dead. One Creole lady said that she usually visits the graves of her mother and of her husband and requests these "between them" to arrange to communicate the message to "the rest of them." Thus although specific dead are often suspected of causing specific afflictions, the mystical sanctions of the dead are ultimately derived from "all of them over there," all the dead. These, of course, are deceased Creoles generally, and just as practically all living Creoles are related within one total moral network, so the dead form a closely interrelated mystical realm.

There are thus conflicting processes operating on the family network all the time, some of them disintegrative and others reintegrative. Although there are utilitarian and manipulative elements in almost every relationship, the relationship cannot last long unless it also contains a moral categorical imperative to support it, or to mystify the contradictions underlying it. Indeed at any one time, an individual's family network should stand as a network of moral relationships which are valued in their own intrinsic right. This is, of course, the case in all kinship systems, where moral and utilitarian elements are locked in a dialectical process.

Kinship systems differ in their capacity to withstand the subversive processes of demographic and social change. An expanded family among the Tallensi peasants of northern Ghana is a discrete social grouping, clearly defined in genealogical and economic terms. The Creole "family," on the other hand, lacks such stability. Hence, I suggest, its need for frequent and intensive family ceremonials. It is these ceremonials and the beliefs that are associated with, or generated by them, that continually develop and maintain the family network in the face of subversive processes of change. This, of course, is not to say that the Tallensi do not need ceremonials of this type to maintain their structures. It is a matter of degree.

What is more, the Creoles are essentially a middle-class, highly differentiated group, which makes the ubiquity and intensity of their ceremonials even more significant. Thus, in the absence of clear, articulating principles of kinship organization, it is the frequent ceremonials which continually define and redefine the egocentric "family."

So far, the Creole "family" has emerged as an egocentric network of kin, whose relative permanence is achieved and maintained by frequent ceremonials. But this picture is in fact an abstraction which is of little structural significance if it is considered on its own. To gain a proper understanding of its nature, it is necessary to place it within its structural perspective, i.e., within the whole extent of Creoledom as a sociocultural group. In this perspective, it will become evident that, although we are talking about different "families," we are in fact arbitrarily selecting and delineating collectivities of people, the groups who attend the respective "family" ceremonials. The same person will be a member of different family networks, and many of the members of one's family are also members of other families in which one is not necessarily a member. The different families overlap and cut across one another.

All this implies that through a person's membership in different family networks and the similar links of the members of his network he/she can have access, when the need arises, to any person within the total network of Creoledom. Thus when a person of significance is mentioned to a Creole, he is most likely to say: "He is my cousin!" The broad, structural picture that emerges, therefore, is that of a large number of families, linked and cross-linked, each of which surrounds an important man. Within this wider network, it is possible for any man to trace a kinship relationship with any other man, either directly or through someone else within his own network.

The Feminine Factor in Elite Organization

5

The Roles Women Play in the Organization of Eliteness
  Economic Production
  Socialization for Eliteness
  Stagers of Ceremonies
  Enhancers of the Universalistic Image
Pillars of the Grand Cousinhood
Conflict and Communion between the Sexes

The structure, definition, and exclusiveness of the network of amity are closely related to a cluster of contradictory roles that women play in elite formation and organization. In all systems of stratification, women play a crucial part in the distribution and maintenance of power between groups. The higher a group is in the hierarchy, the more crucial that part tends to be.

Marriage is therefore intimately interconnected with social hierarchy. In many systems homogamy, i.e., marriage between equals, is combined with hypergamy, i.e., the movement of women in marriage from lower to upper strata. The overall outcome of such processes will be a relative preponderance of women at the top, resulting from the continuous "rise" of women from lower strata, and from the fact that they remain at the upper end of the system. This does not create a significant imbalance between the sexes in the lower groups, because the elite is small in size and the number of women who enter from the other groups is very small. But within the elite itself the problem is dramatic, as it inevitably brings about a great deal of friction and alienation between the sexes. Elite ideology makes women develop and maintain the very systems that restrict their freedom of choice, and that even in some cases subject them to bondage.

Among the Creoles, this contradiction in the position of women has created a serious cleavage between the sexes, and in 1970 there was hardly a sermon in a church service or at a wedding which did not bring this cleavage to the attention of the congregation. Demographically, women among the Creoles outnumber the men. The two sexes are almost equal in number up to the age of twenty-four. From then until the age of forty-five, women outnumber men. (This is perhaps the cumulative result of hypergamy, whereby Creole men, being of high status, have for generations attracted as legal or "outside" wives an increasing number of non-Creole women, who eventually passed as Creole.) This imbalance between the sexes is greatly aggravated by the fact that while females begin their sexual careers and also marry at an early age, well before they are twenty, males marry late, often not until they are about forty and have achieved a high enough status. There is a strong pressure on Creoles, especially on Creole women, to marry Creoles. The net result is that there are far more marriageable women than marriageable men. This is particularly the case because the Creoles are Christians and pride themselves on being monogamous. Their pattern of marriage is, moreover, regulated under civil law, and it is illegal for a Creole to have more than one wife, while according to customary law a Mende or a Temne can do so.

The Roles Women Play in the Organization of Eliteness

Economic Production

Creole women contribute greatly to Creole resources through the income gained from their participation in the wider economy. Their activities as traders have already been mentioned. Far more important is the rapidly increasing number of Creole women working in secure and well-paid "white collar" jobs. In the household survey, of 699 Creoles gainfully employed in Freetown, 278 were females and 421 were males. Of 322 Creoles employed in government establishments, 102 were females and 220 were males. Most of these females were either teachers or secretaries, in steady and relatively well-paid jobs. In addition, there were a number of professional women who were self-employed.

Most of these working women can support themselves and their children comfortably on their own incomes. This potentiality for independent economic existence is enhanced by their ownership or shared rights in inherited freehold property. With the increasing uncertainties of conjugal relationships, even married women living with their husbands now tend to save some of their own earnings and, what is perhaps of great symbolic significance, some of them have started building their own family house quite independently of their husbands. Indeed, some women now prefer to remain unmarried, with or without children. Nearly a third of Creole households in the survey sample were headed by women. Some of these women are maintained by absent husbands or by lovers, and some maintain themselves on their own incomes either from property or jobs or both. Thus, women contribute directly to Creole income and wealth in their own right.

This potential for female independence is much greater among Creoles than among non-Creoles in Sierra Leone. Banton (1957:204) observed the same tendency in the 1950s. In his own survey, 42 percent of Creole households had female heads, as compared with 14 percent among the provincials. Even those women who are not formally employed outside the house make a fundamental economic contribution as housewives, unmarried mothers, widows, spinsters, or elderly women, by running and maintaining the household, and looking after the children of those of both sexes, but particularly of men, who are employed. It is these women who enable Creole professionals to spend years of their lives continuing their university training, and permit them to be sufficiently mobile to take important jobs outside of Freetown. The contribution that these women make indirectly to Creole fortunes cannot be quantified, but its magnitude and significance can be assessed and appreciated.

Some of these economic roles need not be played exclusively by Creole women. And indeed, there are non-Creole women who perform some of them in Creole households, whether as wives, concubines, or domestic help; because of the educational differential, however, there are more educated and professionally trained Creole women than non-Creole women. But there are other roles, more fundamental for the corporate organization of the Creoles as a power group, which only Creole women can and do play.

Socialization for Eliteness
One of these roles is the socialization of children in Creole ideology and style of life, which are fundamental in the education and training of professionals. Success in formal education is related to informal socialization, like articulateness in English, acquaintance with the Christian and European values that inform such education, deep motivation for achievement, self-discipline in systematic work, and so on. (For more details, see E. G. Cohen, 1979.)

Women also socialize men in "decorum," i.e., in the manners, etiquette, and comportment which not only identify the elite and inspire them with confidence in themselves, but also serve as an exclusive "language" of communication—a "hieroglyph"—among them. Their role in staging the ball discussed earlier (see chapter 2), in maintaining a variety of social and cultural societies, and in the

79

inculcation of "civilization" among the men, has already been examined.

Stagers of Ceremonies

All the extensive family ceremonials are initiated and staged by women, who provide the motivation for holding them. It is they who assemble the food and drinks, sew the dresses, issue most of the invitations, and play the most active roles in the procedure. Indeed, in most of these ceremonials, the women are often busy dancing and drinking, while the men sit separately on the side "talking lodge." It is the women who push the men into these family affairs, and who are the driving force behind the cult of the dead in particular. They dream the dreams, receive messages from the dead, and communicate with the dead. Their solidarity is objectified and upheld by these ceremonies, and is expressed—indeed repetitively recreated—by the wearing of a uniform African-style dress (*ashobi*) made of the same cloth, color, and design, and sewn specifically for each occasion.

Equally crucial is the women's role in the churches. As the men became progressively absorbed in Freemasonry, women increasingly assumed more significant roles in church organization and maintenance. Their attendance at services is massive and regular. Every church has its "sisterhood," a sizeable grouping of women who perform different functions in the running of the churches. Here again, their solidarity and identification with the church is expressed by the wearing of a uniform consisting of European-style dress and hat during the services. They collect money, maintain the organ, help in ushering people into the services, and look after the children in Sunday classes.

Enhancers of the Universalistic Image

Women also run a wide variety of associations, societies, clubs, and activities for the wider public, thus developing and sustaining the universalistic image of the elite group as leaders. They operate philanthropic associations to help the poor, the sick, and the ignorant, thus creating an image of universal concern. Many of them work as teachers. They patronize the arts and are active in drama. They also play significant roles as entertainers, hostesses, and masters of ceremonies on state occasions and at receptions for diplomats and other foreign visitors.

Pillars of the Grand Cousinhood

The Creole cousinhood is an alliance which in many ways is developed and maintained through women. The basic family unit is matricentric, consisting of a woman and her daughters and sons. Generally speaking, the relationship between a man and his wife and her children is tense. Men marry late, and are often too preoccupied with their careers, old friends, Masonic lodge, and outside wives, to have much time for their legal wives and children. The legal wife is embittered because of neglect and the threat to her status and material welfare, either currently or in the event of the death of her husband. The children, too, are antagonized by their father because of his neglect or desertion of their mother. Even under ideal family conditions, when no outside wife or children exist, the husband's mobility takes him away from home, either to go abroad on his own for training, or to hold an appointment outside of Freetown.

The Creole nuclear family is thus matrifocal, and the relationship between mother and children is highly intense. This is why in cases of affliction, the first question a man asks himself, or is asked, is whether he ever offended his deceased mother in her lifetime.

Women are not only wives and mothers, however, but also sisters, aunts, and in-laws. Men are, therefore, related to one another through them in a variety of ways, and because of the tendency for the Creoles to marry endogamously, the men become related to one another, directly or classificatorily, patrilaterally, matrilaterally, and affinally. Relationships of affinity established in one generation generate relationships of matrilaterality and patrilaterality in the next. The endogamous group becomes morally exclusive in evolving distinctiveness as a "bilateral descent group." The alliance becomes a cousinhood. As it is only

Creole women who can effect such an arrangement, they become transformed into a potent group symbol, a collective representation. Their different roles in production, reproduction, sexuality, and socialization, and their role in staging the family ceremonials are combined as different significata attached ambiguously to Creole womanhood. The Creole female symbol becomes part of the mystique and cult of eliteness. While some of the aforementioned roles can be played by women from any group, this symbolic function can be fulfilled only by Creole women. There is therefore a strong collective pressure, mediated by relatives and close friends and by Creole public opinion generally, for Creole women to marry Creole men.

In the majority of cases, however, no such pressure is necessary to induce a woman to marry a Creole. Most Creole women value independence and are ambitious and competitive, and many of them strategize their love affairs and matches to gain maximum advantage. They are after economic security and prestige, and in all societies one way a woman can best achieve this is by marrying someone of as high a social status as possible. The ideal husband is an educated man with professional training and a secure, well-paid position, and as many Creole men answer these requirements it is only natural that women will want to be married to them. Many Creole women prefer becoming the illegitimate "outside wives" of such men to marrying lower-status men. Thus, even without external constraint, Creole women will want to marry Creole men.

In addition, however, there are some very serious considerations which inhibit Creole women from marrying provincial men. In the first place, there is the fear of being married to a potentially polygynous man. Creole men, by contrast, are Christian and officially monogamous, their family relationships being regulated under civil law which prohibits polygamy. It is, of course, true that Creole men do nevertheless have "sweethearts" or "outside wives." The status of these is insecure, however, and unless the "husband" goes out of his way to write a will specifying that some of the property should go to his illegitimate widow and children, they will inherit nothing. In 1970 I witnessed a case of a legal wife going to court after the death of her husband to get an eviction order against an "outside wife" who had for years lived with her children in a house provided for her by the man.

Creole women fear the ease with which a woman can be divorced by her husband under Islamic or customary law, as compared with the great difficulty of being divorced under civil law. In addition to the legal sanctions, a woman married to a Creole man has the moral support of the Creole community behind her if her husband wants to divorce her. A woman married to a provincial under customary or Islamic law is likely to lose custody over her children to her husband or to his family if she is divorced or widowed. Children, and under strict traditional customary law the wife herself, are "inherited" by the husband's kin (see Harrell-Bond, 1975:109). The inheritance laws are such that a Creole woman married to a native will inherit nothing from her husband (for details see ibid.: 107–13; Joko-Smart, 1969).

Creole women are also afraid of having to live "upcountry" if they marry a provincial man. The modern provincial elite, who usually live in Freetown, retain close links with their homes, where they have their political backing. They frequently visit them, and may eventually be appointed to an administrative post there. Not only do the provinces lack the sophistication, amenities, and social glamour of Freetown, but they also are the sources of deep fears in the Creole mind, associated with "devils," "cannibalism," ritual murders, witchcraft, and secret societies.

Provincial men are seen by most Creole women as members of Poro, the men's secret societies, and some women informants said they would not like to marry men who harboured secrets from them. It is true that many Creole men are members of the Masonic order, another secret society, but Creole women regard it as an elitist, liberal, democratic, enlightened organization, whose members do not resort to violence. It is also voluntary, while Poro is obligatory.

The heavy obligations which tie provincial men to their extended families in the provinces also discourage Creole women, who almost invariably cite cases of Creoles married to provincial men who had to spend all their time entertaining the many relatives of their husbands, who frequently came to stay with them.

More fundamentally, the Creoles believe that the children of a Creole woman married to a provincial man are likely to grow up in the wrong cultural atmosphere. Such children are likely to be bilingual, and to be brought up in a different style of life, with the wrong ideology, manners, and customs. Creole interviewees would say politely: "We do not marry them because our ways of life differ; we speak different 'languages' and we often cannot really communicate."

Some of these are genuine individually held reasons inhibiting Creole women from marrying out. But they are in addition sustained and exaggerated by Creole public opinion generally. They are inculcated in a variety of ways through the socialization of the Creole girl. A Creole girl marrying out is disgraced, and is often likely to lose touch with her family and to become absorbed into a separate social circle, unless she manages to wean her husband away from his own circle and succeeds in bringing him into hers.

Pressure comes not only from the living but also from the dead. Sawyerr (1965:54–55) gives the full text of a typical libation speech by a woman who had married a Muslim provincial against her mother's advice. Her husband eventually drove her out of the house, and she had come to her mother's grave for help:

> Mother, I have come to seek your forgiveness. I acknowledge the mistake I made. You did advise me, but I did not pay any heed to you. . . . Moslems and Christians cannot make *rapport*. . . . So, please mother I have come to cool your heart. You must forgive me. . . . I bring some cold water. Here it is. . . . I have come to you and (so) I am preparing your kola-nuts. . . . Let me know whether your wrath has cooled off. . . . Please direct me how to proceed.

Cases of this sort are often quoted by Creoles to indicate that, though they are not prejudiced against any group, cross-ethnic and cross-religious marriages do not succeed.

To avoid marriages with "the wrong men," occasions for Creole girls to meet and date non-Creole men are minimized. Why do some Creole women, nevertheless, marry provincial men? The explanation given in 1970 was that these were mainly inexperienced Creole girls studying abroad, falling in love with provincial boys, and ending up marrying them abroad, where no pressure could be applied or advice given to them by their relatives.

Since the mid-1950s an ever-increasing number of provincials, predominantly males, have been acquiring higher degrees of education and becoming professionals, and the "danger" of Creole girls going out with them and eventually marrying them has increased. But even this has not resulted in an increase in the incidence of intermarriage. Though nearly 40 percent of the students in Fourah Bay College, Freetown, were male provincials, there was in 1970 no evidence at all of an increase in the number of Creole girls dating provincial boys.

A significant role in insulating Creole girls from intimate contacts with provincial boys was played by an all-Creole sorority formed in the mid-1950s, which organized exclusive dancing parties and emphasized good behavior, "manners," and refinement. Indeed the sorority was so successful in its role that provincial boys urged students generally to boycott its activities and functions, describing its members as snooty and snobbish.

In 1970 I attended a dinner-dance party organized by this sorority. A four-page invitation gave the names of the members, of the "senior friend," of givers and responders to various toasts. There were about 200 people present, including students, a few members of the academic and administrative staff with their spouses, and some visitors from town, mainly relatives and friends of the members. Everything was organized with taste, sensitivity and propriety. People talked in low voices and there was emphasis throughout on good manners and politeness. The food was exquisitely prepared and served. The dancing was genteel and very "proper."

About half an hour was spent on formal toasts. First, the social secretary of the sorority introduced the chairman of the session, dwelling on his high status and remarkable achievements. Then one male academician proposed the toast to the sorority, in the process giving a short speech.

85

The president of the sorority responded formally. This was followed by the proposal of a toast to the outgoing members, and one of these responded. Finally, a member of the sorority proposed a toast to the guests, and one of the guests responded. All this was done with tact, wit, and charm.

The sorority was originally founded by an American woman who was married to a Creole academic. It has fifteen members only. Each year, graduating members are replaced by more junior girls. Potential candidates are chosen secretly during the previous session and, without their knowledge, are for many months subjected to close, careful observation by the current members. They should prove themselves to be intelligent, industrious, and proper in dress and relationships. They do not "sleep around" with men, do not dance too close with boys, do not drink alcohol excessively. A girl who, after becoming a member, does not live up to these expectations, is forced to resign.

The sorority has a so-called senior friend, who is usually a middle-aged professional. In 1970 the incumbent was a highly respectable, socially active educationalist, happily married to an academician, with several children. The sorority met at her house once a month to discuss current issues and make plans for future events.

Members of the sorority keep in touch with "old girls," and ex-members are always keen on helping younger members materially and in finding jobs. Two such "old girls" with whom I talked at the time said how nostalgic and proud they felt about their past membership in the sorority.

The principle underlying the existence of the sorority is that the select members should serve as an example for non-members to emulate. Female students who are not members are always potential candidates for the sorority, or are invited guests at its social functions. The emphasis is genuinely on good character, irrespective of ethnic or social background. The secretary was at pains to point out that the sorority was not, in principle, exclusively Creole. In fact, during that session the first non-Creole member was chosen. The girl was intelligent and well-mannered, with a strong character, and came from a very good Aku Muslim family. She had been fostered by a well-known Creole professional couple, who supervised her academic career and provided her with help in many respects. In the past, such a girl might have passed as Creole, but now she went out of her way to emphasize that she was non-Creole.

These sentiments and practices inhibiting Creole women from marrying out are, in fact, paralleled, though in a different manner and for different reasons, by ideologies advanced by provincials to inhibit provincial men from marrying Creole women. A Creole woman is thought to be snobbish, and might assume an air of superiority and "lord it" over her husband and in-laws. She would estrange her husband from his people and from his religion, and convert him to Christianity. The children might be brought up as strangers to their father's people, and might eventually become identified as Creoles. Creole women are not initiated into the native women's secret society, Sande, and are therefore not real women. They do not know the secrets of womanhood, and are not sufficiently instructed in their duties towards their husbands. A provincial girl, a student at Fourah Bay College, explained to me with much conviction that Creole women are not really African, "because it is only when a girl goes through the weeks of instruction and initiation in the bush that she comprehends what being African means." Indeed, a provincial women's sorority, which was in many ways a rival of the Creole one mentioned above, was formed to distract provincial boys from Creole girls and encourage them to associate only with provincial girls.

Conflict and Communion Between the Sexes

A number of points emerge from the previous discussion. Creole women are, to a large extent, the basis of Creole social corporateness and status. There are strong forces that prevent them from marrying out, and because of hypergamy they outnumber men. They contribute significantly to economic production, ensure biological continuity through reproduction, and maintain the Creole lifestyle through the socialization of the young and through the staging of ceremonials that develop Creole status. The numerical imbalance between the sexes means that relatively older and fewer high-status men have to attend to the sexual, social, and sentimental needs of a larger number of women. But because the Creoles are officially monogamous, the problem is solved mainly by the institution of "the outside wife," and by leaving a high proportion of unmarried widows and spinsters. Many Creole women prefer being unmarried mothers, and the mistresses of relatively important men, to being married to non-Creole men or remaining spinsters. There is no serious stigma attached to illegitimate children in Sierra Leone, and some eminent men are known to have many children of such status.

On the individual level however, the system inevitably engenders a great deal of tension between the sexes. A woman is always gripped with anxiety, insecurity, and uncertainty. If officially married, she is in fear of the "outside wife," who is a threat to the material resources of the husband, both in life and in death, as well as a competitor for his sexual and sentimental attentions. If she is an "outside wife," her rights and those of her children are always precarious and questionable. Women thus become the victims of the very system which they struggle so hard to develop and maintain.

Cults of Secrecy 6

An Embattled Group
The Tradition of Ritual Secrecy
The Lodges
The Incidence of Membership
Collective Constraints
Exclusive Organization

All state elites are subjected to pressures by their wider publics. In the development of their particularistic interests, as well as in the performance of their universalistic functions, they are forced to coordinate their activities behind masks of secrecy, communalistic as well as official.

An Embattled Group

For about twenty-five years the Creoles have been under threat from a variety of factions and groups. This is not just because they are relatively privileged, but also because they have progressively become an integral part of the new state elite, and thus a target for the kind of public pressure to which all "establishments" are exposed. Every opposition has attempted to exploit past anti-Creole sentiment in its fight against the government of the day. What is more, even the conservative elements, the politicians and chiefs of the provinces, have adopted the same tactics to suppress popular movements against them. Thus, in successive elections during the 1950s and 1960s, progressive national parties from Freetown were branded "Creole parties" and ruthlessly prevented from operating in the hinterland.

Early in 1970, a "Creole Convention" was organized by a Creole barrister, and held two meetings (one on February 1 and the other on March 6). In the speeches at these meetings, and in printed leaflets that were widely distributed, alarm was expressed at the growing danger to the Creoles. Two sources of danger were stressed. One was the temptation leading some Creoles to sell land to non-Creoles. The other was the growing threat of unemployment among educated Creole youth as a result of discrimination against them. The Creoles were urged to refrain from selling land, and also to set up Creole business enterprises in order to provide employment for Creole youth.

One of the main factors leading to the organization of the convention was the activities of a group of opposition politicians from the provinces, who had a few weeks earlier formed an anti-Creole association that came to be known as the "Provincial Committee," led by a well-known former cabinet minister. In meetings held by the committee, many allegations were made about the extent of Creole influence on the government. Photographs of public appearances of the prime minister were shown in which he was seen consistently surrounded by Creole officials.

The formation of the Provincial Committee and of the Creole Convention in 1970 were brought about by a complex set of factors which will become clear in due course. What must be stressed at this stage is that the emergence of these two groupings was not an isolated political event, but yet one more dramatic manifestation of what had been going on in Sierra Leone during the preceding two decades. All through that period, provincials would attack and agitate against Creole power and influence, and the Creoles would react by yet another attempt to mobilize their forces and coordinate their strategies to meet the challenge.

During the 1947–57 period, the major political cleavage in the country was that between the Creoles and the provincials. Indeed the SLPP, which ruled Sierra Leone from 1951 to 1967, came into being essentially as an anti-Creole alliance, and succeeded in unifying the whole country, chiefs and politicians, Mende and Temne and others, in opposition to the Creoles.

Throughout this period, the Creoles were continually challenged as property owners and in their dominant position in the civil service. The challenge came from different combinations of forces at different times, principally from the two dominant ethnic groups, the Mende (30.9 percent of the population) and the Temne (29.8 percent of the population). By their sheer voting power, these provincials have dominated the executive and the legislature, and their politicians have frequently denounced Creole influence and endeavored to reduce Creole power by a variety of strategies.

The Temne have every now and then argued that the very land on which the Creoles developed their society and culture, i.e., the Freetown peninsula, was originally theirs, and that their forefathers were tricked into selling it to the British for a trivial price, for the purpose of settling the Creoles on it (see Fyfe, 1964: 112–23). They point out that their chiefs *did* accept "payment" for giving the land to the British for settlement, but that this could by no means be described as the absolute alienation of that land. The transfer of freehold rights is alien to the traditional system of landholding in Sierra Leone. Indeed, even today all land in mainland Sierra Leone is still tribal land, held by the chiefs in trust. It can be leased, but cannot be sold or bought as freehold. The Creoles have always been aware of this argument, but sought either to dismiss it as a "thing of the past," nearly two centuries old, or to attribute it to the will of God, who gave the land to the Creoles to fulfill their "mission" (Spitzer, 1974: 70).

This threat by the Temne has always been made in the sporadic rhetoric and agitation against the Creoles, but has never been seriously translated into practical action. Nevertheless, it lurks in people's minds on both sides.

A similar kind of threat occasionally aired by various factions is the suggestion that the capital of Sierra Leone be transferred to the interior of the country. Some provincials argue that such a step would deal a death blow to Creole power. The value of Creole land would be severely diminished, and the whole of Creole society would be disrupted. The bulk of the Creoles work for the government in the capital, and in the event of the transfer of the capital they would have to move away from their traditional home. The Creoles do not like to live in the hinterland. Creole businessmen, missionaries, and officials were massacred in Mendeland during the Hut Tax War of 1895, and the Creoles have since developed a traumatic fear of the interior. Furthermore, the Creoles have all their churches, schools, clubs, societies, and lodges concentrated in Freetown, and if they moved away they would suffer grievously in the very bases of their cultural and social life. On the other hand, if they chose not to move with the capital, they would lose the basis of their political and economic power. In either case, they are likely to be dislodged from their privileged elite position.

This, of course, has always been in the realm of talk and, some people say, fantasy, although during the colonial period, the town of Bo was transformed by the British into a kind of administrative capital for the protectorate. Apart from being the capital, Freetown is also a sea port of paramount importance to the country. Furthermore, the establishment of a new capital would require a great deal of investment in new buildings, roads, institutions, and facilities, and this would require a great deal of capital, planning, and organizing, which are not available at present. What is more, a move of this kind would require that the provincials, particularly the Mende and the Temne, stand united on the issue, and this is highly improbable. And if the Creoles chose to stay on in Freetown to develop some kind of autonomy, and to withdraw from the leading positions which they occupy, the State would probably sink into chaos. It would be difficult for any one of the major ethnic groups to rule the country without the services of the Creoles or the mediating functions of the Creole culture. The fact remains, however, that at least some Creoles are apprehensive about the threat, which is often made by provincials in all seriousness.

But the actual threat to Creole land in recent years has come from the sharp rise in the value of property in the Freetown peninsula, and the growing temptation among Creole landlords to sell at a time when no Creole can buy land elsewhere in the country. Very few have succumbed to the temptation, but the threat of alienating property to non-Creoles, with resultant weakening of their status, is always present, and is still regarded as a potential source of danger. This is why the 1970 Creole Convention expressed alarm at the sale of property by Creoles. Admonition by leaders in this respect has been significantly mediated in terms of individual motives by the beliefs and practices of the cult of the dead. Indeed, as the temptation to sell and the dangers thought likely to result from selling have grown stronger over the years, so the cult of the dead has gained in strength and intensity.

The second major threat to Creole power which was emphasized at the 1970 Creole Convention is the rapidly increasing number of educated provincials who are competing with Creole candidates for positions in the civil service. There is growing concern that more and more trained Creoles will have difficulty finding jobs in the public sector, and the convention urged that Creoles develop their own private businesses to absorb their young.

The Creoles have also been subjected to political threats and challenges of various kinds. In 1970 there was a great deal of agitation in some of the papers against the power of the permanent secretaries in the administration, who were predominantly Creoles. Some articles in the papers spoke of the "insubordination" of permanent secretaries to the authority of ministers. A picture was presented of cunning Creole senior officials scheming and determining policy behind the backs of outwitted, unsuspecting provincial ministers.

The Creoles are officially regarded as "non-natives," although they have been in the country for about a century and a half. Their family relationships are regulated under British civil law, those of the provincials under customary law. They are frequently described as "foreigners" and even as "whites" by provincials.

In the face of such pressures, the Creoles have attempted to coordinate their actions by means of a formal corporate organization, and to establish regular channels for communication, both for decision making and for concerted action. During the colonial period, they did not have any such organization, because they were secure in their positions under the protection of the colonial administration. The provincials posed no serious challenge to them. Indeed, the Creoles' most bitter struggle during that period was with the British, whom they accused of racial discrimination against them. Despite their education and Western ways of life, they were not treated as equals. Creole doctors, for instance, were given a lower grade and lower pay than British doctors with the same qualifications.

Like the middle classes in Western societies, the Creoles during the colonial period developed numerous types of formal associations, cultural societies, youth clubs, men's clubs, old schoolboys' and schoolgirls' associations, churches and church societies, and ratepayers' associations. But these were voluntary, small-scale organizations, and had no fundamental corporate organizational functions. A die-hard Creole once complained bitterly that the British had deliberately fractionized Creole society to prevent them from developing an all-Creole organization. It should be mentioned here that the British administered the affairs of the non-native Creoles differently from those of the indigenous populations. The colony of Freetown was administered centrally by the British, while the provincials were administered on the basis of indirect rule. The result was that while the Temne, Mende, and the other ethnic groups had their own local and paramount chiefs, whose authority was upheld by the colonial administration, the Creoles had no hierarchy of authority of their own, and were not organized corporately as Creoles.

Not only was Creole society highly individualistic and

competitive, it was also divided on the basis of class and origin, and sometimes of church denomination, with these cleavages essentially overlapping.

Creoles made sporadic efforts at achieving formal power, seeking greater representation than warranted by their ratio in the population, independence for all or parts of the Freetown peninsula, or to develop a formal political party of their own, but all these efforts were frustrated. They failed not just because of the resistance of the provincials, but because the overwhelming majority of the Creoles soon realized that any formal grouping they might develop would be fatal to their privileged position. Their numerical weakness meant that their representation on state level would inevitably be insignificant, and would in the long run mean that their adversaries would insist on reducing the proportion of Creoles in the civil service and their access to other privileges accordingly.

The Tradition of Ritual Secrecy

Like all elites, the Creoles have coordinated their activities informally through a variety of mechanisms, but in their case particularly through the development of a fraternity within the framework of the Masonic order.

During the colonial period, the Creoles had great potential for developing informal organization. They lived in a small territory, were few in number, and interacted intensively with one another. They met in their churches, and in clubs and societies of all sorts. And apart from such external symbols of identity and exclusiveness as accent, dress, and general style of life, they were linked together through the network of the Grand Cousinhood.

But all these provided only a very loose kind of organization, which was incapable by itself of coping with the emerging political realities associated with independence. The Creoles were now operating within the framework of the new state, confronting formal political organizations. What they lacked above all else was a system for the regular articulation of corporate organizational functions, for deliberation, decision making, and the exercise of authority to ensure compliance and implementation. And it is against such a background that we should consider the development of the Masonic order among them.

On the face of it, this process of Freemasonization appears to be dramatic and innovatory. However, it is essentially a continuation of the indigenous cultural tradition among both Creoles and provincials of organization into so-called secret societies. Throughout the nineteenth century, the Creoles had their own secret societies, whose beliefs and practices derived from the countries of origin of liberated Africans, particularly from Yorubaland. The provincials, on the other hand, had their own male and female secret societies, whose pervasive beliefs, rituals, and organization played fundamental political roles in the precolonial, colonial, and post-Independence periods. Indeed, Freemasonization among the Creoles in the last twenty-five years has been in many ways a reaction to the manipulation by the provincials of the symbolism and organization of their own traditional secret societies in political mobilization within the framework of the modern polity of Sierra Leone, often directly against the Creoles.

The reference here is not to purely political societies of a conspiratorial nature, but to associations based on ritual beliefs and practices that are formally non-political. Their manifest aims are essentially symbolic, though their organization has always had great potential for the articulation of political groupings of various sorts, on different levels of organization.

For the provincials, the Poro all-male secret society has always been a major traditional institution, particularly among the Mende and the Temne. But our information about it is still fragmentary and confused. Most of the accounts that are available in the literature provide only an eclectic, clouded picture, made up of bits of information taken from different types of sources, at different periods and from different culture groups in the area. This is only partly because of the secrecy surrounding its rituals and the fear of native informants of the severe punishment that may be meted out to them for disclosing its secrets. However, the contents of the secret rituals themselves are of no great sociological significance. What is crucially important is the process by which these rituals affect the relations of power in a community, and this can be studied without detailed accounts of the rituals themselves. From the available information (see Little, 1948; 1951; 1965; 1966; Harley, 1941; 1950; d'Azavedo, 1973), it is possible to establish a number of points regarding the potential of the Poro for the organization of political action. (For a brief account of the women's secret society, Sande, see MacCormack, 1975.)

The Poro is rooted in the deep traumatic experience of initiation to which all males are subject at puberty. Initiation into the society is the rite of passage from boyhood to manhood. It takes place in the "secret bush," where the boys are taken and placed in the custody of Poro officials. Rituals are performed to signify the death and subsequent rebirth of the initiates, who in the process undergo physical pain, and are imbued with a fear of the horrors that the masked spirits of the society may afflict on wrongdoers. At the same time, the novices are instructed about sex and the procreation of children, duties to one's tribe and obedience to its elders, and about the meaning of life and death. The anxieties of passage to adulthood, physical pain, dramatic rituals, and the horrors behind the masks, combine to make a deep psychic impact on the initiates, which remains a source of emotional and affectional agitation that can be triggered off and kept alive by display of the symbols of the society and the performance of its rituals. In the process of initiation, a powerful bond of loyalty is created between the newly initiated and their Poro masters, who are thus loved, revered, feared, and unquestioningly obeyed. This bond is of great significance for the structure of authority and leadership, and for political mobilization.

While the overwhelming majority of the initiates remain ordinary members of the Poro, a small minority continue to pursue a ritual career by undergoing further courses of instruction, and are subsequently initiated into higher ritual degrees within the order. To achieve this, they have to pay high fees and costs, and this means that only the wealthy and the influential will rise in the hierarchy of leadership. There is no agreement in the literature about how elaborate this hierarchy is. Harley (1941; 1950) writes of 99 degrees, while others mention a smaller number. But it is evident that the procedure allows of a great deal of flexibility, and that the depth of the hierarchy depends on external factors, such as the size of the community and the nature of its political system. The ritual Poro hierarchy is formally independent of the secular political hierarchy. The sources are confused and often contradictory on the question of which of the two hierarchies wields the greater power. Some authors attribute the upper hand to the "inner circle" of the Poro, whose members are said to be the supporters and arbiters of chiefly authority, sometimes checking its excesses even to the extent of dismissing the secular chief. Other sources would make the Poro hierarchy subordinate to the secular political authority. Little (1965; 1966) says that, among the Mende, the Poro supplies the mystical element in the otherwise purely secular authority of the chief. Here again, it is evident that there is a great deal of flexibility. The two hierarchies are only nominally autonomous, but in fact overlap in roles and in personnel. The powerful men in the one tend to be the powerful men in the other. The hierarchies are complementary, and should be seen as together forming one composite system of authority. What is clear is that Poro leadership is not elected, but essentially imposed from above. It is the "inner circle" of the Poro, together with the secular chief, who take decisions and expect obedience from men.

This makes the Poro a powerful weapon in the hands of the chiefly families, particularly when their own interests are concerned. This occurred on a number of occasions during the colonial period and after Independence, one of these being the Hut Tax War of 1898.

When the British established the protectorate in 1896, they took a number of measures which hit hard at the status and interests of the provincial chiefs. They restricted the judicial authority of the chiefs within narrow bounds, and directed a severe blow at their economic interests by abolishing the institution of slavery, as slaves had been the principal medium of exchange for other forms of wealth. The chiefs reacted to this by mobilizing Poro loyalties and sanctions against trading in palm kernels with the colony. The Government responded by issuing an ordinance prohibiting "all Poro in restraint of trade." Commenting on the effect of this proclamation, Chalmers (1899:52) states: "Poro being practically the means by which the chiefs govern their country, this Ordinance . . . had the effect of taking away the chiefs' power of governing."

The prohibition of Poro economic sanctions was closely followed by the imposition of the Hut Tax on all householders, and this proved to be the final straw. Violence broke out simultaneously across Mendeland on 26 April 1898. There is a great deal of circumstantial evidence to suggest that the mobilization of forces on such a scale and with such a degree of coordination could not have been achieved by the secular political organization of the chiefships alone. A number of authorities maintain that the rising was planned in a specially convened Poro meeting. The whole country was put under the Poro oath, and the war signal was given by dispatching special messengers, who carried the Poro war symbol. Although such evidence of a direct link between Poro and the organization of the uprising is not definite, it is almost certain that Poro organization facilitated the coordination of military activities through the use of the Poro system of communication and reliance on Poro leadership, loyalties, and sanctions.

The role of Poro organization in the riots of 1955–56 is more clearly noted by Sir Herbert Cox (1957) in the report of the commission of inquiry into *The Disturbances in the Provinces during 1955–56*. He states that the strength of the society had been openly displayed, as had their dresses, signs, and tokens, and that the commission were quite satisfied that Poro played an important part in facilitating the disturbances, which might well partly account for the extreme secrecy which shrouded the prevailing discontent. The influence of the Poro society was subtle, profound, and universal. It was a cult which almost at will could become the basis of a native government of its own.

When the British began to hand power over to representatives who were elected on the principle of one-man–one-vote, they were in effect handing the country over into the rule of the chiefs. The provincial politicians operating in Freetown were mostly the sons or close kin of the provincial chiefs (see Barrows, 1976), and because the contending political parties were only loose coalitions, without any organizations in the provinces, it was left to the chiefs to mobilize support for their sons there. In successive elections there was a great deal of evidence indicating that Poro organization probably played a crucial part in mobilizing votes for provincial representatives. Sir Milton Margai adopted the traditional Poro symbol as the SLPP party symbol in 1951 (see Kilson, 1966). More directly, Margai, himself the son of a chief, manipulated Poro obligations in his relations with chiefs and other traditional notables.

Scott, who carried out an intensive field study of the 1957 elections, writes that he found secret societies to be a political force that deeply penetrated the life of the country (1960:173–74), and describes the Poro as "probably the most important political force in the country." He quotes a provincial politician as having suggested that the Poro was politically most effective in keeping Creoles and other outsiders in the dark, and that the mere fact of non-membership would make it difficult for such people to get a sympathetic hearing in the protectorate.

A survey of the newspapers from that period indicates frequent complaints in Freetown against the shady, unlawful activities of secret societies of provincial origin, particularly the Bundu society (the all-female society which parallels the Poro) and the Alikali society. It is significant that Bankole-Bright, the leader of the die-hard Creoles, raised the issue in a speech which he gave in the Legislative Council, in which he dwelt at length on the need to stamp out "cannibalism," and singled out the Bundu society for attack (see the Sierra Leone *Daily Mail*, 2 December 1954). This was rejected in the same council by Sir Milton Margai, who maintained that the Bundu society was an integral part of the social life of the people. An editorial in the *Daily Mail* (6 December 1954), while conceding Margai's assertion, objected to some of the "primitive" practices of these societies. In Freetown their activities seem to have continued almost unabated, and in front-page stories the *Daily*

Mail claimed that Freetown citizens were afraid of going out at night because of the danger of "cannibalism."

What emerges from all this is that secret ritual groupings have played a significant part in the traditional political systems of the Mende, the Temne, and other tribes in what d'Azavedo aptly calls the "Poro Belt," as well as in the resistance to the British during the colonial period, and later in mobilizing support in the political confrontation with the Creoles during the period of decolonization. In neighboring Liberia these societies—particularly the Poro—played similar roles, and were banned by the Americo-Liberians; subsequently, seeing the futility of the attempt, the latter began to penetrate the secret societies from the top by having President Tubman made the head of the Poro (see Libenow, 1969).

Consistent with traditional cultures in West Africa, the Creoles themselves had their own secret societies, which were active in the villages of the Freetown peninsula during the nineteenth century. Foremost among them was the Agugu, which had been brought by Aku recaptives from Yoruba country (see Peterson, 1969:20). It thrived on the mysteries of death and on curative medicines (see Banton, 1957:20).

A more advanced secret society was created in the colony and came to be known as the "Hunters' Secret Society," a distinctly Creole organization, which for many served as a replacement for the Agugu. Peterson (1969:268–69) writes: "As the Creole became increasingly a Freetown-based person, and as the wild life in the Colony grew scarce, the Hunters Society transformed itself into a secret organization of Creole civil servants." Kreutzinger (1966) gives extensive details of the beliefs, organization, and activities of this society on the basis of field inquiries and observations carried out in the early 1960s. The society had a hierarchy of officers headed by a "field marshal," and over sixty branches in Freetown and the rest of the colony, federated in the "Hunting Amalgamation." Nearly all the members were Anglicans, and most of the officers were also church officials. The local branches met once a month, on a Sunday, as most of the members worked during weekdays in

Freetown as clerks, government officials, drivers, electricians, or railway officers. The meeting began with a brief Christian prayer and the reading of a passage from the Bible, and ended two hours later with a second prayer. Each society was represented by two men at the "Amalgamation," which held one meeting every three months.

In 1970 the Hunters' society was still functioning, but mainly in the villages. The members were rural Creoles and junior clerks and technicians. The bulk of the civil servants and professionals were affiliated within the Masonic order. Some Freemasons who were traditionally members of the Hunters' society kept their membership in it for sentimental reasons.

Thus, there was nothing fundamentally new in the dramatic, massive affiliation of Creole men to the Masonic order. What was new was the strict bureaucratic type of organization and discipline which the order introduced within the modern polity.

The Lodges

There are about six million men in the world today who are the members of what has been described as the largest secret society on earth—Freemasonry. The overwhelming majority of these men live in the highly industrialized societies of Western Europe and America, and almost all are members of the wealthy and professional classes.

In Britain alone, there are about three-quarters of a million Freemasons (see Dewar, 1966:46–47). They are organized in local lodges, which are ritually, ideologically, and bureaucratically supervised by the grand lodges of England, Scotland, and Ireland. They meet periodically in their local centres and, behind the locked and well-guarded doors of their temples, wear their colourful and elaborately embroidered regalia, carry the jewels, swords, and other emblems of office, and perform their "ancient" secret rituals.

The bulk of these rituals are concerned with the initiation of new members, or the promotion of existing members to higher degrees. These rites of passage involve the enactment of lengthy dramas, in the course of which candidates go through phases of death and rebirth, are entrusted with new secret signs, passwords, and hand-clasps, and are made to take oaths, under the threat of horrifying sanctions, not to betray these secrets to outsiders. Recurring within these rites of passage are episodes from the life and career of a mythological hero, Hiram Abiff, who is said to have designed the Temple of Solomon. In the face of continual criticism and opposition from the Church, Freemasons go out of their way to emphasize their faith in the Supreme Being, to whom they refer as "The Great Architect of the Universe," or, at times, "The Grand Geometrician," and prominently display the Holy Book at all their meetings.

There is a vast literature on Freemasonry. A large part of it is concerned with controversies about the origins of the cult and the sources of its mythology and rituals. The long essay in the *Encyclopedia Britannica* is purely historical. Another section of this literature consists of attacks, particularly by Roman Catholic clergymen, against the movement, or of defensive reactions by Masons to these attacks. A third section consists of speculations about or disclosures of the secret rituals of the order.

Although a great deal is now known about its history and rituals, very little is known about Freemasonry's social significance, or its involvement in the distribution and exercise of power in society. Our ignorance is only partly due to the secrecy in which the movement is enveloped. Freemasons repeatedly point out that they are not a secret society, but a society with secret rituals. By this they mean that it is only their rituals that are secret, and that membership is not secret. But the paradoxical situation in Britain is that while these rituals are no longer secret, hardly anything is known about membership. Legally, every lodge is obliged by law to submit a list of its members to the local clerk of the peace. But neither clerks of the peace nor the Masonic authorities are obliged to make public the full list of members (see Dewar, 1967:103–4). Some scanty bits of information appear in the newspapers every now and then about individual Masons, and some Masons may also in one way or another reveal their membership to friends, but on the whole the majority do not go out of their way to make their membership known.

Even a casual look through the pages of the year books of the Masonic grand lodges will be sufficient to show that relatively large numbers of Masonic lodges exist in nearly all the new states of Africa and Asia. (In 1970 there were 44 in Nigeria, 43 in Ghana, and well over 100 in India, to take only random examples.) There is practically nothing whatever known about the social significance of these lodges.

There are (1970) seventeen Masonic lodges in Sierra Leone, all in Freetown. Seven of these follow the English Constitution of Freemasonry. They are organized under a district grand lodge, and are ultimately supervised by the grand lodge of England. The remaining ten lodges follow the Scottish Constitution of Freemasonry, are organized under a separate district grand lodge, and are ultimately supervised by the grand lodge of Scotland (see table). There are no Masonic Lodges in Sierra Leone which follow the third "sister" constitution, that of Ireland.

There are between 1,500 and 2,000 members in these lodges. Only a handful of these are Europeans, mainly British, although it was originally British officials in the colonial administration who established Freemasonry in Sierra Leone. Most of these Europeans are today concentrated in one particular lodge, along with Africans. Some of the British members were in the movement in Britain before going to Sierra Leone, and want to continue their membership through affiliation to a Freetown lodge. A few have joined in Sierra Leone, mainly in order to become part of the movement in Britain when they return home. These find it much easier to join in Sierra Leone than in Britain. My impression is that on the whole these European Masons play no significant role in the activities of the local lodges at present, and at least some of them seem to be lukewarm in their attendance at the regular meetings of the movement.

The bulk of the Masons in Freetown are thus Africans, and the grand masters and the other important office-bearers in both district grand lodges are African, most of them Creoles.

There is no consciously formulated policy of excluding non-Creole Sierra Leoneans from membership. Many Masons think that non-Creoles are rare in the movement either because they are not interested, because they are Muslims, or because they cannot afford the expense. Many Creoles would also add that the provincials have their own secret society, the Poro, to which they are invariably affiliated. The provincials do not, in fact, need to become members in the Masonic movement. Moreover, while there is a good deal of pressure on Creole men to join the movement, there is a good deal of pressure on provincials *not* to join it. For example, in its agitation against the APC (All People's Congress) government in 1970, an opposition paper claimed that Siaka Stevens had made history being the first prime minister of the country to become a Freemason. This was to imply that he was now deeply under Creole influence.

The Incidence of Membership

As with every other cult, individual Masons mention a wide variety of motives for joining the movement and remaining in it. Some join because they personally want to, but others join because of pressure. Often a man may join initially for one motive, but develops others after joining. The same man may at different times emphasize different motives for being a Mason. A man who joined as a result of pressure may develop motives or sentiments that are individual and personal. If we consider the sentiments, motives, and circumstances of individual members, we will find that each is a unique case. When questioned, however, Masons often offer reasoned justifications for their membership.

This, of course, is only one side of the story, and by itself does not tell us anything about Freemasonry as an institution in its own right, or about the structural circumstances which keep it alive as a going concern. The structural consequences of Masonic activity are certainly largely unintended by individual Masons, as each individual's first concern is his own interest. But there is a dialectical relationship between the individual and the group; although members seem to be acting freely and rationally, their actions are nevertheless conditioned, largely unconsciously, by structural factors which to some extent constrain a man to behave in certain ways. The collective and the individual are thus closely related, though for analytical purposes they should be kept apart if we are to understand the social significance of the movement. As I want to avoid discussing this problem in the abstract at this stage, I shall proceed to consider briefly the multiplicity and complexity of the factors underlying membership.

Like many other ritual systems, Freemasonry offers a body of beliefs and practices which have intrinsic value. It provides a world view which includes a conception of the place of man in the universe. The literature of speculative Freemasonry contains a large number of treatises on metaphysics and theology written by men who are passionate in their search for what they believe to be the truth. In Freetown I met young Masons who spent a good deal of their spare time reading Masonic literature for their own satisfaction out of sheer intellectual curiosity.

Some men join the movement in the belief that the secrets which they will acquire contain vital intellectual and mystical formulae. This belief is sustained for a long time after joining, as more and more secrets and rituals are unfolded to the Mason when he passes to higher degrees within the order.

Many of the Masons in Freetown with whom I talked stressed the personal satisfaction which they derived from the regular, frequent, and extensive rituals and ceremonies of the lodge. Some of these Masons said, in explanation, that after all they were Africans, and thus fond of the type of drama that the movement provided. A particularly powerful attraction in this respect is the Masonic ceremonial connected with the death of a "brother." Lodges under the English Masonic constitution are prohibited by special rules of the grand lodge of England from going out in regalia to attend a public funeral, although they are given special permission to appear in regalia within the church for the funeral service of a brother. But this prohibition does not exist in the Scottish Constitution, to which the greatest number of Freetown lodges belong. Many of the members of English lodges are, however, also affiliated to Scottish lodges, so that their funerals are often attended formally by their lodges of affiliation in regalia. The deceased man is "laid out" in his formal black suit, bedecked in his full Masonic regalia, for hours before the funeral service, and large numbers of people file past. When the coffin is finally covered, the regalia are taken off the body and placed on top. Masons under the Scottish Constitution proceed in their regalia to the burial ground, and when the Christian burial service is over, the Masons perform a special service at the grave to send their deceased brother off to the "highest lodge." It was, indeed, the dream of many Creole men with whom I talked to be buried with all the pomp and colour of the Masonic ceremonial, and there is no doubt that this is an important source of satisfaction for members of the movement. Some of the obituaries in the newspapers also carry photographs of the deceased in Masonic regalia.

A second body of intrinsic values that men find in Freemasonry is the "system of morality" that it offers. A great deal of the organization and ceremonial of the movement is concerned with the development and maintenance of a true brotherhood among its members. Members are asked specifically to "fraternize" with one another, and a good deal of the time and resources of the lodges are devoted to this end. The regular ritual sessions of the lodge are followed by lavish institutionalized banqueting and drinking. The Creoles generally drink heavily, and many cynics in Freetown say that men take to Masonry primarily for "boozing." The lodge is indeed very much an exclusive club.

One important aspect of Freemasonry as a brotherhood is the elaborate organization of mutual help which it develops, and there is no doubt that the welfare and social security benefits that it offers attract some men to the movement. Masonic welfare services in Britain are indeed among the most lavish and efficient. Many of their benevolent institutions are patronized by members of the royal family. In the United States, this aspect of the movement is even more pronounced. In Freetown, no formal benevolent institutions have been established yet. Such institutions take time to develop, and nearly all Masons have a network of kin who are under the customary obligations to help in the hour of need. Nevertheless, the lodges have provided help in many instances, and their care for aged members is particularly noteworthy. Every lodge has an almoner who attends to cases of need and has at his disposal for the purpose a special welfare fund to which each member contributes regularly at a fixed rate. Thus, although a Creole may expect help in the time of need from his kin, he may still join a lodge in order to secure for himself and his family an additional measure of support or security without the burden of kin obligations.

Some Masons also mentioned the importance of contacting "brothers" in foreign lands. Creoles very frequently travel to Britain and the United States in the course of their educational and professional careers, and they see in Freemasonry an organization that enables them to find helping and welcoming brothers wherever they go. These brothers abroad tend at the same time to be people of means and influence, and their help can be substantial. I met a young Creole on his way to Britain for the first time to study who told me that he was a member of a Scottish lodge, but that shortly before he left he had affiliated himself with one of the English lodges in order to be able to make contacts with brothers in both England and Scotland.

Freemasons are required by special rules to harbour no enmity against one another, and to settle misunderstandings or tension between brothers promptly and amicably. This must be particularly significant for many Creole Masons, who in ordinary secular life are caught up in the tensions of competition for appointments and promotions and the estrangement resulting from involvement in the hierarchical bureaucratic structure of the civil service or the professions.

One of the moral principles of the brotherhood which is particularly stressed by Creole Masons in Freetown is that no brother should flirt or commit adultery with the wife of another brother. This "private" piece of morality is one of the mechanisms meant to reduce potential sources of tension and enmity between members, and is widely used in the organization of many kinds of fraternities. Women are seen in many contexts as a source of tension between men. This is probably one of the main reasons why Freemasonry and other secret societies of this kind are exclusively male. Indeed, one of the indirect consequences of lodge membership among the Creoles is that it serves as a mechanism to institutionalize the weaning of men from their wives. Wives and female relatives are invited only once a year to a ladies' night which each lodge holds. Even if a man belongs to only one lodge, he may spend two or three nights a week away from his wife in ceremonial sessions, meetings of committees, or visiting other lodges. A substantial proportion of the members of a lodge are office bearers, and their various duties necessitate frequent meetings. And as many Creole Masons in Freetown are not only members of one lodge, but are also affiliated to one or more other lodges, their absence from their wives is indeed frequent and prolonged. Most Masonic meetings in Freetown start at about 6:30 P.M and go on in ceremonial and banqueting until about 2 A.M. While often sharing some of the benefits of Freemasonry with their husbands, wives are annoyed by this. Many think that their husbands use lodge meetings as an alibi for visiting other women.

Apart from these ritual and moral values, some individual Creoles find in Freemasonry more "practical" and mundane advantages. Non-Mason cynics in Freetown claim that men join in order to establish informal links with their superiors in the civil service or the professions, as the case may be. It must be remembered that many of the most eminent judges, lawyers, permanent secretaries, heads of departments, doctors, engineers, and others are members of the Masonic lodges in Freetown. In a society where rank and patronage count for a great deal, this must indeed be an important factor attracting men to join. In 1970 one often heard gossip in Freetown society to the effect that all appointments and promotions in certain establishments were "cooked" in the lodges. Similar charges have also been made against Freemasonry in Britain, America, and elsewhere. But one need not assume their validity in order to appreciate that men seek to establish primary relations with their superiors, irrespective of possible material gain. Many of the Masons are involved as superiors and subordinates in bureaucratic hierarchies outside the movement, and a great deal of tension arises between them in various situations. It is natural that they should welcome an institution which alleviates the effects of this tension. Members go out of their way to show that the order enjoins strict moral standards, and that there is no nepotism or corruption involved.

Association with "high-ups" through Masonry leads many non-Masons in Freetown to complain that Masons are snobs and behave in a superior manner. Masonry is certainly synonymous with high status in Freetown, for the simple reason that a man cannot become a Mason if he cannot afford to pay the relatively high expenses of membership and of the very frequent and lavish banqueting. In 1970 the annual cost of membership for an initiate into the entered apprentice degree was about £50, excluding the cost of a formal suit, transport, and so on. At promotion to the second degree, the cost was higher, and when one was eventually "raised" to the third degree, that of master, the cost during the year of one's "reign" in the lodge was between £400 and £500. Although both kin and lodge brothers contribute towards such expenses, the bulk of the cost is borne by the man himself. The regular payments that members make annually include fees for registration, contributions to benevolent funds, and some other minor items. The regalia for the initiate cost over £25, and as the Mason rises in degree so does the cost of his regalia. Most of the lodges in Freetown include the basic cost of banqueting for the whole year in their annual fees, so that whether a man attends a banquet or not he will have paid the costs.

Quite apart from the expenses of membership, a man must also have the right connections if he wants to join the order. Freemasons do not proselytize, and candidates are nearly always nominated by kin and friends who are already members. There is an initial period of investigation by a "committee of membership," during which inquiries are made about the candidate and he himself is interviewed and questioned at length. When the committee is satisfied, the candidate is proposed for election at a general meeting of the lodge. Election is by secret balloting. If more than one blackball is cast, the candidate will not be admitted. This means that only "the right people," who are acceptable to nearly the whole lodge, will be admitted. Membership is thus taken as a privilege, and Masons are to a great extent proud of it. Perhaps largely unconsciously, the Creoles generally see in Masonry a mechanism for the development and maintenance of the "mystique" which marks and enhances their distinctiveness.

Collective Constraints

But by far the most important factor driving Creole men to Freemasonry is pressure from kin, from friends, and from wider groupings. Indeed many of the benefits that individual Masons are said to gain from membership are elaborations or rationalizations developed *after* joining. A great deal of insight into the structural forces that constrain Creole men to join can be gained from talking to men who are not yet Masons.

Some join because their fathers are or were Masons. A Mason regards it as a duty and a source of pride to bring his sons into membership, often within the same lodge. As sons reach the age of twenty-one, their fathers begin to press them to join. I knew of at least one case where a man, who was eminent in both Freemasonry and in the political organization of the state of Sierra Leone, took the trouble to ask the higher Masonic authorities in Britain for special permission to have his eighteen-year-old son admitted as a member. I talked to men in their twenties and a few in their thirties who told me they had been putting off joining the movement by telling their fathers or other related Masons that they were not yet "really old enough" for it. Even when the father is dead, older brothers or other relatives urge their younger brother to respect their father's wish that his son should join. Pressure also comes from other kin who are already in the movement.

Most important of all is the pressure of friends and colleagues. It must be remembered that we are here discussing a few thousand men who were born, brought up, and had their schooling and most of their university education in a relatively small town. Men spend most of their leisure time in cliques of friends, and when most of a man's peers join one after the other, and become absorbed in Masonic activities, a great deal of pressure is exerted on him to join. If he does not, he is likely to lose his friends. A young engineer told me that his Masonic friends would sometimes request him to leave the room so that they could say something in the confidence of Masonic brothers. He was in fact not sure, telling me this, whether it was not done deliberately by his friends in order to induce him to join.

Although only about a third of Creole men are full members of the Masonic lodges, the other two-thirds are to a large extent structurally involved with the movement. For although only the relatively well-to-do are in the lodges, these are in fact the patrons of those who are not members. Patronage involves both privileges and obligations, and it is difficult for a man to remain in this position without keeping in close relationship with the other patrons who occupy strategic positions in the society. Masonic membership is an important feature of the lifestyle of any Creole of importance. It is a collective representation to which a man will subscribe in order to partake in the network of privilege. A patron is indeed under strong pressure to join if he does not want to forfeit his role and his power.

On deeper analysis, it will become evident that this pressure by relatives, friends, and status groups, operating on the individual, is itself a mechanism of constraint, whose source is the wide cleavage between Creoles and non-Creoles in Sierra Leone. To appreciate the nature of this structural constraint, we must view it developmentally. I have for this purpose drawn up a list of the Masonic lodges in Freetown, by name, year of consecration, and constitution. The establishment, consecration, and continuity of a lodge are supervised and administered by the "mother" grand lodge in Britain. No lodge can be established unless it gets a special charter from the grand lodge to certify that it has been formed in accordance with all the regulations of the

Masonic Lodges in Freetown

ENGLISH CONSTITUTION		SCOTTISH CONSTITUTION	
Name	Year of Consecration	Name	Year of Consecration
Freetown	1882*		
St. George	1894*		
Rokell	1899*	S. L. Highland	1905*
Loyal	1914	Academic	1914*
Progressive	1947		
Wilberforce	1947		
		Tranquillity	1949
		Harmony	1950*
		Travelers	1950
Granville	1952		
		Mount Aureol	1965
		Sapiens	1966
		Delco	1966
		Leona	1968
		Earl of	
		Eglington	
		and Winton	1968

*Lodges granted Royal Arch status.

movement. This charter must be displayed in every lodge at every one of its meetings, and without it the meeting is invalid. Moreover, the charter must be renewed annually. Each lodge has a special serial number in the constitution and its name, address, and other details are formally listed in the year book of the mother constitution.

The first point to be noted from the table is that the proliferation of lodges in Sierra Leone has not been a gradual process, but has occurred in bouts. We can divide the development of Freemasonry in Freetown into three major periods. The first is from 1882 to 1914, when six lodges were formed, four under the English Constitution and two under the Scottish Constitution. Most of the members were British officials, and I am not concerned here with that period. For the following three decades, from 1914 to 1946, no new lodges were established. This was roughly the period of indirect rule in British West Africa, which came to an end in most British colonies shortly after World War II. Then in the course of four to five years, from 1947 to 1952, the number of lodges in Freetown doubled, from six to twelve. This was a period of new political developments, leading eventually to Independence in 1961.

There followed a standstill period of about thirteen years, which roughly coincided with the stable premiership of Sir Milton Margai, terminating in 1964 with his death, and the succession to the premiership of his brother, Sir Albert Margai. This ushered in a turbulent time, which came to an end with the coups d'état of 1967 and 1968. In the course of less than three years, the number of lodges leapt by nearly 50 percent, from twelve to seventeen, with all the increase occurring in the Scottish Constitution.

We thus have two phases of concentrated and intensified "Freemasonization," the 1947–52 period and the 1965–68 period. What is significant in both periods is that each involved a direct, serious threat to Creoledom. This emerges clearly from a wealth of documentation of all sorts, and from the detailed studies of the politics of Sierra Leone since World War II by political scientists and other scholars (see particularly Kilson, 1966; Fisher, 1969; Cartwright, 1970). I can here give only a brief outline of the relevant events.

The developments of the 1947–52 period still remain the most traumatic experience in the psychology of the Creoles. Until then they had been securely entrenched in the colony, despite the British policy of restraining them from dominating the provincials from the protectorate. Their ascendency in the civil service and in the professions was overwhelming. Even as late as 1950, there were at least seventy Creole doctors, as against three from the protectorate (Cartwright, 1970:24). In 1953, 92 percent of the civil servants were Creoles. In 1947 the British government presented proposals for constitutional reform in Sierra Leone aiming at unifying the colony and the protectorate, and setting the whole country on the path to independence. The proposals at that stage were not revolutionary for the country as a whole, but they dramatically affected the balance of power between colony and protectorate. Among other things, they stipulated that the fourteen African members of the new legislative Council should be elected by the people. This virtually meant the beginning of the end of Creole political influence, even within what they had hitherto regarded as their own home, the colony.

Their reaction was frantic. In 1948 all the major Creole political groupings, including the Combined Ratepayers' Association and the Sierra Leone Socialist Party presented a petition to the secretary of state for the colonies attacking the colonial government for intending to give power to illiterate "foreigners"; i.e., the people of the protectorate. The Creoles demanded that only the literate should be given the right to vote.

There were bitter exchanges across the deepening cleavage between the Creoles and the natives. Dr. H. C. Bankole-Bright, the Creole political leader at the time, described the Creoles and the natives as "two mountains that can never meet." In a letter published by the Creole *Sierra Leone Weekly News* (26 August 1950), he recalled that the protectorate had come into being "after the massacre of some of our fathers and grandfathers . . . in Mendeland because they were described as 'Black Englishmen.'" For the other camp, Milton Margai, soon to become the prime minister of Sierra Leone, described the Creoles as a handful of foreigners to whom the natives' forefathers had given shelter, who imagined themselves to be superior because they aped Western modes of living, but who had never breathed the true spirit of independence (see Protectorate Assembly, 1950:28–31).

What is important to note here is that although the more conservative Creole elements fought a desperate battle for a long time, and still continue to try to put the clock back,

115

most of the Creole moderates and intellectuals recognized the futility of this stand, and tried to adjust to the times and make the most out of the new opportunities. The latter soon recognized that any attempt by the Creoles to organize politically on formal lines would be disastrous because of their hopeless numerical weakness.

It should be emphasized that, in their determination to leave Sierra Leone, the British pursued a consistent policy in the Africanization of their administration. This entailed the replacement of British officials by Africans, and as few natives were educated enough to qualify, it was inevitable that the bulk of the new recruits would come from among the Creoles. Moreover, as landowners in the colony, the Creoles began to reap the benefits of impending independence in the shape of a rise in the value of their property. All this meant that the Creoles would lose everything if they stood as a formal solid political bloc within the new state structure. On the other hand, if they cooperated in the maintenance of a liberal regime on the basis of individual equality, they would gain a great deal because of their superior education and cultural sophistication. The Creoles who were thinking along these lines eventually cooperated with the native-dominated Milton Margai government. Milton Margai, who was a shrewd politician, grasped that he could not establish a government without the Creoles, and he also recognized the immense contribution that the Creoles had made and could still make to the country. He therefore included many Creoles in his party's representation, and retained Creole men in key administrative positions. Thus, despite the grumbling of some Creoles every now and then, a period of cooperation and stability prevailed throughout Milton Margai's regime, ending with his death in 1964.

His brother, Albert Margai, who succeeded him, was different in character and in style of government. Within a short time he made a serious attempt to change the constitution in order officially to establish a one-party system. He could not do this without the close cooperation of the civil service, the judiciary as well as the legislature. But his attempt was immediately opposed by almost all the Creoles, who now shifted their support to the opposition party. Opposition papers began to agitate against Albert and to expose his alleged corruption. The government brought the agitators to court. But the courts were presided over by Creole judges, and verdicts were in the hands of juries who, because of the requirement that they be literate, were also Creole. Most of the accused were acquitted. This outraged Albert Margai, who in his speeches ominously began to attack the "doctors, lawyers, and lecturers of Freetown" who were wilfully refusing to see the blessings of the one-party system.

Events during the following one or two years show what an influential small minority elite can do against an established government supported by a large section of the population. Creole heads of trade unions, clergymen, lawyers, doctors, teachers, and university students used every shred of influence they had to bring about the downfall of Albert Margai. An opportunity presented itself in the 1967 general elections, when the majority of Creole men and women threw their influence and their organizational weight behind the opposition party. The governing party, the SLPP, was defeated, though by a narrow majority (for details see Cartwright, 1970; Fisher, 1969).

Thus in both the 1947–52 and 1965–68 periods there was a sharp, dramatic turn of events which brought about a serious threat to the continuity of Creole power and privilege. The very men whose power was most threatened in this way, mainly the civil servants and members of the professions, were those who filled the Masonic lodges of Freetown. Unless we assume that these men had split personalities, we can easily see that the two processes of change, i.e., the developing threat to Creole power and the increase in Freemasonic membership, are significantly interrelated. Nearly all the names of the Creoles who were involved in the struggle against Albert Margai in 1966 and 1967 were those of well-known Freemasons. The varied forms that Creole action took to bring about the downfall of Albert Margai showed a remarkable degree of overall coordination, which no formal political party or association was at the time capable of achieving.

Exclusive Organization

Largely without any conscious policy or design, Masonic rituals and organization contributed to the development of an informal structure which helped the Creoles to protect their position in the face of increasing political threat. It did this in a number of ways, the most important being in providing an effective mechanism for regular communication, deliberation, and decision making, and for the development of an authority structure and an integrated ideology. Although the members are divided into two constitutions and further, within each of these, into several lodges, there is a very great deal of intensive interaction among the whole membership. This is done through the manipulation of some of the institutions of Masonic organization.

A Mason can become a member in only one lodge, his "lodge of birth," into which he is initiated. But he can seek affiliation with other lodges, whether of his own or of the other constitution. Many Masons are affiliated to one or more lodges, depending on their ability to meet the high expense in both time and money. Affiliation to a lodge costs only slightly less than membership. When a man is affiliated to a lodge, he enjoys the same privileges and shares in the same activities as its members. I know of some men who are affiliated to five lodges. On the individual level, men seek affiliation for reasons identical to those mentioned above in connection with membership. They may want to associate with eminent men who are the members of other lodges, to interact socially, to enjoy eating and drinking more frequently. Others seek affiliation with lodges where they have better prospects for early promotion to the degree of master Mason.

Another institution, which is probably even more important in establishing channels of communication between the lodges, is that of visiting. A Mason can visit other lodges, where he may or may not have friends. All except the Royal Arch lodges are open to members from all degrees. Royal Arch lodges are, however, open only to reigning or past master Masons. I understood from Masons in Freetown that on the average nearly a quarter to a third of those present at any lodge meeting are visitors from other lodges.

Sociologically, the most important feature of lodge ceremonials is not the formal rituals of the order but the banqueting following their performance. It is here, amidst heavy drinking and eating, that Masons engage in the process of true "fraternizing." This informal spontaneous institution within Masonry is the most fundamental mechanism in welding the members of all the lodges into a single, highly interrelated communal organization. The seventeen lodges meet within less than one square mile; in some cases many lodges have their temples in the same building in the center of town. What is more, the members are also already related to one another as relatives, affines, or friends, attending one another's weddings, funerals, and other family ceremonials.

It is obvious that the wealthier a man is, the more mobile he becomes within the lodges, and this brings us to a second and a most fundamental structural function of Masonic organization. This is that although there is emphasis in Masonry on equality and true brotherhood, Masonic organization provides effective and efficient mechanisms for the establishment of a strong authority structure. Formally, this is achieved by ritual promotion through the three degrees of the craft, the entered apprentice, fellow of the craft, and master Mason. These degrees are the same under both the English and the Scottish Constitutions, but the English Constitution has further degrees within what is known as the royal arch.

Initiation into the first degree, then promotion to the second, "raising" to the third, and further promotion in the royal arch degrees, are marked by very elaborate ritual dramas. Each stage is also marked by new regalia, with additional signs of office. It is also marked by the acquisition of further secrets, by new duties and new privileges. Apart from these ritual degrees, there are also in each lodge a large number of office bearers of all sorts, who are concerned with its running and organization. And paramount

119

among the lodges in each constitution, there is a district grand lodge, headed by a district grand master, with his deputy and secretary. A master is always addressed as "Worshipful Master." A grand master is addressed as the "Most Worshipful Master." The higher a Mason's degree, the greater his mobility within, and access to, the lodges. A master Mason can enter even the Royal Arch lodges without permission or invitation.

All promotions within the order are formally on the basis of attainment in Freemasonic theology and ritual, and require devotion to the movement in regular attendance. But as each promotion to a higher degree necessitates spending more money in fees, on regalia, and especially in providing banquets, only those Masons who can meet these expenses, and who have the necessary backing in the lodges, will seek promotion. Promotion usually takes time, and it may take a man over ten years to become a master Mason. But the process can be greatly speeded up, and there are cases in Freetown of men being raised to the third degree within three years.

In this respect, the Scottish Constitution is more flexible than the English. Promotion can be quicker. Masons from Scottish lodges in Freetown said they thought the Scottish Constitution was more democratic than the English, which they described as conservative. In a Scottish lodge, it is the members of the lodge who decide on who will be raised to the positions of master and deputy, while in English lodges the decision comes from above. On the whole, the Scottish Constitution seems to adapt more easily to changing situations than the English, and I believe that this is the main reason why, as the table shows, the Scottish, rather than the English Constitution, is now predominant among the Creoles. In a rapidly changing situation, it is important for a group to have a more flexible articulating ideology and organization. For the Creoles, this is indeed crucial.

Within the hierarchy of degrees and offices of the Masonic organization there is thus a close relationship between wealth and status in the secular sphere on the one hand, and ritual authority within the order on the other. The prominent men in the Masonic order are prominent men in Sierra Leone.

Individual Masons often manipulate various factors to gain authority and power within the movement. A man who has just joined a lodge, and who would normally have to take his place in the queue behind many other "brothers" until he can be raised to the coveted status of master Mason, will either seek affiliation to another lodge in which more opportunities exist, or will combine with other members—who should include at least seven masters—in order to push through an application for the foundation of a new lodge. If he is a member of an English lodge, he may discover that his chances are better in affiliation with a Scottish lodge. Within the lodge he will try to gain the affection and support of various cliques of friends.

Even at the level of district lodges, the two Masonic organizations are closely interrelated, and, taken together, they merge in effect into one unified Masonic hierarchy. In 1970, the district grand master of the Scottish Constitution, for example, had originally been initiated into an English Constitution lodge, was then affiliated to other lodges from both constitutions, and ultimately became founding master of a Scottish lodge. Other eminent Masons in Freetown had had similar careers within the order.

This integrated hierarchy of authority is of immense significance for the Creoles as a corporate interest group. Like the middle classes in many countries, the Creoles are in general notoriously individualistic, and no sooner does a leader begin to assume leadership than a number of other men begin to contest his claim in the spirit of "why he, and not me?" It must again be emphasized that during the colonial period, while the Temne, Mende, and the other tribes of Sierra Leone had their own local and paramount chiefs whose authority was upheld by the colonial administration, the Creoles were without traditional leadership.

The difficulty in developing a unified leadership and system of authority was further increased by the fact that, outside the formal political arena, the Creoles had several, often competing, hierarchies of authority within different

121

groupings. One was the church hierarchy, others were in each one of the major professions, including the teachers. Furthermore, there was strife within each grouping characterized by intense competition for promotion to higher positions, and by perpetual tension between superiors and subordinates in the bureaucratic structure. But when the members of all these groupings were incorporated in the Masonic order, they became integrated in an all-encompassing authority structure, in which members from the higher positions of the different non-Masonic hierarchies were included. The different types and bases of power within those groupings were expressed in terms of the symbols and ideology of Freemasonry. A unified system of legitimation for a unified authority structure was thus created. This has not been, of course, a once-and-for-all development, but a continuing dialectical process between ritual authority within the order and the various authority structures outside it.

Freemasonry has thus provided the Creoles with a medium for the articulation of the organizational functions of a political group. The organization that has emerged is efficient and effective, and is thus in sharp contrast with the loose, feeble political organizations in Sierra Leone generally. As Cartwright (1970) points out, the political parties of Sierra Leone are loose alliances between various groups, many of which shift their allegiance from one party to another unpredictably. But Masonic organization is strictly supervised by the two grand lodges, which enforce strict standards of organization evolved in an advanced and highly industrialized society. This is why it has thus partly made up for Creole numerical weakness. A small group can indeed greatly enhance its power through rigorous organization.

Although I have here been discussing the political functions of a ritual organization, I am not implying any kind of reductionism which aims at explaining, or rather explaining away, the ritual in terms of political or economic relations. Nor am I imputing conscious and calculated political design to the men who observe the beliefs and the symbolic codes of such an organization. Like many other ritual systems, Freemasonry is a phenomenon sui generis. It is a source of values in its own right, and individuals often look at it as an end in itself, and not as a means to an end. A Creole Mason will be genuinely offended if he is told that he is joining the movement out of political considerations. More fundamentally, the Masonic movement is officially opposed to the discussion of political issues in the course of its formal meetings. There is certainly no conscious and deliberate use of Freemasonry in political manoeuvring.

But the Creoles generally have been under severe pressure during the past twenty-five years, partly as a privileged group and partly as an important state elite which is identified with "the establishment." They have had to put up with threats of various sorts, in the street, in the courtrooms, and in Parliament. It is inevitable that they should be aware of and often discuss these problems. When they gather in the Masonic temples, they do so to perform the prescribed formal rituals. But when they adjourn to banqueting, or when they meet informally outside the framework of Freemasonry, they talk about current problems. In consequence of the sharing of the same sign language, the same system of beliefs, the same rituals, and the same organization, and through frequent banqueting, strong moral bonds develop between them, which often transcend and become stronger than many other bonds, so that when they meet outside the lodge framework they talk together more intimately than they would if they were not brothers in the same movement. Attend any of the frequent ceremonials staged by the Creoles in their ordinary social life, such as weddings, christenings, or graduation ceremonies, and you will not fail to see that while the women are busy dancing on their own to the wild beat of the *Gumbe* band, the men sit quietly in cliques on the side drinking and talking. If you ask the women what their men are doing they will say, "They are talking lodge."

Through these intimate and exclusive gatherings, within and outside the framework of the lodge, men pool their problems, deliberate about them, try to find solutions, and eventually develop formulae for appropriate action. Perhaps it is because of all this deliberation, communication, and coordination of decision making that there is a remarkable unanimity of opinion among the Creoles over major current problems. Talk about any public issue on any day with different Creoles in Freetown, and you will most probably hear the same comments, phrased in almost identical words. Many expatriates in Sierra Leone have remarked on this uniformity of response to major issues on the part of the Creoles. In the course of a few months, I followed a number of public issues, concentrating particularly on two of them. One issue was raised by three different men in different situations within two to four days of each other, and was the subject of an article in a daily newspaper. On enquiry, all three men turned out to be members of the same lodge. In a few days' time the statements about the issue became stereotyped, and truly became the "collective representation" of a whole group of men and, later, of their women.

Freemasonry generally offers two major functions to its members: an exclusive organization and a mechanism for the creation of a brotherhood. Through upholding the principle of secrecy, or rather of the monopoly of their secrets, Freemasons are able to develop, maintain, and run a vast, intricate, efficient, and highly complex organization, with its symbols of distinctiveness, channels of exclusive communication, structure of authority, ideology, and frequent socialization through ceremonials. Through its networks of lodges, its ritual degrees and hierarchical structure, its institutions of affiliation and visiting, and the existence of different constitutions, it is particularly suited to operating in the highly differentiated and complex structure of industrial society. For it is capable of articulating different occupational and social categories of people, allowing for both unity and diversity.

As men join the organization, the impersonal character of a social category such as an elite gives way to the rapid development of moral bonds that link its individuals. Through the sharing of secrets, a common language of signs, passwords, and hand-clasps, experience of the same humbling ceremonials of initiation, mutual aid, frequent communion in worshipping and eating together, and the rules inhibiting disputes between them, the members are transformed into a true brotherhood. This combination of strict, exclusive structure, with the primary bonds of a brotherhood, makes an association like Freemasonry a powerful organization in contemporary society.

Freemasonry has different structural functions under different social conditions, and in its history in Europe it has served to organize conservative as well as progressive movements. Its functions are determined neither by its doctrine nor by its formal organization, but it is definitely especially suited to the well-to-do. What is more, because of its secrecy and its rules of recruitment, it is so constituted that once it is captured or dominated by a strong interest group, or by a number of related interest groups, it tends to become an exclusive vehicle for promoting group interests. Through secret balloting and the requirement of almost complete consensus for admitting new members, it can easily exclude outsiders.

The material presented in this discussion may give the impression that Freemasonry has been evolved by the Creoles into an informal corporate organization by which they seek to protect and advance their own sectional interests. This is true to some extent, but it is only part of the truth. For it is important to realize that during the past two decades the Creoles have been transformed from a predominantly particularistic group to a predominantly "universalistic" one. The men who are affiliated in the lodges are senior public officials and professionals who are responsible for the running of state institutions. They are part of a state elite, and like all state elites are forced to coordinate and regulate important public issues in confidence and secrecy. As Mills (1956:69) would put it, in their inner circles the most impersonal problems of state have become fused with their own personal worries and deliberations.

The Universalistic Mystique

7

The state is based . . . on the
contradiction between *public* and
private life, between *universal* and
particular interests.

KARL MARX (1944:412)

Mediating Cultures
From Particularism to Universalism
Objectification of the State
Protagonists or Functional "Strangers"?

An elite is an interest group, and its culture develops as a
means for the coordination of its corporate activities to enhance and maintain its power. Its culture is thus to that extent particularistic. But because its members are at the
same time the heads of different public institutions and the
leaders of different national groupings, the very organization that articulates their sectional activities functions at
the same time to bring about the close coordination of
these national institutions and groupings and their overall
integration. In this way the elite offers solutions to some
significant organizational problems on the national level,
and to that extent its culture is universalistic. In time, its

126

universalistic organizational needs affect the culture in their own right and eventually transform it. Thus, the particularistic and the universalistic factors in the culture affect one another in a dialectical manner.

Mediating Cultures

This process can be seen in an extreme, dramatic form in segmentary, acephalous societies evolving centralized political institutions in a relatively short time in order to mobilize their forces in the struggle against monolithic exterior forces. When the Nuer confronted the British, they pushed their traditional ritual prophets into assuming positions of leadership that united the traditionally feuding groupings. The process can be seen in greater detail in the case of the Sanusis in Cyrenaica (Evans-Pritchard, 1949). The Sanusiyya was an Islamic mystical order that penetrated the segmentary tribal organization of the bedouin in Cyrenaica. It succeeded in doing so mainly because it was represented by stranger "holy men" who took no part in intertribal feuding, except when they were called upon to act as mediators. The tribes gave the Sanusis land and protection, and the Sanusis provided the tribes with ritual services of various sorts. Then the whole population faced a serious threat to its very existence when the Italians invaded the country. Because of the segmentary nature of the tribal structure, the tribes needed a centralized political authority to mobilize the population for war and to coordinate corporate activities. But, as no such authority could arise out of the political order itself, the tribes turned to the Sanusis, who, with their network of local lodges and centralized ritual authority, had the means of providing channels for communication between the various parts of the population, and also offered leadership, ideology, and mechanisms for decision making. The hitherto purely ritual order became highly politicized. In its turn, the order reacted on the political structure of the tribes, transforming it from a segmentary to a centralized polity. The ritual order and the political structure of the tribes became one, and their unity came to be symbolized by the ritual head of the order, who eventually

127

was to become the king of the whole country. This politico-ritual interdependence was so strong that in order to crush the tribes, the Italians had to crush the order. In the final stages, they even sought to capture the Sanusi leader and to crown him officially as king, in order to dethrone him later and thereby symbolize the destruction of the resistance movement of the tribes. The order was thus transformed by events from a particularistic group serving sectional interests to a universalistic elite entrusted with the coordination of the corporate activities of the whole population.

The discussion here is focused not on the skills and technical expertise that the members of a specialized elite possess, but on the distinctive style of life and sub-culture—the mysterious qualities that Cardinal Newman (see chapter 1, above) said could not be learnt from books—which the elite develop. The network of interpersonal relationships which they form among themselves becomes the instrument through which the various specialized sectors of public life which they serve are informally or invisibly coordinated. In other words, the members of such an elite use their private personal relationships and the idioms of their sub-culture in the coordination of public functions.

No society can be organized as an on-going concern on purely rational, bureaucratic lines, and all public politics involve inevitable compromises, extensive informal dealings, secrecy and concealment. This is true of all societies, developing or developed, simple or complex, communist or capitalist, totalitarian or democratic. Every state is governed by a "village at the top," a group of men and women who interact largely informally—some elitists would say conspiratorially—in the day-to-day running of public affairs.

This kind of covert coordination, although informal in the sense that it is not done according to an institutionalized blue print like a constitution or a bureaucratic structure, is nevertheless conducted according to some unwritten rules, norms, beliefs, and practices that are maintained through elaborate symbolic performances which constitute the particular culture of the elite. This culture is usually acquired by an individual through a long period of informal socialization in inner circles, such as the family, the peer group, the club, the church, the lodge, the party. It often requires socialization from an early age, and this is one of the reasons why there is a tendency for an elite to become a corporate group with not only lateral cooperation but also perpetuation through internal recruitment.

The same elite cult is simultaneously both particularistic, serving the private interests of the group, and universalistic, serving the interests of wider publics. These two functions of the cult are combined in different proportions in different cases, or at different periods in the same case. When the cult becomes exclusively particularistic, the elite loses its legitimacy as the holder of power in the name of the public.

From Particularism to Universalism

Creole men, who are linked through the cousinhood network and meet and interact regularly at Masonic lodges, churches, clubs, halls, and social functions, are also permanent secretaries, heads of departments in various ministries, regional administrative secretaries, the bulk of the country's doctors, lawyers, judges, journalists, writers, teachers, surveyors, engineers, church leaders, and trade union chiefs. The very system of beliefs and practices, or cult, which articulates their informal organization as Creoles, also brings them together as functionaries in the different institutional spheres of the state of Sierra Leone. This cult acts as a mediating system of communication between leaders and functionaries from different sectors and levels of the country. It is the language of the "establishment" and the instrument of "statecraft." Their style of life is instrumental in the coordination of their activities both as Creoles and as administrators and leaders in Sierra Leone. Their culture is both particularistic and universalistic, serving both sectional and state interests.

In the course of the past twenty-five years, the Creoles have been transformed—or have transformed themselves—from an exclusive, aloof, separatist ethnic minority to a functional "stranger" group guarding the authority structure of the State by upholding the independence of the ju-

129

diciary, the neutrality of the civil service, free opposition, free expression, and free competition between rival political groups. They have used their informal corporate organization to develop and maintain these functions, sometimes even against their own immediate interests. The fact that, despite their hopeless numerical weakness and the continual challenge and threat they have encountered during all this time, they have not only retained their power and influence but even increased them in a variety of ways, indicates that their adversaries see in them an indispensable group, who provide a measure of stability and continuity to the State. Their particularist interests and universalistic functions have been so intertwined that sometimes it is difficult to disentangle the one from the other. For example, in their sustained struggle to keep the judiciary independent, it is hard to tell to what extent this is because nearly all the high court judges and most of the lawyers are Creoles, or because the judiciary is the basis of legitimate authority on which the whole State is based.

Until the end of World War II, the Creoles identified themselves with the British, and went out of their way to demonstrate that they had no affinity with the "aborigines" of the protectorate. In their ideology, the peoples of the protectorate were wild, superstitious, wicked, ungodly, primitive, polygynous, and affiliated in devilish secret societies; in contrast they themselves were civilized, Christian, literate, and monogamous. The peoples of the protectorate, in their turn, saw the Creoles as agents of the white man, with the same arrogance and air of superiority. At times they described the Creoles as "white" and as the children of slaves (Spitzer, 1974:84).

This dissociation from the peoples of the protectorate was dramatically expressed by Bankole-Bright when he referred to the Creoles and the provincials as two hills that could never meet. Another Creole leader, Hotobah During, stressed (*Weekly News*, February 1951) that the Creoles, who were British subjects, had nothing in common with the "foreign" people of the protectorate, as the two groups hardly intermarried or ate the same food or wore the same style of clothes.

Creole anxiety during that period was to try to persuade the British that they, the Creoles, were indeed their partners in English culture and British citizenship. "No honest Englishman would deny that he does not see even in the Creole today his own opposite number with a not dissimilar way of life," wrote the Creole paper *Weekly News* (April 1951).

But even during that early period, a small number of Creoles attempted to establish links and common cause with the provincials. This was particularly the case because the Creoles felt that they were spurned and rejected as equals by the British. Other Creoles were imbued by a missionary zeal, taking it as a sacred duty to bring faith and civilization to the "heathens" of the protectorate. As part of this mission, many Creole families took provincial children under the ward system, educated them, and proselytized them. Bringing civilization to the provincials was for them synonymous with Creolization.

Other Creole intellectuals genuinely believed that they had more affinity with the provincials than with the British. Their views were forcefully expressed in the writings of Edward Wilmot Blyden (see Fyfe, 1962; Porter, 1963; Peterson, 1969).

The 1930s saw the rise of a Creole radical, Wallace-Johnson, a Moscow-trained labour organizer, who founded the West African Youth League and formed a strong anti-colonial movement in Sierra Leone. Although he appealed to both protectorate and colony peoples, his followers were mainly Creoles. Eighteen of the twenty-one lawyers in the colony were active in the league (see Spitzer, 1974:180–216).

But, for a variety of reasons, this tendency among progressive Creoles to develop a common cause with the provincials did not gather momentum. There was no provincial proletariat, and hence there were no encouraging responses from the protectorate. The provincial elite came from chiefly families and were not particularly anti-colonial or progressive. Moreover, the rest of the Creoles were alarmed at the threat to their own city, Freetown, posed by the masses of provincial immigrants. Although disappointed and spurned by the British, they enjoyed British protection and remained aloof in their Western way of life. Then World War II broke out and halted the movement temporarily, while Wallace-Johnson was detained in an internment camp for enemy aliens until the end of 1944.

Political events after the war led to the development of the deep cleavage between Creoles and provincials (see above, chapter 6). After initial resistance to the new constitutional changes introduced by the British, the Creoles were ready to share power with the provincial elite. But the latter were the sons of chiefly families, and had no access to the provincial masses except through the local chiefs. The chiefs and the provincial elite from the hinterland thus formed an alliance directed against the Creoles.

Although there were Creole hard-liners who demanded extra-proportional representation or agitated for the independence of the colony, there were many other Creole leaders who sought alliance with popular forces from the hinterland with the aim of establishing a democratic progressive system of government. But the few parties such leaders formed lacked the capacity to operate in the provinces in opposition to the chiefs. With the tacit support of the British and the backing of the chiefs, the SLPP succeeded in denouncing these parties as "Creole parties," and systematically prevented their agents from operating among the masses (for details, see Cartwright, 1970). The bulk of the Creoles did indeed support these "national" parties, but like the predominantly Creole party of Bankole-Bright, they failed dismally in the 1957 election, Creoles being only a small proportion of the total population. For the following decade, state power remained in the hands of the SLPP, with the full backing of the chiefs. But the Creoles were still in control of the civil service and the judiciary, and the government could not function without their full cooperation. For this reason the SLPP, under the shrewd leadership of Sir Milton Margai, sought to accommodate the Creoles, who eventually gave him their full support.

The situation changed dramatically, however, between 1964 and 1967 during Albert Margai's regime. This period, already outlined in the last chapter, saw the culmination of processes that had been going on slowly under the surface during the previous years. One such process was the development of what may be roughly described as a class cleavage in the country. In the provinces, the chiefly families, who enjoyed the full backing first of the British, then of the SLPP, had become progressively more corrupt, extorting money from their subjects, abusing power, and accumulating wealth for themselves. The diamond rush of the late 1950s exacerbated the situation, as it brought about the movement of populations from one locality to another, and the increasing circulation of money, with the result that in many areas allegiance to the local chiefs became weaker. Anti-chief and anti-government passions mounted during the tax riots of 1955–56, partly as a result of disclosures about the corruption of the prime minister and some of his cabinet. The growth of illicit diamond digging and smuggling and the activities of armed bands that roamed some of the provinces demoralized the population. In Freetown there had been riots and strikes organized by the trade unions, and labour unrest generally was exacerbated by the growth in the numbers of the unemployed, half-educated proletariat and the steady increase in the number of immigrants from the provinces.

This developing "class" cleavage overlapped with—indeed in many ways was articulated by—a deep ethnic polarization between the Temne and the Mende. Numerically, the two ethnic groups were almost equal in strength, the Mende comprising 30.9 percent and the Temne 29.8 percent of the total population. But their fortunes had been unequal since the start of European penetration. The Mende lived in the southern provinces, and were thus nearer than the Temne to the coast and to Freetown, with the result that they had greater access to educational facilities. During the colonial period, the British developed Bo, in Mende country, as capital of the protectorate, and established the first secondary school in the protectorate there, catering mainly to the sons of chiefly families. The first provincial doctor and lawyer, Milton and Albert Margai, were

Mende. During the early 1960s, the Mende had four times the educational facilities of the Temne. Economically, too, Temne country remained highly underdeveloped.

During Milton Margai's regime, even at the height of co-operation between Temne and Mende in opposition to the Creoles, fewer posts were given to Temnes than to Mendes. When Sir Milton died, the Temne hoped that their leader, Karefa Smart, would succeed him. According to rumour, however, Albert Margai, with the support of the then chief of the army, threatened to take power by force if the premiership were not given to him. And when he assumed office, Sir Albert systematically dismissed Temne ministers and filled many senior positions with Mendes. He also replaced some Creole permanent secretaries with Mendes. In due course Mendization was carried into the army by the training and commissioning of Mende officers, who in 1967 reached a proportion more than twice that of the Mendes in the total population of the country (see Thomas S. Cox, 1976:72–76). Thus the ruling SLPP came to be identified with the Mende, and the opposition with Temne and with some other ethnic groups in the same region, like the Limba, who were equally embittered against the Mendes.

These two overlapping cleavages, of class and of ethnicity, brought about dramatic growth in the ranks of the APC, the All People's Congress, which stood in opposition to the ruling party. The Creoles joined—and in many ways led—this opposition, for particularistic as well as universalistic reasons. During the previous few years, the Mende had been developing into a challenging elite, with their own "mystique," based on ties that had been developed at Bo, and on the growth of a Freetown-based Mende "network of amity," comprising some senior civil servants, politicians, and army officers. This Mende elite was growing daily both in numbers and in unity, and with the proposal to institutionalize a one-party system and to turn the country into a republic, the danger to Creole status and power became real.

But it was also for "universalistic" considerations that they joined the opposition. Albert Margai threatened to destroy the major principles for which the Creoles had stood: a neutral civil service, free judiciary, free press, and free competition between a plurality of interest groups. He attempted to force civil servants to operate as SLPP agents, and those who objected were dismissed, demoted, or transferred to other places. He made the chiefs suppress the activities of opposition politicians or of their agents in the provinces. He instructed the national radio service to give no news about the opposition, and in 1965 the major daily newspaper in the country, the *Daily Mail*, was bought by the government from the British *Daily Mirror*, and its freedom of reporting and commenting was curtailed. For the Creoles, the greatest threat of all was government interference with the judiciary and the removal of judges who did not cooperate with the prime minister. The change to republicanism contained particular dangers to the judiciary. Some Creole lawyers explained that under the British monarchy, the Privy Council in England provided some kind of safeguard of justice in Sierra Leone. They pointed out that people in Sierra Leone, and particularly in the small society of Freetown, were very much involved with one another in multiplex relationships. Sometimes judge, lawyer, jury, plaintiff, and defendant were linked and cross-linked by primary relationships which would inevitably affect the process of justice. Indeed, at the time when these statements were made, a number of members of the Freetown elite, including some individual Creoles—one of them the former attorney general—were being tried for their part in a recent attempted coup d'état. Under such circumstances, the lawyers maintained, the very thought that when the need arose a case could be referred to the scrutiny of judges from a different society, in a country thousands of miles away, would help in ensuring the independence and neutrality of the judiciary.

Thus it was for these "universalistic" issues, as much as for the direct threat to their interests, that the Creoles threw their weight behind the opposition. Or, expressed differently, by pursuing their own sectional interests, the Creoles were at the same time pursuing the more general interests of the public.

A number of interrelated points emerge clearly from this

brief historical survey of the past two and a half decades. During all of this period, and amidst all the changes and the shifts of power and of alliances among different types of groups, the Creoles maintained their control of the civil service, of the professions and, most important of all, of the judiciary. Their culture was the main mediating instrument that made possible the continual coordination of the activities of the various institutions of the nation-state. They provided the country with stability and continuity despite the fluidity and erratic nature of the political system. Their own particularistic or informal organization was far more efficient than the loose political alliances in the country. They consistently stood for the major liberal principles: a free press, free speech, rule of law, independence of the judiciary, and neutrality of the civil service.

Almost all the progressive political movements were initiated by Creoles, and the Creoles generally were consistently associated with every democratic or socialist progressive movement in opposition to the chiefs and their rule. To some extent events thus transformed them, as in the case of the Sanusis, into a stranger group, whose culture articulated the emergence of the Sierra Leone State.

Objectification of the State

Creole cultural traits have, in the last twenty-five years, been made to serve the maintenance of the state system. Typically, Creole skills in the arts of decorum, etiquette, comportment, rhetoric, mastery of ceremonies, and all the manifestations of what is vaguely called "culture," like the qualities of the "gentleman" listed by Newman (see chapter 1), have been universalized as intrinsic national values. The Creoles, or rather any elite group that masters these skills, are assumed therefore to be indispensable to the ordering and continuity of the state structure.

It must be remembered that "the State" is an abstraction whose reality is socially constructed in terms of a body of symbols and ceremonials: flag, national anthem, national language, national history, national education, national holidays, state ceremonies, courtly receptions and parties for diplomats and foreign visitors, and gatherings of all sorts. Next comes the bureaucratic structure, which has its own symbolism and mythology, regulating public life and integrating all regions and groupings in one organization. Underlying and permeating all these is what MacIver (1947: 39–58) called the Myth of Authority, or the Central Myth, by which authority is sanctified, set apart, and stabilized.

In Sierra Leone the role of the Creoles in the development and maintenance of this symbolic construction of the State has been immense, and should be analytically distinguished from particular professional skills and specializations, which can be attained through formal education and training by any person with sufficient intelligence and opportunity.

Krio, the lingua franca that the Creoles developed and disseminated in the country, is perhaps symbolic, as well as instrumental in bringing the various ethnic groups of the population together. English is the official language of the State, the language of schools, offices, and Parliament, but not of ordinary people in everyday life. Tribal groups in their own provinces use their own native languages in communication, the Mende speaking Mende, the Temne speaking Temne, and so on. But in the mixed towns generally, and throughout the Freetown peninsula in particular, Krio is the "national" language. It is the language of the market place, of the street and of various other spheres of public life. The Creoles themselves speak it at home, although for generations they have attempted to teach their children to speak English even in the home. And from time to time there have been attempts to develop Krio into a written language with its own literature, grammar, and "civilization" (see Jones, 1968).

The Creole role in developing the "national" literature and arts has been overwhelming. In an article in a special supplement to *The Times* (4 May 1974), Professor D. E. Jones of the University of Sierra Leone surveyed all the national literary works, both fiction and non-fiction. Nearly all the authors turned out to be Creoles. Almost the same list of names is given in another article which the same author contributed to a symposium on Freetown (Fyfe, 1968).

137

Thus Freetown Creole literature is at the same time the national literature of Sierra Leone.

More strikingly, Creole history has indirectly come to punctuate and to give a basic structure to the history of Sierra Leone. Anthropologists have developed the concept of "structural time" (see Evans-Pritchard, 1940:94–138), which articulates not an objective historical sequence but political relationships between contemporary groups. Thus Nuer structural time, for example, is built into a genealogy covering a span of ten to twelve generations. This is not an objective chronological time span, but that necessary to conceptualize relations between the major political groupings.

In a similar fashion, the present structure of the Sierra Leone political system is often explained in terms of the history of the Creoles in the country, although both histories were made by colonialism. In the Creole-provincial cleavage that dominated Sierra Leone politics during the period 1947–57, the Creoles talked about "our fathers who built this land," while the provincials talked about "our forefathers" who gave refuge to the Creoles (see chapter 6, above). This ideological history is not confined to political leaders, but is the popular history expressed in everyday life in the country. People explain the present relations between ethnic and regional groupings in terms of the time span of the history of the Creoles. This is the case not just with ordinary people and committed ideologists, but also among academic historians, for a variety of technical reasons. Open any book on the history of Sierra Leone and you will find that its starting point is the story—which by now has acquired legendary character—of the settlement of the emancipated slaves in the country towards the end of the eighteenth century. The most authoritative academic history of Sierra Leone to date, *A History of Sierra Leone* by Christopher Fyfe (1962), starts with an introduction of 12 pages covering the earlier history of the country, and then devotes the remaining 760 pages to the history of the Creoles and the colony. This, of course, is dictated partly by the lack of documentation covering the earlier period, and by the fact that the very formation of Sierra Leone as a political entity occurred only during the colonial period. But it does not change the fact that this is the history of "the nation" as it is today, and it is certainly the history that is taught in schools throughout the country and which filters from the schools into popular ideologies.

Thus, Creole skills, education, values, norms, and symbols have been developed from a particularistic style of life, serving sectional interests, to a "universalistic" culture offered on the national level. Through various processes, its distinctively Creole character has been progressively diminishing, and it now appears as a universalistic, national culture for the whole country. Despite pressure and opposition, the Creole way of life nevertheless remains the ideal pursued by the rising provincial elite. Again, it is necessary to remember that the small group of people being discussed have no executive political power, and no means of exercising physical or economic coercion. Yet their symbols have been powerful and efficacious in influencing the formation of a whole nation-state.

Protagonists or Functional "Strangers"?

By 1970, Sierra Leone had evolved a "segmentary system" consisting of two major fronts, associated with the two major ethnic groups, the Mende and the Temne, with the Creoles at times being pushed, and at others manoeuvring themselves, into the position of the functional "strangers" who maintain the unity, stability, and continuity of the polity.

This was possible partly because no viable political culture has been evolved by the provincials to replace that of the Creoles. The provincials are divided into about sixteen ethnic groups, with different languages and traditions. More significant is the fact that the two major ethnic groups, the Mende and the Temne, are of almost equal numerical strength. Each has formed the core of one of the two national parties, the SLPP and the APC. Temne and Mende elites have been inhibited by traditional laws of land tenure, inheritance, and chiefly authority, from developing a

139

native elite culture which could have competed with that of the Creoles. The nearest approach to the development of such a culture was during the Margais' regime, when a fairly large number of Mende politicians and civil servants formed the core of a circle of men who shared the same cultural background and who were linked loosely by a network of amity. But this was only a beginning, and the elite core was tied to the old traditional chiefs and torn between Freetown and the tribal hinterland. Neither qualitatively nor numerically could it rival the Creole mediating culture. Moreover, its identification with one of the two major ethnic groups posed the threat of that group dominating the whole country, with probably disastrous effects for the neutrality of the judiciary and of the civil service. The Creoles are not tied to any of the traditional chiefs and had a good apprenticeship for nearly a century and a half under European administrators. Fourah Bay College, from which generations of Creole men and women have graduated, was founded in Freetown as early as 1848.

Many Creoles cooperated with the Margais' regimes without ever losing their identity. They were content with their control of the civil service and prominence in the professions. They jealously guarded the neutrality of the civil service and the independence of the judiciary. When these were threatened in 1967, they dissociated themselves from the SLPP and put all their support behind the APC. And again, judging by developments between 1967 and 1970, their links with the men of the new regime have been mostly formal and single-stranded. Already in 1970, only three years after the APC came to office, there were tensions and strains between the Creoles and their recent allies in and out of the government. Indeed one of the leading APC politicians, who had worked hand in hand with the Creoles to bring about the downfall of Albert Margai, was among the leaders of the anti-Creole Provincial Committee of 1970 (see chapter 6).

The important point here is that whichever of the two political "segments" came to power, it would have to have the full support and cooperation of the Creoles. On their part, the Creoles cannot afford to ally themselves with either of the segments on a permanent basis to the extent of integrating with it socially and culturally. What they have, in effect, succeeded in doing so far is to develop their structural position into that of the "mystical strangers," like the Sanusis of Cyrenaica or the prophets of the Nuer, who maintain the administrative and ceremonial structure.

A number of factors have helped them to achieve and maintain this central position. They are not in a position to be economically dominant. They have not been directly involved in the diamond bonanza and the scandals of the mainland. They have progressively lost control of, or abandoned, business and commerce. They have no association with the land-controlling paramount chiefs. While they do own a substantial amount of freehold land and housing in the Freetown peninsula, the significance of these resources has so far been more political than economic. The rent they collect from native tenants, whether on land in the villages of the peninsula, or on houses and shops in Freetown, is by no means high, though they do collect high rents for luxuriously furnished houses which they let almost exclusively to foreign businesses or diplomatic missions.

Like the Sanusis and the Nuer prophets, they have no physical force of their own. Creole men, for a variety of reasons, have shunned service in either the army or the police. Their voting power in elections is negligible, and moreover they have often boycotted elections in a mood either of resentment or despair. At the same time, they continue to be imbued with a missionary spirit to serve, whether in religion, politics, or generally in "civilizing the masses." And on the whole, their political record during the last twenty-five years has often shown them to be in the forefront of practically every progressive movement in the country.

Their small number, while being the source of their weakness in formal politics, is at the same time the source of their organizational strength in informal politics. Not only does it make the provincials less afraid of them, but the informal political organization which their culture articulates has proved to be far stronger and more effective than any of the

141

loose alliances formed by the provincials. The sociological significance of this factor of smallness is pointed out by Simmel (1950:90–93) in his discussion of aristocratic groups:

> There is an *absolute* limit beyond which the aristocratic form of the group can no longer be maintained. . . . If it is to be effective as a whole, the aristocratic group must be "surveyable" by every single member of it. Relations by blood and marriage must be ramified and traceable throughout the whole group. Thus the tendency of extreme numerical limitation, characteristic of historical aristocracies from Sparta to Venice, is not only due to the egoistic disinclination to share a ruling position but also to the instinct that the vital conditions of an aristocracy can be maintained only if the number of its members is small, relatively and absolutely.

Creole society and culture in Freetown provided Sierra Leone with its "village at the top," and, like the politically neutral strips of territory held by the Sanusis in Cyrenaica, Freetown has provided a neutral arena for the "tribesmen" of the interior.

Behind their culture, the Creoles' main strength lies in their advanced education and training. But as the provincials are progressively catching up with them in this respect, they are gripped with anxieties about their status, and seek to enhance their distinctiveness by developing their mystique of excellence, by means of which they continue to set themselves apart from provincial educated elite. This is a common strategy on the part of all elites who are faced with rising "counter-elites." In a way, the British themselves experienced it in relation to the Creoles. Throughout the nineteenth century, British missionaries, administrators, and philanthropists patronized the development of Creole society and culture, and helped the Creoles to acquire the education, religion, and style of life of the West. This was done in a spirit of equality and comradeship between Britons and Creoles. The British lived in Creole neighbourhoods, socialized with Creoles, and worshipped in Creole churches. The Creoles became as sophisticated as their British partners, and Creole men were appointed to many of the most senior positions in the administration of the country. But by the end of the century, the British had changed their attitude and their policy. British officials began to segregate themselves residentially, socially, and culturally from the Creoles. There were many reasons for this change of policy. Some were certainly political, but others were also cultural. As the Creoles became more and more anglicized, identifying themselves with the English and claiming equal partnership in English culture, Britons in Sierra Leone began to express irritation at this claim to equality of status and began to pour scorn on the Creoles' "aping British ways." D. E. Jones (1968) quotes Graham Greene in *The Heart of the Matter* portraying the petulant Englishman's reaction to a nation of people who aped English manners:

> Look at them, look at the one in the feather boa down there. They aren't even real niggers. Just West Indians and they rule the coast. Clerks in the stores, city councillors, magistrates, lawyers—my God. It's alright up in the Protectorate. I haven't anything to say against a real nigger. God made our colours. But these—my God!

But the Creoles are also helped in emphasizing their distinctiveness vis-à-vis the provincials by the reluctance of provincial elite to identify with them, mainly in the belief that being "natives," they stand a better chance in getting privileges through the numerical support and political might of their countrymen.

The Creole cultural "mystique" thus remained dominant until 1970 as the main body of ideological beliefs and practices supporting the structure of the State. If that culture did not exist, it would have been invented—probably through a long and costly process, as has been the case in other African countries. Indeed, to a very large extent the Creoles themselves, as an entity, have been created by the evolving Sierra Leone polity, for their alleged distinctiveness as descendants of former slaves or as non-natives is essentially mythological. It is significant that when the army took over in 1967, it soon found that it could not rule the country and, after a counter-coup, handed the reins of power to civilians—the APC and the Creole-operated administration.

Drama and the Chain   8
of Sociocultural Causation

The history of the Creoles in the last three decades or so is the story of the formation of an informally organized state elite. This has entailed fundamental changes in Creole culture, as expressed and embodied in a series of dramatic performances of different types, employing different symbolic forms and techniques to achieve basic organizational functions. In an effort to analyze this process of sociocultural change, I discuss a number of such performances in this chapter, attempting at the same time to probe the methodological potential of this dramaturgical approach for the study of sociocultural causation.

Power relationships and patterns of normative culture are dialectically related, the one continually acting on and modifying the other. The process is not clear-cut and uniform, but highly complex and dynamic, involving different types of process that vary in their pace of change, and operate on different levels of social organization. A change in power relationships may lead to a change in one symbolic form, and this may in turn lead to a change in another. Sometimes a change in symbolic techniques may lead to a change in symbolic forms that may in the short run affect power relationships. Sociocultural causation therefore operates in series, or chains, of different processes that are mediated through different types of dramatic performances. Analysis of change cannot, and need not, cover all processes on all levels, but rather selects a number of key dramatic performances involving different issues, actors, audiences, and techniques of theatricality.

The correlations between power and cult that have been developed in the previous chapters are inevitably based on conjecture. Two processes may operate together epiphenomenally, without any necessary direct causal connection between them. It is therefore essential to analyze the nature of mediation between the two variables. How are political and cultural processes mediated so that a change in the one will affect the other? The two variables differ fundamentally in nature, even though they are intimately related. Power relationships are manipulative, technical, contractual, instrumental, non-moral. Symbolic patterns of action, on the other hand, are moral, governed by categorical imperatives; they are affective valences, and involve the totality of the selves of the actors. The two also differ in their pace of change, and as a result the relations between them are dynamic and complex.

In the history of the Creoles of Sierra Leone during the past 25 years, two different processes of change have been isolated and analyzed: the one in the relationships of power, the other in the forms, functions, and techniques of cultural symbolism.

On the power front, more Creoles have been recruited to

the middle and upper echelons of the civil service and to the professions, and Creole freehold estates in the Freetown peninsula have greatly appreciated in value. This has been achieved despite the fact that the Creoles are less than 2 percent of the population, have no corporate executive power and no control of the army or the police, and have had to put up with a great deal of pressure and incessant animosity directed against them.

On the cultural front, the period has seen the emergence of the Masonic order as a major institution, and the development of subtle patterns of behavior in manners and etiquette. The Creoles' religion has seen greater intensification of ritual, and marked homogenization of Anglican and Methodist practices and organization. Their family ceremonials have gained in intensity, particularly in their cult of the dead. At the same time, the more external traditional symbols of Creole identity, such as naming and clothing, have been de-emphasized.

The previous chapters attempted to point out some correlations between these two broad processes. Because of the cleavages that divide the provincials and prevent the domination of one segment or another within the State as a whole, the Creoles have been transformed, or have transformed themselves into a group of "structural strangers," mediating between different groupings within the state, maintaining the central myth of law and authority, objectifying national history and national institutions, and ensuring some measure of institutional continuity in the face of various types of subversive processes and organizational weaknesses. The very particularistic, informal organization which they have developed to protect and advance their own power and privileges enables them also to serve the more "universalistic" functions of coordinating the activities of the various national state institutions.

How have the two processes affected one another? How have they been mediated? And what is the nature of the sociocultural, more specifically of the politico-symbolic causal relations between them?

The Organizational Factor

To deal with these and with related questions, a distinction should be made between forms, functions, and techniques in the symbolic process. A change in the form and techniques of symbolism need not automatically entail a change in its organizational functions, because these can be fulfilled by different forms. On the other hand, a change in the relations of power need not necessarily lead to a change in symbolic forms and techniques, because the same form can satisfy different organizational functions.

During the latter part of the colonial period, the Creoles lacked a corporate organization, formal or informal. They were sharply divided on class lines, reinforced by divisions in terms of origin (mainly as settlers and recaptives), and by denominational and church affiliations. Under the protective umbrella of the British colonial administration, there was little occasion for confrontation with the provincials. There were also no serious confrontations with the British. On the contrary, the Creoles identified with the British, and worked to convince them that they subscribed to the same values and norms, were truly their partners in civilization, and in no way inferior to them. The Creoles' family relationships were regulated under British civil law, and most of their values derived from Christianity. The churches provided the framework for their social and cultural life. Mission schools and Christian ideology and connections ensured the continuous recruitment of Creole youth to the literate and professionally trained strata. Creole society as such was highly individualistic, with only a weak sense of communal cohesion and hardly any unified leadership to articulate its corporateness.

With the beginning of decolonization after World War II, leading eventually to independence, there was a dramatic change in Creole fortunes. On the one hand, they made substantial gains in appointments to high civil service positions and came to command a great deal of bureaucratic state power. On the other, they had to put up with mounting pressure and threats from various provincial groupings. The two developments were obviously related, and they created two sets of organizational "needs," the one set for universalistic purposes, the other for particularistic purposes.

On the universalistic side, there was increasing pressure on the many Creoles in responsible positions to coordinate the activities of the various state administrative units and public services. This called for the regular, speedy exchange of information, both horizontally, between the various units, and vertically, within the same unit. Such information had to flow with speed and without "distortion." It also had to be "stored" without records. Public services, like education, medicine, development, and the judiciary, had to be continuously coordinated. On occasion, compromises involving bending the rules here and there had to be made, as indeed is the case everywhere in the world. And it was important to ensure the stability and continuity of these activities, and to maintain the authority of the State. At least as important was the need to ensure, as far as possible, the neutrality of the state apparatus between the major sections of the population, specifically, as it proved later, between the Mende and the Temne. Furthermore, the state needed regular connections abroad.

Such informal types of organizational transactions and arrangements can be performed most easily and efficiently between personnel who speak the same "language," trust one another, subscribe to the same norms, values, and beliefs and can operate informally and confidentially. As studies of various bureaucratic systems indicate, this will call for the development of a special "culture," an elaborate mystique regulating administrative power. The continuous pressure by both the executive and the public at large for speedy, efficient, and effective administration creates pressures on the administrators to develop this kind of mystique. Inevitably, the mystique will have to be exclusive, and hence to some extent particularistic. Thus if a culture like that of Creoledom, which was accommodated to satisfy some of these needs, did not exist, it would have to be developed.

On the particularistic side, the Creoles came under pressure from various quarters, and increasingly needed corporate organizational mechanisms to maintain, develop, and defend their interests and privileges. They had to close ranks in the face of stiffening competition from provincials in education, and hence in recruitment to the bureaucracy. This closure could not be based on any formal principle, and had to rely on a yet more subtle and more elaborate lifestyle, marking new heights of "civilization" and excellence. They were therefore forced to achieve a higher degree of unity across internal status, sex, and "descent" lines of cleavage, bringing about greater homogenization of culture in the process. New types of leadership were needed to infuse the group with corporate consciousness, to find solutions to new problems, to take decisions, and invent new symbols and slogans. A new, more elaborate ideology had to be evolved to reintegrate the culture in a meaningful way, to interpret it in terms of the needs and aspirations of the individual, and also to convince the Creoles of their excellence and the importance of their "mission," and to give them confidence in playing their new roles. A corporate internal authority structure, with sufficient ability to exercise constraint, and even to impose "sanctions" on individuals to make them abide by decisions, had to be set up.

These two sets of organizational needs are felt by the same set of people, and thus overlap sufficiently to lead to the production of one unified, highly integrated body of symbols, comprising a culture which is both universalistic and particularistic. This is a process aptly discussed by Marx (1956:215–17) and Mills (1956).

In discussing organizational *needs* in this way, one runs the risk of reifying corporate organizations by endowing them with almost anthropomorphic qualities. One also runs the risk of engaging in circular arguments, particularly in interpreting events retrospectively, by explaining culture in terms of organizational needs and inferring organizational needs from the observation of culture. The only justification for this is that one is attempting here to analyze a very complex set of sociocultural phenomena from different angles, in the hope of achieving clarifications that are not otherwise possible.

Limited Symbolic Repertoire

In response to these universalistic-particularistic organizational needs, pre-Independence Creole normative culture, with its dominant symbols and ideologies, has undergone changes in a variety of ways. The processes involved have been long, slow, subtle, and complex. In order to understand them, we have to keep in mind that the forms of normative culture tend to be more stable than relations of power. Cultural norms and the symbols which objectify them are systematized not by a special logic inherent in symbols, but by an ideology reflecting the disposition of power within a polity. The symbolic repertoire is nevertheless significantly limited, because it is rooted in basic human *and* social organizational requirements.

An axiomatic human requirement is the continuous creation and recreation of selfhood, of the "I," the oneness of an integrated psyche, in the face of subversive processes from within, as in the demands of conflicting roles, and from without, as in facing death and the singularity of misfortune. (For a more detailed discussion, see Cohen, 1977.) Selfhood is achieved in the course of pursuing primary interaction with significant other human beings, and developing a body of symbolic beliefs and practices forming a world view. In all societies, men engage in primary moral relationships of parenthood, kinship, marriage and affinity, friendship, brotherhood, ritual kinship, and cousinhood. These are the relations of amity (Fortes, 1969) and are one of the constancies of human social life. Similarly, there are general beliefs and symbolic practices purporting to deal with the perennial problems of the human condition. These can have different forms and employ different dramatic techniques in different social groups, or in the same group at different historical periods, but the basic themes are the same, although the psyches of people can to some extent be manipulated in order to deepen or dampen, as the case may be, the inner need for such constructions.

At the same time, the same persons are members of social groups with basic organizational needs like distinctiveness, communication, and authority. Groups may differ in size, composition, and aims, but they have the same basic organizational requirements, which can be met by some basic symbolic constructions. Cultural symbols are thus conditioned by basic human and societal requirements, and their repertoire is thus limited.

What all this means is that despite drastic changes in power relationships, and the almost endless variety of cultural traditions, there are basic symbolic forms that tend to recur in different sociocultural systems, and at different historical periods within the same system. The symbolic repertoire of culture is thus not unlimited. Furthermore, both sets of basic requirements, the existential and the organizational, tend to be met by the same set of symbols.

This is indeed the very essence of normative symbols, that they cater at one and the same time to the two types of requirements. Normative symbols are thus essentially *bivocal*, catering to both individual and social organizational needs. Kinship relationships provide primary, affective moral links with other men, and are thus instrumental in the creation of selfhood. At the same time these relationships may be instrumental in articulating organizational functions, such as the definition of the boundaries of the group, or the provision of channels for the communication of group messages. This bivocality is the very basis of the "mystery" in symbolism. Often a man performing a ritual or participating in a ceremonial is simply unclear, mystified as to whether his symbolic activities express and cater to his own inner needs or the organizational needs of the group to which he belongs. At times he may be inclined this way, at others that. And it is this ambiguity in their meaning that makes symbols such powerful instruments in the hands of leaders and elite groups for mystifying people for particularistic or universalistic purposes, or both.

There is thus a high degree of continuity of symbolic forms, even amidst substantial changes in the dispositions of power. But the functions of such forms within a new political context may be different. This change in function is usually effected through their recombination in a new ideology. In the process they will undergo changes in weighting. The significance of some forms will be heightened and exaggerated, and that of others de-emphasized. It is through these subtle changes in symbolic forms, and their restructuring in new ideologies, that a great deal of organizational change is effected, though a few new forms may appear here or there. A great deal of organizational change is thus often effected through continuities of old forms.

During the colonial period, the Creoles had distinct cultural characteristics by which they displayed their identity and exclusiveness. But with the rise of the provincials to power after Independence, the continued assumption of that distinctiveness became a threat to their privileged position. They began to play down the external markers of their identity and to attack "tribalism," whose origin they even attributed to colonialism. Many of them today emphasize and convincingly demonstrate kinship links with provincials. Christianity is now less of an index to Creoledom, particularly as many of the new provincial elite are also Christian. Indeed there is a studied avoidance in Sierra Leone of formally politicizing religion, which is likely to backfire, inasmuch as there are substantially more Muslims in the country than Christians. It is also possible that in the last census (in 1963) a number of Creoles registered as non-Creole. This is certainly the case with people who had earlier "passed" as Creoles. Thus, to many, Creoledom has been dissolving. Even European observers, among them social scientists, have begun to talk about the steady integration of the Creoles into the native population.

Yet even as some of the traditional symbols of Creole identity have lost their significance, other symbols, both old and new, some conspicuous and some not, have been slipping in to articulate, not just the same, but a more enhanced identity. Creole family ceremonials during this period have gained greatly in intensity, elaborateness, and exclusiveness, even though informants have tended to explain this in terms of increasing wealth leading to a mounting degree of conspicuous consumption.

These kinship relationships existed during the colonial period, but did not create the same tight, intense network which exists today. "Class" differences within Creoledom were sharper than they are today, but there was no external pressure to force the Creoles to close their ranks. More fundamentally, the role of patronage within the Creole network was not as significant as it is today. During the latter part of the colonial period, the Creoles were denied appointment to senior positions in the civil service. All power in the various departments of government administration was in the hands of British senior officials, and Creoles had little influence on appointments, promotions, and scholarships, or in providing administrative facilities.

The situation changed drastically with the Africanization of the civil service, when Creoles came to occupy prominent senior positions in the bureaucracy. As a result, family relationships, or cousinhood generally, began to articulate more fundamental interests than ever before, and the ceremonials that create, develop, and sustain them were intensified.

The strengthening of "family" relationships and the intensification of their ceremonials have enhanced the exclusiveness of the Creoles, in that they have left scant time and resources for the Creoles to cultivate similarly intensive primary relationships with non-Creoles. Thus the overall network of amity, created by the overlapping and cross-cutting networks of the few hundred Creole families, is characterized by dense moral relationships within the group. There is a great deal of symbolic continuity with the past, but in the present situation these continuities have come to fulfil new functions, under drastically changed circumstances.

This continuity of symbolic forms can be detected even in apparently new forms. The most dramatic innovative change among the Creoles during the last twenty-five years has been the massive adoption of Freemasonry by a large proportion of their men. Yet this change, though innovative in a number of respects, and fulfilling new organizational needs, both universalistic and particularistic, is essentially simply a *new combination* of diverse old symbolic forms and practices.

Secret societies generally are a tradition in Sierra Leone and in many other parts of West Africa, and many Creole men had been affiliated to traditional secret societies like

153

the Hunters' societies. The Masonic order itself was introduced into the country during the colonial period by British civil servants and army officers, and a few important Creole men became Masons at that time. The relationship of brotherhood created by the order among its members is yet another version of the more traditional forms of amity relationships, like those of family, cousinhood, godparenthood, and friendship, which already linked many Creoles. Commensality—eating and drinking together—which is an essential part of the activities of almost every lodge, has always been an elaborate tradition in Creole culture. The initiation of new members, and the promotion of members to higher ritual grades within the order, are celebrated in dramas of death and rebirth that are familiar to the Creoles. The exhibition of the Bible and the singing of hymns at every meeting are all standard Christian practices of the sort that have played such a crucial role in the formation of Creoledom. Regular attendance at lodge meetings resembles regular attendance at church, and the existence of two hierarchies in lodge organization, the one ritual and the other administrative, echoes the organization of the Christian churches. The wearing of formal clothes, badges, and regalia were nothing new for the Creoles, and skills in public speaking and sophisticated rhetoric, so pronounced in the dramas of the lodges, have always been part of the culture in Creole churches. Moreover, the organization and administration of the lodges involve skills no different from those already familiar to the Creoles in the organization of their clubs, societies, and other types of voluntary associations. Finally, the links with the higher authorities of the order that Freemasonry entails are qualitatively no different from the links of the different Creole Christian denominations with their international organizations. Thus, most of the basic symbolic forms involved in Freemasonry are parts of traditional Creole culture.

What is new is that these symbols have been restructured in accordance with a new ideology to create a more rigorous and effective organization, linking some of the most important mature males as the patrons—the decision makers in many walks of life—in a close-knit, confidential brotherhood, in order to serve new organizational functions for both particularistic and universalistic purposes. On the particularistic side, post-Independence Creoledom sought an integrated corporate leadership, supported by a unified authority structure, to take decisions and to ensure the compliance of individuals. The order in effect linked at a higher level a chain of authority running from the grass roots of Creole society to the top: members of a "family" would abide by the authority of their head-patrons, and these subscribed to the ritual authority structure of the order.

Simultaneously, these "family" heads occupy important positions in the state bureaucracy and the major public professions. The order solves the problem of the rapid and effective exchange of information necessary to coordinate state institutions and services, as within the confidentiality of the brotherhood public problems are discussed and tackled. The secrecy of the order is indeed to a large measure the secrecy of all bureaucracies in all states, where different types of groupings, such as clubs and old school contacts, perform similar functions.

The Structure of the Drama

There are thus basic cultural continuities amidst even some of the most radical social changes. The study of sociocultural causation can therefore be pursued by tracing the slow and subtle modification of old symbolic forms, and their recombination in response to changes in organizational requirements. One way of doing this is to explore the dramatic process underlying the rituals, ceremonials, and other types of symbolic activity in social life. For it is mainly in the course of such key dramatic performances that the symbolic order and the power order interpenetrate one another within the self to produce, and repetitively reproduce, the bivocality, and hence the mystificatory nature, of the major symbolic forms. In these performances, selfhood is recreated in terms of the symbolic forms that articulate the changing organizational needs of the group; and organizational needs are thereby transformed into categorical imperatives that impel the individual to action through the inner dynamics of selfhood. In this way, the study of sociocultural causation and change becomes the analysis of the creation or transformation of dramatic forms—their production, direction, authentication, techniques, and performance—and of the transformation they bring about in the relationships between the men and women involved in them.

A drama is a limited sequence of action, defined in space and time, which is set aside from the ordinary flow of purposeful social activity. In this sense the drama is not an imitation of life, but a selective composition. Ordinary social life consists of complex processes of events, involving a multiplicity of actors, themes, variables, issues, and purposes in a never-ending sequence. The drama on the other hand selects a few elements that are not obviously related in ordinary life, indeed that are often contradictory, and integrates them within a unity of action and of form, a "gestalt" that temporarily structures the psyches of the actors and transforms their relationships. The more disparate the parts, the more intensive the drama.

This usage of the term "drama" is thus narrower than the metaphorical sense in which "all the world's a stage" and the ordinary phenomenological flow of ongoing social life and social crises is treated as "theatrical" events. Turner's (1957:19) social drama encompasses both a series of actual events occurring over a long period of time and involving a number of people in their daily quarrels and alliances, and the performance of ritual dramas in the narrower sense of the term, within an overall analytical framework for which Gluckman (1961) coined the phrase "extended case method." I am here using the term in its more restricted sense in order to highlight a number of issues involved in the analysis of sociocultural causation. The two senses of the term "drama" are, of course, not opposed to one another, but mark differences in emphasis. For, as I show later, even a "pure," formalized, highly conventional drama, like a church service, a wedding reception, or a ball, is always interpenetrated in its procedure by non-dramatic events that are not formally designed as parts of the original "dramaturgical script."

156

The remaining part of this chapter will deal with a number of specific, concrete dramatic performances which I witnessed at different times in the course of field study. The performances were of different types, were concerned with different issues, and appealed to different sentiments. They involved audiences of varying sizes with different degrees of active participation, employing different techniques of staging. Because of the ease with which they can be detached from the ongoing chronological and spatial processes, and the different social and historical contexts within which they occur, they are multivalent in their import and can thus be arranged in different sequences, classified on the basis of different criteria, and analyzed to highlight different social issues.

Here they will be surveyed to explore the processes by which the corporate organizational requirements of the group are repetitively converted into "oughts," into moral imperatives that govern, shape, and reshape relationships between the actors, and thereby structure the sentiments, attitudes, beliefs, and ideas of the individual. From the other end, they will be examined to show how the individual creates and recreates his selfhood, the unity of his being, in terms of the agreed symbols of the group—how individual problems are tackled in terms of collective solutions. In this way, the participants engage in a process of "thinking aloud," exchanging views in the search for solutions to collective problems. Different types of "leaders"— clergymen, masters of ceremony, patrons, elders, orators, politicians, organizers, officials, artists—play different roles in exposing the problems, probing them, and heightening the sensitivities of audiences to grasp them, highlighting internal conflicts and contradictions to impress on the actors the necessity of achieving communion. In the process, different *dramatic techniques* are employed: music, dance, dress, poetry, rhetoric, commensality.

The Topicality of the Drama

The first point to highlight is the topicality, the living immediacy and concreteness of the drama (see Esslin, 1976). No matter how old or traditional its script, it is an instantaneous event experienced in the here-and-now reality, tackling current problems that are confronted by real people. The most formal, abstract, and remote dramatic blueprint is authenticated in terms of live contemporary issues. It is always topical, an event affecting social relationships, strengthening or weakening existing ones, modifying and reshaping others, terminating some and creating new ones. It is a vehicle in the social process, effecting continuity as well as change.

To discuss this feature of the drama, I do not take an apt illustration like the ball discussed in chapter 2, which is a particularly "modern" ceremonial, but a highly conventional, traditional, formalized, strictly routine performance—a church service.

This was a thanksgiving service held in a church on Sunday morning to celebrate the restoration of the church organ and furniture that had been vandalized a few months earlier. It was attended by about 900 men, women and children and lasted for three hours, from 9:30 to 12:30, culminating in the administration of communion to hundreds, followed by a powerful sermon given by an ordained retired schoolmaster in which he told the sharply attentive audience tales from biblical times about the victory of the faithful few against ignorant and merciless hordes.

It was a Methodist church located in the East End of Freetown. When it had originally been built, a long time earlier, the neighborhood had been predominantly Creole, but since then most of the Creoles had left for more fashionable areas in the city, and the neighborhood had become a run-down area, densely populated by immigrants from the provinces. There was a sharp contrast between the Creoles, heavily clad in formal, Western-style clothes, arriving in their cars, and the crowds of noisy ordinary people in the adjoining streets, with children, many of them half naked, making taunting remarks at Creole children accompanying their parents.

Some days before the service, an invitation had been sent to hundreds of families to attend. The invitation was in the form of a four-page printed pamphlet, issued in the name of the church's stewards' union, seven of whose officers were named on the cover: the circuit superintendent, the president, vice-president, secretary, assistant secretary, financial secretary, and treasurer. One page covered the sequence of the service, containing eighteen different items. The rest of the pamphlet listed by name and title 233 patrons, arranged in what seemed to be an hierarchical order. Twelve were named in conspicuous print on the cover: first, the grand chief patron, a well-known professor at the University of Sierra Leone, followed by two chief patrons—one of them, again, a professor at the university, the other a top senior civil servant—and their wives. Next to be named was the grand receiver, a woman medical doctor, followed in the next line by two chief receivers, both women, one a teacher and one the widow of a former civil servant, and by four ordinary receivers, all women.

The rest of the patrons were named in small print, in two neatly arranged columns on the fourth page of the invitation, with the first thirteen names preceded by the title "Dr." The list of the patrons had two related aims. The first was to lend prestige, dignity, and significance to the gathering; the second, a more mundane one, was to collect money to offset the heavy expenses incurred in the restoration of the church furniture and organ. A member of the stewards' union later told me that it was known by convention what amount each patron was expected to contribute. The grand chief patron paid 50 Leones (£25). Each of the ordinary patrons paid between 10 and 5 Leones. With each invitation there was a small collection envelope on which the name of the person receiving it was inscribed, so that it was known later what amount each person had donated. I gathered later that many other people whose names were not mentioned in the list had received similar invitations.

One of the reasons why so many people had to be invited in person, instead of relying on their automatic attendance, is that a large proportion of the patrons and the others who were invited did not belong to the congregation. All Creoles—men, women, and children—are registered in specific churches, which they usually attend for regular services and for social functions. A man attends the church of his father, but a wife attends the church of her husband. Thus a woman would say: I am Anglican by birth, Methodist by marriage. Many of the patrons appearing on the list belonged neither to that particular church nor to that denomination. Some were Anglicans, and a few were Catholic.

The seating of the congregation was regulated by ten formally dressed men who were the members of the stewards' union. They ushered people in, and led them to appropriate seats in different parts of the church. The building was a vast rectangular hall, with large stained-glass windows high in the front. Under these windows stood the altar, on which there were multi-layered trays bearing hundreds of miniature wine glasses, already filled before the service. The altar was flanked by a few rows of seats, on which a number of clergymen and dignitaries in black suits sat confronting the main congregation. Next down the hall, on both sides of the aisle, sat the choir, numbering about 80. Next to them, but only on the right-hand side, sat about 60 women, members of the sisterhood of the church. They were mostly middle-aged, and wore white uniform dresses with matching hats. On the left-hand side stood the pulpit, with the leading patrons seated in front of it. In the scores of rows of seats behind these, on both sides of the aisle, sat the rest of the patrons, followed by the members of the ordinary congregation, who also filled the seats in the large balcony above. Thus the congregation presented a cross section of the Creole community in its two major divisions on sex and status lines, with the professionals in the lead.

All those present, without exception, wore European-style dress, including the children. For the grand chief patron this was one of the few occasions on which he did not appear in his specially designed Europeanized African suit. He was one of those Creoles who thought that the Creoles should become fully Africanized. He gave his own children African names and went out of his way to invite provincial guests to his parties. The choir consisted of men only, who wore black suits with white shirts. The clergy, about fifteen in number, wore a variety of gowns indicating rank and denomination. The organ music and the hymn singing were purely European.

The gathering was solemn, dignified, and beautiful, and

everyone conducted themselves in a natural way which was the outcome of years of experience and practice. All were literate and followed the service from the script.

The service started with a processional hymn. Two lessons were then read, one of them by the grand chief patron, dealing with Judas on the night of the last supper. The communion service lasted for about 45 minutes and was conducted by a guest clergyman, who was assisted by junior clergymen. It was a competently organized operation, in which hundreds participated. Members of the choir, followed by the sisterhood, the patrons headed by the chief patrons, the receivers, and then the rest of the congregation were invited to the altar in rows and escorted by the stewards. They knelt, received the sacrament, and returned to their seats. Nearly two-thirds of the congregation took part. Soft organ music played throughout. Otherwise there was complete silence, though the seated congregants seemed to be deeply interested in watching the order in which different groups were called, with seated women furtively inspecting the dresses of the women walking to and from the altar.

Then the secretary of the church, a middle-aged man, read several announcements from a book, giving details of different functions and activities in the church during the following few weeks, in the process mentioning many societies, meetings, and classes. He also announced the presentation of a cantata that evening.

This was followed by the collection, a ceremonial procedure in itself, starting with the grand receiver, who was the wife of the grand chief patron, being called to the stage. She wore an elegant silk dress and a large hat. She stood in the middle facing the congregation and was duly flanked first by the two chief receivers, then by the four ordinary receivers. The congregation watched the procedure attentively. The donations in the special envelopes were collected in impeccable order and symmetry by primly and colourfully dressed young ladies, each standing at the end of a row of pews and handing a tray which passed from hand to hand, with each person or family group adding a donation. In minutes the trays were full, and the collecting girls, each

161

from one side of the aisle, handed them to the stewards, who in turn presented the donations to the receivers. When all the envelopes had been collected, the latter walked in a line to a side room. Like the administration of the communion, the whole operation was executed with skilled dispatch.

In retrospect, the whole procedure seemed to have been leading to the message of the sermon, which in the Methodist church is the culmination of the service. There was an air of expectancy. It seemed as if the congregation was putting its own house in order, so as to create a ritual unity in order to receive the message. The mystery of the communion and the sacrifice in the form of the donation united the congregants with one another, as well as with God. The secular became sacred, and the sacred secular. The mind was temporarily relieved of its burdens, and there prevailed a mood of receptive, enhanced consciousness.

The sermon was given from the pulpit on the left hand side of church. The preacher was in his early sixties, and had been ordained early in life, a fairly regular practice among the Creoles. Until World War II, clergymen commanded a great deal of honor and respect, and many laymen sought ordination as an added accomplishment in life. This was particularly the case with teachers of the older generation, who grew up and taught in mission schools. In 1970, one of these men, who was the headmaster of an important secondary school, was made a canon in the Anglican cathedral.

The sermon was a masterly performance, a great feat of rhetoric, skillfully employing dramatic techniques, repeating significant themes with tension-charged, spaced pauses. It guided the audience in subtle ways to take part mentally and emotionally in "living" the timeless dramatic themes it tackled. The preacher began by announcing his theme: "Take Pura with you," repeating it three times, in differing pitch and intonation. He told the story of Israel, who had sinned against God and as a result stood to be overwhelmed by the might of the Midianites. God called Gideon and told him to assemble the sons of Israel to fight. Thirty thousand rallied to his call. Then Gideon asked that those who were weak in their belief should withdraw. Twenty thousand went home. "Oh yes! Twenty thousand went home!" The remaining ten thousand were asked to search their souls carefully and honestly, so that those of them whose faith was weak should also withdraw. Upon this call, all except three hundred went home. "Only three hundred. . . . Only you, the faithful," he said,—stretching out his arms to indicate that he meant the congregation—"remained to fight." Then, God told Gideon to take the slave Pura with him, who, though of a low status and hence weak, was truly devout, faithful, and therefore strong.

The preacher then skillfully played on the theme: "Take Pura with you," applying it to various situations from the mythical past and from the present life of the Creoles. He related the dramatic story of David and Goliath. Although the story and its outcome were well-known to the congregation, the atmosphere was tense with expectation. David finally triumphed because he took Pura—"faith"—with him. One application of the motto which drew an almost unanimous chorus of "Hear . . . Hear" from the women present, particularly from among the members of the sisterhood, was when the preacher denounced those men who, after the initial wedding festivities are over, neglect their "Puras," their wives, treating them as slaves instead of as companions marching side by side with them through life.

The sermon concluded, and the whole service came to an end. The congregants emerged into the crowded town, perhaps with greater faith in their mission and renewed strength in facing the odds against them.

Thus even a very formal traditional drama is authenticated and made topical, by being worked out in terms of the problems and relationships of the actors within the contemporaneous situation. In the course of the service, the congregation enacted their divisions along the lines of sex, status, age, and denomination, then transcended these through the mystery of the communion, and finally achieved unity in their faith, their enlightenment and their course in life to confront the odds. This was not just a subjective symbolic experience, but an objective reality, involving concrete existing categories and relationships between the worshippers; for the congregation comprised about a tenth of the adult Creole population.

Timeless Motifs

What the above discussion indicates is that, other things being equal, the greater the flexibility of the drama in comprehending changing realities, the greater its mystificatory possibilities, and the more enduring it tends to be. But the true drama encompasses a basic contradiction, in that it will lose its efficacy if it does not, along with this flexibility, have an element of permanence, of continuity, of timelessness— an enduring core that can withstand and contain the vagaries of passing, day-to-day changes. The stronger and the more timeless this core, the more powerful the drama.

Drama is thus most efficacious in shaping sentiments and attitudes, and in impelling men to action, when it tackles perennial problems that are basic to the human condition. Foremost among these is the problem of existence: Why are we born and why do we die? Where do we come from and where do we go?

Death is an ever-present threat to selfhood and is thus a potential source of deep emotions and sentiments. It is an enigma which is not given to "scientific explanation," and is always enveloped in mystery. Men seldom face the mystery alone; it is nearly always defined for them by the corporate groups to which they belong, which also provide them with "explanations" and prescribe "solutions" in the form of world views and of dramatic action. While the problem is universal, faced by men everywhere, social groups differ considerably in their preoccupation with it and in dramatizing it, and the same group may vary in this respect over time.

During the past 25 years there has been a sharp intensification of the cult of the dead among the Creoles. This has had the effect of halting the fragmentation and alienation of Creole housing and land. It has also helped in eroding class and status differences within the group, and has

thus strengthened the bonds and unity of the Creole cousinhood.

Like all other major culture groups in Sierra Leone, the
Creoles have always ceremonialized death and the dead,
following essentially Yoruba traditions that were carried
into the country to Yoruba recaptives. But the past two-
and-a-half decades have seen a great revival and intensification of these ceremonials, as manifested in elaborate burial
arrangements, greater attendance at funerals, lavishness of
wakes, frequency of visiting graves to pour libations, holding of feasts for the dead, and publicizing the relevant
events through the mass media. In the past, the traditional
beliefs and practices relating to the dead were opposed and
denounced as pagan and superstitious by the church. They
are now fully integrated into the beliefs and practices of
both the Christian church and the Masonic lodges, with the
leaders of both often taking an active part.

Some Creoles attribute this intensification partly to a
technical innovation—the refrigeration of corpses, which
was introduced into Freetown during the 1950s by an American funerary company operating from neighboring Liberia,
who also introduced embalming and cosmetics. Until then,
corpses had had to be buried within a few hours of death in
accordance with municipal regulations prompted by the fear
of health hazards in the humid tropical climate of the country. Funerals had, therefore, to be arranged at a short notice,
and the bereaved family, their relatives and friends, had no
time to prepare for any elaborate funerary arrangements.
With the availability of refrigeration, however, there remained no excuse for the bereaved "family" not to arrange
massive and elaborate ceremonials commensurate with their
status.

During the few days following death, detailed arrangements are made for the funeral. These will include the sew-
ing of a special uniform dress (*ashobi*) for the mourning
women, who include relatives of all categories as well as
close friends. In the absence of specific detailed instruc-
tions in a will, the immediate family of the deceased decide
on the colour of mourning to be adopted. Arrangements are
also made for an all-night wake preceding the day of burial.

Large quantities of alcoholic drinks, food, cigarettes, and coffee and tea are contributed by all relatives and friends.

Although "families" differ in status, the intensity and lavishness of the ceremonials tend to be almost identical, as each family group includes wealthy members who will be anxious about their status and will therefore help in ensuring appropriate arrangements.

Some of these and other points will be examined in the course of discussing a few of the many specific occasions I witnessed during 1970. The cases are selected from field notes, not in order to present apt illustrations, but to elaborate a number of sociological issues within a variety of contexts.

First to be considered is a wake, celebrated in a Freetown suburb, which was attended by relatives and friends of different statuses, involving in its symbolic procedure a syncresis of European and African themes. I was taken to the wake by a school headmistress, a "cousin" of the family. We arrived at the house at about 11:00 P.M. The deceased was a ninety-two-year-old woman who had lived alone with her sister, but next door to the houses of daughters, nieces, and other relatives. The wake was held in four separate houses in the same neighborhood. I spent most of the time in the house of a niece of the deceased, a short distance away from the dead woman's house.

Although we arrived an hour before midnight, the gathering had not yet warmed up. Drinks were not yet being served, and the hosts were still cooking inside the house. We sat on benches outside in the front yard. At first there were only a few mourners, but cars presently began to arrive from the city bringing more people. An hour later there were nearly a hundred men and women in the yard. In the corner where I sat, I counted thirty women, mostly middle-aged. My "host" introduced me to some of them, and also told me who the others were. Most were professional women from the capital, although all wore conservative traditional Creole dresses. Almost all were "relatives" of the bereaved family, though a few were just friends of either the family or the relatives. I identified some as the very sophisticated women I had interviewed in government departments and at parties or weddings. But now all looked alike, and there was no way of distinguishing status among them.

Shortly after midnight, cases of beer were distributed. In time, bottles of brandy were passing from hand to hand. One woman who sat next to me brought with her a large thermos flask of chilled "best quality" palm wine. Then various types of food began to circulate. Peppered chicken and shashlik were distributed on skewers straight from open fires.

As the quantity of alcohol consumed increased, the session heated up. First some of the women started to sing hymns and most of the others joined in. Then, as the singing became louder, the soft European tunes gave way to a rhythmic African beat, and many of the women began to move their bodies and limbs. Soon a number of them rose in dance. There were ten to fifteen women dancing at a time, most of them with bottles of alcohol in their hands.

Most of the men sat quietly talking on the side. As the night rolled on, the revelling women began to taunt and shout at them, inviting them to participate actively. There was a brief halt in the dancing, and the men, who by that time had consumed a good deal of alcohol, sang a hymn. Later, when the dancing was resumed, they one by one joined in.

As the night wore on, Western music and Western singing faded and gave way to surging beats and grunts that were, as one woman explained to me, "from the heart of Africa." Sometimes the words of the hymns were changed, but the European tune kept; at other times the words of the hymns were kept but the music changed. Every now and then a woman would halt the procedure for a few seconds shouting "Halleluia," with the rest of the congregation responding "Halleluia" and then resuming the dancing and singing. At one time all those present, men and women, chanted a series of songs in different languages, mainly English and Krio. For a brief two minutes they even chanted in Arabic: *"La Ilaha illa Allah; Muhammad rasul ullah"* ("There is no God but Allah and Muhammad is his messenger"), probably in deference to some Muslims present.

Occasionally there was some solo dancing or singing by some of the women.

Yet more men and women joined in, in an ever-rising crescendo of dancing and singing. As the house became overcrowded, they left the yard in a long single-file column, snaking out through the gate and continuing in noisy merriment along the street. They were soon joined by two similar formations from the other houses involved in the wake. In the meantime, some groups of men and women remained seated in the yard, drinking and talking about the deceased, relating various stories and anecdotes from her life, and appraising her character.

This merry atmosphere develops only when the deceased is an old person. When the deceased is younger, the celebration is more subdued. This is also the case when the house of the deceased is in the city. In these cases, hymn singing is more solemn, and the activities more contained, although probably just as much alcohol is consumed.

Details of the funeral are announced on the radio, giving the time and the address where the body can be viewed, the time of the funeral service, and the name of the church. If the deceased is a Mason, his lodge will usually put a separate announcement on the radio inviting the members to meet at a specific place and time before the service.

One of the funerals I attended took place late in the afternoon. The announcement on the radio stated that the body would be on view for the public at 10 A.M. at the deceased's house and later at the church. The funeral service was scheduled to start at 4 P.M., but I arrived at 2:30 P.M. Well over a hundred men and women were already there. The church had two floors. The body lay in state in the middle of the large ground-floor hall on a raised platform covered with red carpet and encircled with golden ropes. All around were long rows of benches on which men and women sat singing hymns. Outside the church there were scores of men in black suits greeting mourners and directing them to the hall. There was a constant line of men and women moving from the yard to the hall, snaking up the platform and proceeding slowly between the ropes to view the body. The deceased lay in full evening dress in a luxurious, satin-lined coffin. The face seemed very much "alive," skill-fully made up by the expert funeral directors. The body was draped with the full regalia of a master Mason.

It was a very solemn occasion, with the stream of people filing by in silence against the background of the hymns sung by those who were sitting on the side. As viewers moved away from the coffin, they sat on the benches around about for a while, before going out of the building into the front yard.

Within half an hour, hundreds of mourners had gathered around the church, in the yard, and in the adjoining streets. Masons in black suits and regalia began to arrive in groups. Among the first was the district grand master of the Scottish Constitution in Freetown. Members of the five lodges gathered on one side of the yard. All wore black suits, white shirts, and black ties. A few also wore bowler hats. The deceased belonged to the English Constitution of Freemasonry, but was affiliated with a number of Scottish lodges, and it was the latter which had staged a full Masonic funeral service. By about 3:30 there were several hundred people standing outside. Then a procession of Masons formed and walked towards the building, headed by a member carrying a thick book laid on a small cushion, flanked by mace bearers. They went into the now empty hall where the coffin lay, and conducted an exclusive Masonic service. A brass band in uniform played tunes in accompaniment to the hymn singing, with people outside joining in.

Yet hundreds more men and women converged on the church: the streets were jammed with cars, and traffic police frantically tried to introduce order. As the time drew nearer to four o'clock, important people from many walks of life began to arrive, among them some ministers of state and senior clergymen headed by the bishop of Sierra Leone. Then the door of the lower hall was opened, and a procession of Masons headed by the district grand master emerged, followed by the coffin, which by now was covered, with the Masonic regalia of the deceased placed on top.

There were easily over a hundred wreaths carried in by a variety of people and groups. Some were arranged in a cross, some as a ring; a large one carried by two men was in the shape of the Masonic emblem. In the meantime a few men in black had been distributing a pamphlet containing the church service, with a photograph of the dead man on the cover.

Like many other Creole patrons, the deceased had been prominent in the church as a benefactor, in the bureaucracy as a former senior official, in Freemasonry as a master affiliated to many lodges in both the English and the Scottish Constitutions, and in business (after retirement) as an entrepreneur. He was also the patron of a large "family," including "outside" wives and children.

In the meantime, the church had become so packed with people that literally hundreds of men and women had to stand outside to listen to the service. I had to do the same, because although I had arrived early I had been busy watching the going and comings outside. For the scene inside the church, I give here a brief account of the funeral service of another Creole man of equal social standing.

The deceased in this case had been a head surgeon in a government hospital, the patron of a large extended "family," a former master Mason in one of the exclusive English lodges, and a member of the Rotary Club. The service was held in St. George's Cathedral. Although I arrived half an hour before the start of the proceedings, almost all the seats in the vast hall had been occupied, except for six rows on the left-hand side, which were conspicuously empty. Two men at the back told me that these seats were reserved "for the Lodge people."

Within a few minutes, about seventy masons in regalia entered the church and walked in a column towards the reserved seats. They were headed by four senior masters, one of them the grand master Mason, who was also the speaker of the House of Representatives. Apart from the Freemasons, there were several men and women from societies and associations identifiable by their uniforms, badges or ties. The "Guard of Honour," both within and outside the cathedral, consisted of about sixty nurses in prim white uniforms. Many of the important people in town were there, probably including most of the Creole patrons, many of whom I recognized. Most of the men wore dark suits, and the women black, white, or navy blue dresses with matching hats. Despite the presence of possibly over a thousand men and women in the congregation, the atmosphere was serene and dignified, with solemn organ music played in turn by three professional organists. The whole congregation participated in singing hymns. All behaved and acted with the familiarity and certainty of people who were accustomed to such occasions. The sermon—given by a prominent educationalist who was also a high-ranking, ordained churchman and a prominent Freemason, though not in regalia—combined religious, secular, and, I was told later, Masonic themes.

When the service was over, I drove in a very long line of cars to the cemetery. Although it was Sunday, traffic was jammed. Men and women assembled around the grave, which was an elaborate concrete vault painted white. We waited for about forty-five minutes until the coffin arrived, during which time people stood talking in small groups. The Masons, being followers of the English Constitution, had taken off their regalia on leaving the church, and came in plain clothes.

The graveside service was brief. Close members of the bereaved family stood near the grave opening, including the widow, her children (aged seven to ten), and the sisters of the deceased. The coffin was lowered, and many people took their turns throwing earth into the grave.

These funerary ceremonies are but the tip of the iceberg of the cult of the dead among the Creoles, though they play their part in strengthening it and keeping it alive in the consciousness of men and women. The burial is followed by customary ceremonials on the fortieth day and on the anniversary. A customary ceremony observing the third day after death has now been dropped, because often the deceased is not buried by then.

But the bulk of the cult and its most important manifestations consist of the day-to-day observances and beliefs about the dead, and their significance for the living. The dead are very much "alive" among the living, who consult them, implore them, seek their advice, their love, and their forgiveness (see chapter 4, above).

The prohibition against selling property inherited from the dead is a collective value and not just an individual concern. This was clearly and formally stated by the leaflet distributed at the 1970 Creole Convention. "Our fathers built this land," the Creoles say, referring to the Freetown peninsula. Alienating property to non-Creoles is thus a betrayal of the trust of the dead, and can bring about mystical harm. Thus, the sentiments of love, reverence, and fear of the dead by individuals are compounded by a heightened concern for the future of Creole corporate power and privilege. The 1970 convention, predictably, led to no formal steps, but it served as yet a further impetus for Creoles to preserve the "heritage." Conscious corporate policy strengthens non-rational beliefs and practices. The cult of the dead is no longer just an individual or family concern, but is a collective representation of a corporate group. The individual and the group support one another and their interests become fused. The recent intensification of the cult is the result of the constraints exercised by the group over the individual. Collective constraints lead to the intensification of public rituals, and these in turn strengthen and keep alive the beliefs and sentiments of the individual. Collective interest thus becomes ingrained and internalized in an individual's beliefs. In the course of the frequent ceremonies, belief and the action based on it are strengthened and kept alive.

The cult will function and affect social relationships only if men believe in it and act on it. Not all Creoles necessarily subscribe to these mystical beliefs all the time. Some believe in some parts of the ideology and disbelieve in others. Others may believe in the ideology, yet not admit to it in public. Yet others, on the other hand, do not ordinarily believe in it, though they declare publicly that they do so. What is certain, however, is what people actually do, not what goes on in their minds.

It is in this context that the significance of the elaborate ceremonials relating to the dead should be examined. In order to highlight a few points with regard to this problem,

I will briefly discuss a case I observed, involving a young Creole man who occupied a senior academic post when his father died. I followed his activities from the day of death till the day of the funeral. The day his father died, he told me solemnly that he did not subscribe to traditional Creole ideas about the dead, and certainly did not accept the validity of the ceremonials associated with them. He did not, he said, intend to go through all the elaborate funeral arrangements prescribed by current custom.

Within an hour, his cousin, who occupied an important position in a public establishment, telephoned to ask if he had prepared the list of survivors to be read in the radio announcement. When the academician said he was not going to do all that, his cousin thought he was joking. When he said he was serious, his cousin told him he was "out of his mind." How would he face his family and friends!? Consequently he had to spend several hours with his immediate relatives preparing the list to be broadcast. Thereafter he was driven, step by step, by various types of pressure, to arrange for the performance of all the ceremonials in which he had said he did not believe.

About a week later, the funeral was held. Prayers were read, hymns were sung, a sermon was given. I listened to one hymn in particular which went, "There is a land that is fairer than light. . . ." It was sung by all the hundreds of men and women present in a most skillful and moving way, accompanied by the organ, which was played by a senior professional organist. The singing congregation were nearly all Christian, and had been trained in choir-singing since their childhood. They sang softly and passionately. The contrast between the grimness of death, represented by the coffin in the middle of the cathedral, and the promised land "fairer than light" was a sharp one. The genius of the poet, the skill of the organist, the art of the original composer of the music, the men and the women in their sombre yet lavish clothes, the coffin, and the trained voices of the congregation, combined to agitate the mind and to force one to think about the mysteries of life and death, and the destiny of men. I, who am neither Christian nor Creole, certainly experienced this. As I looked around at the faces in the congregation, including my friend the academician, I had no doubt that everyone was moved. The promise of the bright land transformed the subjective experience from the dismal presence of death to a vista of hope. The effect on others must have been equally, if not more, dramatic. This mystical experience is vague and difficult to express.

Death is not merely a physical phenomenon but one of the insoluble mysteries of human existence, like fortune and misfortune, good and evil. These are problems which are perhaps beyond rational solution. In the Jewish burial ceremony, as in those of many other religious traditions, the cantor dramatically poses the conundrum when he addresses the deceased before the grave is sealed: "From where did you come and where are you going?" Modern man, no less than "primitive man," needs a solution to these problems. Such solutions are always symbolic constructions. They are only partly rational.

We do not usually face these mysteries of human existence on our own. For most of us, the major groups to which we belong take care of this side of our life as well as of other sides. They provide us with explanations sharpened by the endeavours of generations of ordinary people as well as by those of expert ideologists. Only a few sophisticated individuals will attempt to find their own formulas for solving these perennial problems. Most people adopt readymade formulations like those of organized religion.

With most people, including saints and prophets, belief is seldom fixed and unshaken. The symbols that express and support it always have technical shortcomings. There is a continuous battle in the mind between individual experience, forms of belief, and symbolic behaviour, which simultaneously support each other. Often it is the symbols and the ceremonials that conjure up belief and mystical experience rather than the other way round. The battle goes on all the time and is never concluded. This is why ritual and ceremonial are not once-and-for-all affairs, but have to be frequent and repetitive in order to do their job at all.

The enigma of death confronts men and women everywhere. It is timeless. So is the singularity of misfortune. So are the problems of transition from one phase of life to another. All great dramas are based on such timeless themes, implicit in the human condition. But they are at the same time loaded with current social meanings. The major groups to which we belong always attempt to seize on these themes to advance their own ends. Thus, a group's particularistic interest is made stable and meaningful to the individual in consequence of being rooted in the human condition, and is expressed in terms of moral and ritual imperatives that impel the individual to act spontaneously and autonomously in the corporate interests of the group.

The transformation, or the link, is achieved through ceremonials. Other things being equal, the more important the interests, the more intensive the ceremonials. In the process, the subjective preoccupation with the perennial problem grows deeper and stronger. Basically, an Englishman is as predisposed to be concerned about death as a Creole. But the ordinary, average Englishman is little exposed to ceremonies concerned with death or with the dead. In England such ceremonies are sparse and shallow because there is no great need to articulate group interests in terms of categorical moral imperatives. There, most of these interests can be articulated in terms of formal associations. A Creole, on the other hand, is exposed to the cult of the dead almost daily. His awareness of the problem, the intensity of his feelings about it, and his preoccupation with it are continuous and constraining.

The Private Made Collective

The perennial problems of the human condition, life and death, fortune and misfortune, sickness and health, passage through different phases of life, all these are first and foremost experienced by the individual. But they are everywhere ceremonialized by social groups—the nuclear family, the extended family, kindred, lineages, castes, sects, factions, ethnic groups, the State. The scale of the social groupings that become involved depends on the dispositions and strategies of power in the society. When an event concerning one individual occurs, a series of dramas are staged in the course of which the concerns of the individual

175

are made the affair of the collective. (For recent developments in this respect in the Soviet Union, see Binns, 1978;
Lane, 1979.)

Thus among the Creoles, the private affair of boy weds
girl is progressively made the affair of the whole corporate
group to which they belong. In the course of a single day,
the major cults of Creoledom—those of the dead, the
church, the family, and of decorum—are staged within a
grand series of dramas, progressively invoking wider and
wider audiences, and culminating in a multiple feast given
by different patrons and held through the night in different
parts of the city, involving people who sometimes hardly
know the couple or their immediate families. The formalized church service, which accommodates the new union
within the grand design of the universe, involves few active
participants. The congregation remain almost passive wit-
nesses, constrained by high formal rituals. The reception
which follows accommodates the couple within the social
structure, as mediated by some major social actors. The
guests still play little part, being constrained by the formal
rules of decorum. In the evening's multiple feasts, the main
actors of the morning's dramas recede from the stage, and
the Grand Cousinhood comes to life in an intensive primary
communion, free from formal constraints, but greatly enhanced by eating, drinking, dancing, and socializing together. In an average wedding about 10 percent of the
whole adult Creole population of Freetown take part, representing a cross section of the community, recreating patronage, reconciling men and women, wealthy and less
wealthy, superior and subordinate. The ceremonial provides an opportunity for people to "survey" one another, to
think aloud about current issues, and serves as yet another
occasion for the repetitive creation and recreation of the
Grand Cousinhood.

The wedding of Zara and Harry was typical, in its essen-
tials, of five weddings I observed and of others I collected
information about during 1970. It started at dawn with separate gatherings of the close relatives of the bride and the
groom to make offerings to the dead. Holes were dug at the
entrance to the house and a specially cooked food, *okara*,

was poured into them, with members of the small congregation symbolically partaking in the feast. Senior men and women made short speeches addressing a number of the dead by name, informing them of the impending wedding and imploring them to bless the couple. The ritual lasted for about forty-five minutes.

A few hours later, the church ceremony started in accordance with a program contained in an invitation in the form of a small, twelve-page pamphlet that had been sent to hundreds of families a few days earlier. On the decorated cover appeared the title: "SOUVENIR of the WEDDING between Miss Zara Large and Mr. Harry Williams [pseudonymns] at Holy Trinity Church, Kissy Road, Freetown on Saturday 20th June 1970 at 11:00 A.M." Lower down, the names of four officiating clergymen were given. (At another wedding, seven were listed, one of them a professor of theology.) The next page, inside the pamphlet, gave the names of two chief bridesmaids, two best men, and two groomsmen, followed by the names of three organists, in the case of one of them listing his academic degrees. Page 4 outlined the order of the ceremony, listing fourteen items. The next six pages gave the programme in detail, including the hymns and prayers, and the final page gave the details of the reception which would follow in a separate hall a few blocks away immediately after the service.

By 11:00 A.M. the church was only half full, but in the following five minutes a stream of guests poured in, and it was soon packed to capacity. Probably about 800 guests were present. (In 1970 audiences at wedding services fluctuated between 300 and over 1,000; the variation had very little to do with the status of the families concerned, but was related to the timing of the ceremony—on weekday mornings most people are busy, but on Saturdays they are free.) The entire congregation wore European clothes, with the women displaying a spectacular array of colour and pageantry. These preliminaries took place in complete silence, with great dignity and solemnity, against a background of soft, melodious organ music. Throughout, the two best men, in formal dress, directed the guests to their seats in a prearranged order.

The clergymen wore their festive gowns, and every movement they made throughout the ceremony was prescribed and well rehearsed. The hymns were sung by the whole congregation, many of them reading the lines from the invitation pamphlet, and the singing was beautiful and serene. The service followed its course in accordance with the program. The address was given by one of the clergymen, emphasizing three issues. First, fidelity, condemning men who seek other women in adultery. (This was accompanied by some laughter and grunts of approval from many of the women in the audience.) Second, that marriage should last till death, and even after. Third, that the procreation of children was the most important function of marriage. The speaker also mentioned that both bride and groom came from "good Christian families" and that the father was a well-known school headmaster. Finally, he stressed the importance of the role played by the congregation in the solemnization of marriage.

The hymn—"Immortal Love"—was followed by a communion service. About thirty close relatives of the bride and the groom went forward to the stage and knelt in two wings behind the couple, relatives of the bride behind the bride and those of the groom behind the groom. One of the clergymen distributed bread, uttering a short prayer and crossing the head of each of the communicants. Another clergyman went around from the other side with a cup of wine, helping each to a sip, with an assistant refilling the cup every now and then. A hymn was sung: "Here O my Lord would I feed upon the bread of God . . . drink with Thee the royal wine of heaven."

After "Concluding prayers and Benediction," there was a hush in the congregation and an air of expectancy developed. This was the stage of "Signing the Register." Formally, only twelve persons needed to sign, but in Freetown the occasion has been transformed into an important social institution. Scores of guests were invited to sign. It was a matter of honour and prestige, not just to be invited to sign, but in what order. This phase lasted for a full forty-five minutes, against the background of continuous organ music.

The register was in a room on one side of the altar. First

to enter were the bride and groom, followed by the choir, then by the bridesmaids and best men and a few close relatives. The two best men then came out of the room, each with a list in his hand, and began to invite men and women, some individually and some in couples, to go in to sign the register. I was told that it was the bride and groom who fixed the list and the order, and that people were often offended if they were either not asked to sign the register or if were asked to sign after others without clear justification. This phase resembles the reading of the list of survivors in death announcements on the radio. (At two other weddings, the acting governor general was a guest, and he and his wife were among the first to sign the register.) Although the procedure lasted a long time, no one seemed to be bored. The formal ritual had ended, and people began to talk in low voices, commenting on the comings and goings. Signing the register was described to me as "an extremely sensitive operation," which required a great deal of planning and tact.

After that there was a recessional march, and the bride and groom and their entourage walked out of the church, with the congregation following. Outside everyone crowded around in a dense circle in the street to watch as the couple and relatives posed for photographs. Traffic came to a halt and over twenty policemen desperately tried to regulate it. After fifteen minutes of this, the couple and their company headed the line of cars driving to the hall, a few streets away, where the reception was to be held.

The atmosphere at the reception differed from that in the church. It was a different type of drama. Freed from the dignity and constraints of holy rituals, people were now behaving in accordance with the rules of decorum. Now came the opportunity for people, especially the women, to look one another over. There were about 300 of them, all dressed in individually designed dresses, with matching hats, gloves, and handbags; nearly all wore elaborately coiffured wigs.

The newly wedded couple, flanked by the bridesmaids, sat at a table facing a huge wedding cake. The rest of the audience sat at small circular tables arranged in a semicircle, and also in rows on the sides. The reception lasted just over an hour, following in its procedure the detailed programme given on the last page of the invitation pamphlet.

The first item, "The Introduction of the Chairman," took a relatively long time, about twelve minutes. Although everyone knew from the invitation pamphlet who the chairman was, the introducer kept the name "secret" and proceeded to extol the virtues of "this chairman that I am going to introduce to you." He gave an outline of his biography, listing his academic degrees, appointments, travels, achievements, and virtues, building up his greatness and fame. The man himself hid in an adjoining balcony, waiting to make his dramatic entrance at the appropriate time. The introducer went on to say that "this chairman" was the head of an important institution of higher learning, where he, the introducer, had studied under him. The chairman was a geographer, he observed, and as geography was related to demography and to the proliferation of the population—here there was great laughter—he was an ideal man to chair such an occasion. By now, the suspense was high, and the expectations of the whole gathering were greatly enhanced, and when the introducer finally announced the name and the chairman made his entry into the hall and took his place at the central table, there was loud applause, followed by an expectant hush.

The chairman began by outlining the programme, then gave a brief speech in which he congratulated the bride and groom for wisely choosing one another—the groom for choosing a bride from the "Large" family, as this augured well for the development of a large family, and the bride for choosing a man from the "Harding" family, thereby judiciously selecting a firm head for her future family. (Laughter and applause.) He harped on the solemnity of marriage, and on its most important function—the procreation of children.

The chairman then said he would "proceed with the business of the day without delay," starting with cutting the wedding cake. He made a few remarks about the symbolic significance of the cake, and wished that this would be the one and only wedding cake that either of the couple would cut. With the whole audience counting "one, two, three . . . go," the bride and groom, assisted by the chairman, cut the cake, and everyone applauded. The bridesmaids and best men also ceremonially cut the cake. Two layers of the cake were then rushed by two ladies to an adjoining serving room where they were sliced into small pieces that were immediately distributed by six mini-skirted young ladies. In the meantime, waiters distributed champagne in shallow glasses in preparation for the highlight of the occasion—the toasts.

All the proposers of toasts and the responders to them were mentioned by name in the invitation pamphlet. In all, five toasts were proposed: "To the health of the bride and bridegroom," responded to by the bridegroom; "To the health of the bride's parents," responded to by a relative who represented them; "To the health of the bridegroom's parents," responded to, again, by a relative representing them; "To the health of the bridesmaids," responded to by one of the bridesmaids; and "To the health of the guests," responded to by a professional lady representing them. Each proposer then made some witty closing remarks, and called on one of the guests to read the benediction.

The ceremony outlined the social significance of the event: the passage of the wedded couple to a new status, the founding of a new household and the nucleus of a new "family," and the forging of new relationships involving at least four large "family" networks. The marriage established new linkages strengthening and maintaining the Grand Cousinhood, concretely represented by the participant audience, which probably included members from almost every family network in Creoledom. The speeches only *signified* these developments; their contents were not so important. The medium was indeed the message. It was later that evening, when the Grand Cousinhood took over the affair, that the medium was used to transform concrete reality, developing new relationships, renewing old ones, strengthening others, occasioning the exchange of news and views, and the deliberation of current problems, all culminating in *actual*, as opposed to symbolic, grand communion.

When the reception was over, the bridal couple and their close relatives moved to one of their "family" houses, where lunch was ready. A *Gumbe* band was already in the house filling the air with deep rhythmic music. (At another wedding I observed, the *Gumbe* band was waiting outside the church to escort the wedding entourage first to the reception hall, then to the house.)

When evening came, the whole character of the ceremonial changed radically. No less than fourteen—in some other weddings during 1970, as many as twenty—patrons of the couple staged grand celebrations, each in his or her own home for his or her own relatives and friends, many of whom were hardly related to the bridal couple. At one wedding, this stage in the celebration involved as many as 1,700 men and women, well over a tenth of the adult Creoles in the city.

Many weeks before the wedding day, the couple had approached a number of prominent men and women and requested them to be their "patrons." Each of the two had at least two patrons, a godfather and a godmother. These need not be the original godparents who were so named at the christening, although if these were still alive and capable of meeting the colossal expense, they would be the first choice. Thus a minimum of four different feasts are conventionally expected for every wedding. It is, however, very rare that a wedding be celebrated on such a small scale. The couple try their utmost to mobilize as many patrons as possible. Apart from original godparents, they approach uncles, aunts, cousins, eminent friends, former teachers and headmasters, with the request in each case: "Please be my patron." On the face of it, what the couple seek is the status and prestige resulting from having so many feasts, with so many people celebrating the wedding. More fundamentally, however, the multiple feasts will in due course give them access to the patrons and to the members of their "families," each of which will inevitably include important people in the bureaucracy and in other spheres of life. These will be a potential source of support in the years to come, both for themselves and for the family they raise.

On their part, patrons think twice before declining a request to stage a party. In a few cases during 1970, one patron or another reacted to such a request by offering the couple the option of accepting a substantial gift of money instead of a party, although at the same time expressing an unquestioning willingness to give a party. It seems, however, that this option is a recent development and is only rarely taken. A patron will more often seize on the opportunity to emphasize and develop his status and to consolidate his "family" and friends. For the "family" lacks clear boundaries and definition, and such feasts are periodically needed to provide occasions for relatives and friends to come with presents in hand to confirm their affiliations and allegiance. At the few wedding feasts which I attended, some of the participants had only a vague idea about the specific purpose of the feast. The only association with the wedding was the brief appearance of the bride and groom at the party.

The symbolic structure of the feast is radically different from the ceremonies of the day. After the constraints of church rituals and of the rules of decorum governing the reception, there is now an air of release. Most of the guests change into African-style dress, and instead of the serene and polite behaviour of earlier on, there is now deafening music and uninhibited noise. There is also heavy alcohol consumption. The women, in particular, undergo a dramatic transformation in their appearance and behaviour. While the men sit on the side and "talk lodge" most of the time, the women, sweating in the heat and from the effect of alcohol, dance vigorously to the incessant beat of *Gumbe* drumming or highlife music played over amplifiers. In 1970, there were only four *Gumbe* groups in the whole of Freetown, and they were all fully booked weeks in advance. In the idiom of dramaturgy, the majority of the people were spectators during the events of the day, but now they took to the stage as active participants in a true drama of primary communion.

The different parties, being given by different patrons from different walks of life, with different sets of colleagues and friends, differ in their structure. Some are more tradi-

183

tionally Creole; others more modern. Typical of the "traditional" type was one of the feasts which I attended on the evening of the wedding day. My wife and I were invited to the party by a cousin of the bride, a well-known dressmaker who had sewn the dresses of many of the women who attended the wedding celebrations. The party was given in a very large, neatly painted house in the East End of Freetown, where more traditional Creoles lived. The patron, the owner of the house, was a cousin of the bride's father. He was a lawyer, and many of his colleagues in the profession were among the guests. His wife was a school teacher, and many of her colleagues attended too.

We arrived there at about 7:30 in the evening. A *gumbe* band was already playing a deep rhythmic beat. It consisted of three men. One sat on a hollow wooden box, which he beat on the two sides. A second bestrode a cylindrical drum and beat its skin in front. The third held a large, ordinary, trapeze-shaped saw and produced a great variety of notes by scratching a knife against its teeth and by bending it in different curves. The saw is the main instrument, and without it there can be no *Gumbe* band. Many women had already begun dancing. I set a recorder on the windowsill to tape the music, but when the leader of the band noticed it, he abruptly asked his colleagues to stop playing, and for a few seconds there was an embarrassing silence, with the dancers looking about in consternation to see what had happened. The leader started shouting that my recording was an infringement of their copyright. Our hostess, who immediately realized what was involved, rushed to the leader and put some money into his pocket. I did the same. After that the band leader and his two colleagues became very friendly, and whenever they rested from playing, leaving the gramophone records to fill the gap, I sat next to them and chatted about their life and their music.

There were between 150 and 200 men and women present, the number varying over the course of the evening. Most of the women and some of the men were dressed casually. About 40 of the women, mainly the middle-aged but also some young ones, were dressed uniformly in *ashobi*. They were all dressed alike, and it was these women in particular who drank a lot of alcohol, and who seemed for the greater part of the evening to be seized by the ecstasy of dancing. Later on I discovered that some of them were professional women, many being the wives of important patrons. In fact, most of them were the very women who had appeared in church and at the reception in elegant Western clothing. But that evening there was no way of telling from their appearance which women were "elite," and which were "poor." Many of them drank beer, which they frequently augmented with French brandy from bottles that were circulating from hand to hand. Later in the evening, each obliged the gathering with a solo dance, while the others stood around and clapped.

In contrast with the Western-type snacks provided at the reception, the food was Afro-Caribbean. It was served at about 9:30 on disposable plates: chicken, beef, rice, and vegetables, all heavily spiced. After midnight, sharply peppered soup was served in bowls, followed by peppered meat, grilled and served on skewers.

Drinks were lavishly provided throughout the night. While glasses were still full, more chilled beer was placed on tables and windowsills near the guests. This was real drinking; in contrast, the communion wine at the church service and the glass of champagne at the reception were only symbolic.

Most of the dancing was by women, as was the serving and catering. Only occasionally did some of the men join in. Most of the other men lingered on the sides in small groups talking.

As the night wore on, the music became louder and more deafening. The women, many of them heavy, danced with even greater vigour. On the whole, the occasion allowed no distinction between actors and audience. All were actors engaged in a true primary social communion, which seemed to be the sole purpose of the celebration.

At about 11:30, while the dancing, music, and noise were going on, there was some unusual activity in a room adjoining the hall where we sat, and where most of the action was taking place. The bride and the groom had just come in, on their "round" of the different parties given in their honor, having changed into ordinary clothes. They looked haggard and washed out, and appeared bewildered as they sat uncomfortably on the edge of a settee, seeming very much out of place in the ongoing activities and not at all in the spirit of the party. The bride's uncle, who was giving the party, made a short speech, which was heard only by those who happened to be in the room. He proposed a toast to the couple, and then there was a chorus of "For he's a jolly good fellow," after which the newlyweds apologetically bade farewell and left to resume their round of the other parties. In all, they had stayed no more than ten minutes. Many of the people dancing or talking in the main hall did not even know that the couple had made an appearance, and continued with their activities.

Not all the other parties were similar to this one. Some were more Western in character. I attended one such party, which celebrated another wedding. It was held at the house of a niece of the bride, in an area where senior civil servants lived. Most of the people were civil servants or university teachers with their spouses. There was no *Gumbe* band, but the highlife music and beat were no less deafening. There was a similar pattern of drinking and the same type of food was served. But dancing tended to be in couples and was more of the European type. A few days later I discussed this type of party with a woman who criticized it as "elitist" and "stiff and formal." For a while she was convincing. Later I found the same woman participating in both kind of party, and indeed in both cases the same people were involved. The Creoles are "dualistic" in their culture, with the same men and women partaking in both types of symbolic activity, even though they may express criticism of the one type or the other, betraying an underlying contradiction in their cultural and social life.

For the relatively small Creole elite, a wedding is an event that ultimately affects the whole group because of its implications for recruitment, distinctiveness, the network of amity and of privilege, and the status and power of the collectivity in general. Through a series of dramatic performances, the whole symbolic order of the group is activated to create new links, strengthen existing ones, sharpen

boundaries, and seize the opportunity of informally delib-
erating the current problems of the collectivity in small,
overlapping groups chatting about solutions. Thus, through
the magic and the mystificatory powers of the drama, a
transformation in relationships and in the structure of the
collectivity is effected.

The Universal in the Particular: Dramatizing the Educational Process

The ball, the thanksgiving service, the ceremonials relating
to the dead, and the rites of transition—these dramas were
staged largely for Creole audiences, with the same people
being both actors and audience. But, like other elites, the
Creoles stage dramas directed at the wider society in order
to render universal what is essentially particular. A significant case in point is that of education. The educational process, the ladder to the power, security, and prestige of
eliteness, is throughout its various stages interrelated with
a series of dramas that are mounted daily to objectify values, norms, and beliefs. These impel pupil and teacher to
greater effort and achievement, proclaim to the wider public the supreme significance of learning for the nation, and
bestow a universalistic mystique on those who have reached
the top—the professionals.

In Freetown society, indeed throughout Sierra Leone,
the highest honour, prestige, financial security, and fringe
benefits are associated with civil service appointments and
with professionalism. The only road to these statuses is
through the acquisition of higher education. As business is
mainly in the hands of foreigners, education is the sole ladder to upward mobility within the system, and is therefore
coveted by all. Education is idolized not only as the means
of individual achievement but also—indeed primarily—as
a national value deemed essential for economic development, enlightened social planning, efficient administration
of public affairs, and general progress in the scientific, cultural, and artistic fields. This is a goal pursued by all na-
tions, communist and capitalist, developed and developing.
Everywhere, education is power. And this is essentially the

187

basis of Creole status. Formal education is almost universal among them, and every one of its stages is heavily ceremonialized. Education and professionalism are a way of life for them, and are built into the very structure of their households and of the Creole cousinhood generally.

Until recently, education has been closely associated with Christian ideology, practice, and organization. Indeed the whole success of the Christian missionary enterprise among the Creoles and other educated sections of the population has been attributed to what one Christian theologian and missionary (Olson, 1969) called "the School approach." This has been true for most African societies, and where Christian missions were prevented from operating— for example, in Hausaland in Northern Nigeria—modern education seriously lagged behind, sometimes with serious political consequences. The liberated Africans (the recaptives) succeeded in achieving the same high status as the settlers when they invested the money they earned from trade in the education of their children, and adopted Christianity. It is not simply that the missions opened schools and made the acquisition of education possible. Christianity also provided values, norms, and an ideology that subjectively predisposed pupils to achievement. For the Creoles it evolved into a way of life and an ideology—a body of norms and beliefs which the growing individual acquired through socialization in the home, at church, and later in school, and success in school indirectly depended on this ideology.

The first drama ritualizing education is baptism. In this ceremony the child is given a Christian name, and is affiliated to the church. More fundamentally, the child is also linked to a godfather and a godmother. These are chosen by the parents, and are almost invariably highly educated men and women, very often prominent academics, headmasters, or teachers. The child is thereby ritually linked to two exemplary adults whom she or he can respect and emulate. The godparents in their turn become bound by ritual obligations to look after the welfare of the child as he or she develops. The formal religious obligation is that they ensure that the child grow up to be a good Christian. This is, however, socially interpreted as an obligation to see to it that the child is given good education. By convention, the godparents often pay the first fee instalment when the child starts schooling, even though the parents may not need any financial help. The institution thus implies that the child will always have godparents who are professionals, often with higher academic attainments than its parents, concerned with its education and general development. The arrangement holds even for children born out of wedlock.

In 1970, I attended the christening ceremony of such a child, born out of wedlock to Angela and John. It began at 4:00 P.M. in an Anglican church, and lasted for an hour. There were only about thirty men and women present. I was told that many had been invited, but that because it was a weekday most of them could not come. The father of the baby stood at the entrance to the church hovering restlessly, perhaps anxiously expecting guests who had not arrived. He entered the church after the ceremony had started. The service was conducted by two clergymen, one of whom distributed copies of the prayer book to those present. Half the service was conducted around the altar; the other half around the baptismal font. The congregation sang hymns. The child was named Jonathan, the headmaster of a school being named the godfather, and a civil servant the godmother. The child "promised" through the godfather to have nothing to do with the devil.

After the service we drove to the house of the baby's mother's mother. It was built of stone on top of a hill amidst one of the most densely populated slums in the city. Naked children interrupted their play at a communal water tap, and looked curiously at the strange procession of elegantly dressed men and women, complete with hats, wigs, and white gloves, one of them carrying the baby, which was heavily clad in white robes and wrap.

When we entered the living room, there were a number of people waiting, including the grandmother and a clergyman. The latter immediately started conducting a service which lasted for fifteen minutes, in which he blessed the house and its people. We were then served with drinks—beer and whisky—and cake. There was also the traditional rice cake, served in small slices. The baby was stripped of what must have been an irritating stiff, white baptismal gown, and a girl of about eighteen took him in her arms and danced with him to the highlife rhythms from the huge radio in the room.

In the meantime, I was given a detailed account of a feast for the dead which had been held the morning before. A hole had been dug in the yard near a wall, into which an offering of food was placed. The offering was made principally to the founder of the family house in the name of the baby, who would in the future inherit a portion of the property. The baby's father took me to a room on the other side of the house, where a small table was neatly laid out with offerings to the dead. There was a small bottle of whisky, a bottle of 7 Up, a glass full of a special milky drink, a bowl containing baked beans and some other ingredients, and four kola nut halves, two red and two white, placed in the propitious arrangement of two up and two down. The 7 Up was offered because the founder of the house did not like alcohol. While we were in the house, women came individually or in pairs and brought presents and offered congratulations.

In the evening, a proper, lavish celebration was staged in the house of the baby's father's mother in a different part of the city. There was some ambiguity in the celebration, in that it was said to celebrate John's recent promotion at work as well as the christening of the baby.

The christening of a child born out of wedlock has been intentionally chosen to show the child's prospects of acquiring education. John was a university graduate and had a good income, and although he had a legitimate family as well, he acknowledged fathering Angela's child and assumed responsibility for its future. Angela herself was employed as a teacher, and her mother would be looking after the child. The new godparents were a distinguished man and woman with comfortable incomes, each prepared to help in the child's education when the time came.

Christening also signified that the child had become associated with a church, his "church of birth." A male remains a member of his church of birth throughout his life. He is registered in it, and dues are paid first on his behalf and then by himself when he is an adult.

Soon Jonathan would join special classes at the church, in which he would continue to receive instruction till adulthood, along with his formal schooling. Although the main concern of such classes is religion, their impact on his educational attainments in the years to come would be dramatic. He would learn to pray in English, to speak in front of his age-mates, and to sing hymns to European music. In short, an essentially Western ideology, with the emphasis on individualism, liberalism, education, "proper" dress, and "proper" behavior, would be inculcated in him.

This kind of informal education, strongly supported and contributed to in the home, gives the child a significant advantage in acquiring basic skills in formal education. Thus, even though children from the same "class" background and the same degree of intelligence come to study within the framework of the same school, the Christian child has an advantage over the non-Christian.

All through the educational process, ritual drama goes hand in hand with the acquisition of knowledge and skill, serving to objectify values, change moods and attitudes, orient the children to the refinements of culture, and motivate them to achieve. With Creole children, this goes on together with—and is greatly supported by—additional orientation, stimulation, and prompting in the home. Home and school are both shaped by Christian values and institutions, and both cooperate in developing the child. With the non-Creole child on the other hand, the home experience is often different from that of the school in many crucial ways.

One of the ceremonials of the school year is prize giving. In March 1970, I attended such an occasion at the Annie Walsh Memorial School, now called the Sierra Leone Grammar School for Girls. This is the oldest girls' school in the country, having been established on its present premises by the Church Missionary Society (CMS). At the time, the daughter of a Reverend Walsh donated £2500 towards its foundation, and the school was named after her. In 1970, it had about 500 girls, of whom nearly 60 percent were Creole. About 60 of the girls, mostly from important families in the provinces and almost all non-Creole, were boarders. The rest were day-pupils whose homes were in Freetown. Admission was on the basis of qualification and merit, but other things being equal priority was given to girls whose mothers had been pupils at the school. The governing committee was overwhelmingly Creole, and the CMS still retained some role in the running of the school.

I did not at the time appreciate how serious and how solemn the occasion was for most of the parents and the other guests who attended. I was given a lift to the school ceremony by a senior Creole faculty member of Fourah Bay College who was also invited. When I came out of my house, he looked me over with surprise and anxiety and asked: "Are you going like this?" I looked at my clothes— long trousers, a long-sleeved shirt, a tie, and proper shoes. I thought I had been particularly careful about my appearance, and I asked what the matter was. "This is an extremely formal occasion which is attended by many important dignitaries from various sections of Freetown society and one is expected to dress formally," he said. He himself had a navy blue suit on. He advised me to go back into the house and put on a proper suit, but I had locked the door and the key was with my wife, who had gone to town. Although he was a close friend, I felt that he was annoyed, and that he probably thought my appearance without a jacket indicated disrespect for the ceremony. To allay his fears, I suggested that once we arrived at the school I part company with him so as not to embarrass him in front of the other guests by our appearing together. This we eventually did; he went to the front rows and I went to the back.

The ceremony was held in the open playgrounds of the school. There were between 1,200 and 1,500 people seated in long rows on chairs facing a high wooden stage. The streets leading to the school were lined with hundreds of parked cars, with scores of policemen keeping order. The ladies wore colourful dresses with hats; most of the men wore dark suits, many of them woollen, even though the temperature was in the nineties and the sun was still blazing fiercely. Although 40 percent of the students were non-

192

Creole, the audience was overwhelmingly Creole. The occasion was staged on a national scale in the sense that among those who attended it there were government officials, foreign diplomats, and representatives of various Christian denominations. There were also a few score Europeans, who either represented organizations or were parents of girls attending the school or teachers there or at other schools in Freetown. There were also representatives of the press and professional photographers. Most of the girls of the school, wearing dark green uniforms with orange fringes and matching hats, sat in rows on the right-hand side of the field.

The procedure lasted for two and a half hours; the audience was patient and most people seemed attentive and fully absorbed. The program included the performance of two short plays, one in French and one in English. All the actors were girls, some of them appearing in male roles, and the acting was excellent. The time between the different parts of the programme was filled with songs by a well-trained choir accompanied on the piano by a teacher.

The artistic part of the programme was followed by the report of the principal, a dignified lady of immense character, the wife of a high-court judge. She spoke for about twenty minutes, surveying the development of the school, giving extensive figures, and expressing her gratitude to the many societies and foreign missions who had contributed to it in various ways. Among those thanked were USAID, for providing funds for a whole new building; the British VSO (Voluntary Service Overseas), for providing some teachers; and many others for contributing books to be given as prizes. The principal also mentioned the substantial help given by numerous societies of "old girls" of the school, who had faithfully given a lot of their time, energies, and material resources towards maintaining the school at such a high standard. Finally, she praised the Parents-Teachers' Association for doing so much in the coordination of the educational progress of the young between the school and the home. The aim of the school, she concluded, was "to produce women of integrity and responsibility. . . . to serve in our heterogeneous society."

This was followed by a short speech, delivered by a British-born professor of education then teaching at the University of Sierra Leone. It was brief, but even so was rather out of place in the ceremonial context.

Then came the distribution of prizes to a long list of girls who had excelled in one or another activity or subject. The girls were called to the platform one by one to receive the prizes. All but a few of the names were Creole, and the applause was overwhelming. The professional photographers went into a frenzy trying to capture the appearance of every girl as she came on stage.

After that, the school song was sung, with many of the women in the audience joining in enthusiastically, being themselves old girls of the school, which in many ways can be described as the "cradle of Creoledom." Finally, the benediction was recited over the microphone by a senior Anglican clergyman. He requested the audience to lower their heads, which all did silently and obediently, and then gave the blessing, in the name of the Lord.

Four days later, the school had its Thanksgiving Day. The service was held at an Anglican church, and was followed by a march along the main streets in the centre of the city to the music of brass bands. Not only the girls and teachers, but also mothers and "old girls" marched. The onlookers wildly cheered a number of three-generation groups consisting of pupil, mother, and grandmother, all graduates of the school.

In all Freetown schools, parents take an active part in the running of the school, and especially in its ceremonials. I attended the "Sports Day" of a primary school where our three children were enrolled for the year, held in the afternoon on a large sports field. It was very well organized, and was massively attended by parents (mostly civil servants and faculty members of FBC). A police band played throughout. Many of the parents were involved in the organization.

The sporting events included a competition among the teachers, one for the mothers, one for the fathers (in which I took part), and a fourth among the old boys and girls of the school. One of the school's important patrons, the wife of a Creole professor, and president of many women's and dramatic societies, distributed the prizes. One of the girls later presented her with a bouquet of flowers.

Two months earlier, the same school had held its Thanksgiving Day at St. George's Cathedral in the centre of the city. I attended, and our three children participated. About 500 people were present, of whom two-thirds were women. It was a solemn ceremony, with soft organ music, a children's choir, and a sermon by a canon. The service lasted for an hour, after which we all went outside to see the children starting off on their march in the main street of Freetown, headed by their headmistress and teachers, and accompanied by the brass band of one of the city's main secondary schools. We waited in the Secretariat Court Building with other parents until the procession came back. Photographs were taken, and the headmistress gave a short speech thanking everyone for helping, and praising the children for their endurance and cooperation.

These ceremonials probably occupy as much time as does the actual learning process. Sometimes teaching in school is halted for a whole week in all classes so that children and teachers can prepare for an event. Large resources are expended. Drama is indeed part of the educational process itself, and is the way the mystique of eliteness is created and recreated. Through a succession of ceremonial events, the schools also succeed in involving many sections of the population—among them parents, old boys and girls, designers, musicians, ministers, and foreign representatives. School "events" are frequent in Freetown society, taking the shape of thanksgiving ceremonies, speech days, prize-giving days, graduation ceremonies, and massive marches to the sound of brass bands through the short, narrow streets of the capital. The parade in the street proclaims a message—the supreme significance of education, the universalistic value of which is thereby acknowledged and celebrated by society. And the concern is not individual, but public on a grand scale, at state level. This is manifest as much in the ceremonials of a small primary school as in those of the national university.

In November 1969, I witnessed the holding of Congregation at Fourah Bay College of the University of Sierra

Leone, to celebrate the weaning of the college from the patronage of the University of Durham. Fourah Bay College was founded by the Christian Missionary Society in 1827 to train African clergy and teachers for schools. In 1876, it was affiliated to the University of Durham, which made it possible for its students to sit for their examinations in Freetown and get an English degree. The affiliation with Durham had officially come to an end the previous year, the occasion being commemorated at the time by another grand celebration at which the University of Sierra Leone was established, incorporating the two colleges of Fourah Bay (in Freetown) and Njala (in the provinces), and a Sierra Leonean, Sir Samuel Bankole Jones (a high-court judge at the time), was installed as chancellor. But the students who were at the time in their final year before graduation had been registered with Durham University, and their final examinations had to be conducted by Durham. As the 151 graduates who were to receive their degrees from Durham that year were the last to do so, the 1969 graduation ceremony was, as the principal of the college put it, a historic occasion.

Preparations for the ceremony had started many months earlier. A large (10″ x 8″), expensive invitation pamphlet, with a hard cover elaborately decorated and inscribed in gold, was distributed to literally thousands of people from every walk of life in the country. The roads leading from the centre of Freetown to the college and within the campus were substantially repaired, and their edges painted stark white. The terraces of the amphitheatre where the ceremony was to be held were repaired and consolidated with the help of a gift of £1,000 from the United Africa Company. Traffic police made arrangements, days ahead, for the large number of cars expected to come, and a number of reserved special parking areas were marked for the VIP's. Both newspapers and radio and television services anticipated the day as an important national event. A week beforehand, all teaching in the college stopped and rehearsals of the processions and of parts of the program were held.

The ceremony started at 5:00 P.M., with the arrival of the acting governor general, who appeared in the role of deputy visitor, the visitor of the college being the queen of England. An important clergyman represented the president of the college, "The Most Reverend and Right Honourable A. M. Ramsey, P.C., M.A., D.D., Archbishop of Canterbury." Apart from the students and their relatives, and faculty members and their families, there were hundreds of important men and women present, including ambassadors, ministers, members of Parliament, representatives of various Christian denominations, of Muslim community organizations, of various business concerns, and of different societies, associations, and institutions. It was a drama on a national scale, meticulously planned and staged by experienced masters of ceremonies.

The program started with the first procession, consisting of a marshal, the graduates, representatives of the students' union, graduates of the university of Durham, representatives of the old students' union, another marshal, the academic staff, the chaplain, bursar, medical officer, and estate officer, the academic board, the registrar, the librarian, and the council.

When these took their seats on the large stage in the amphitheatre, there was a fanfare and the entire congregation rose to honour the deputy visitor's procession, consisting of the university mace bearer, a marshal, an honorary graduate, the minister of education, the prime minister, the vice-principal, the university vice-presidents, the principal, and the deputy visitor. The congregation sat when the deputy visitor had taken his seat, and the principal declared it open "for the conferment of degrees of the University of Durham." One by one, the deans of the various faculties then presented the candidates who were to receive degrees. It was a great occasion for the graduates, their teachers, and their families, who rejoiced and cheered continuously.

But the culmination of the drama was the forty-minute speech given by the principal of Fourah Bay College, a prominent Creole clergyman, academician, author, and administrator, and a well-known national figure. He was a remarkable performer, and his speech was delivered with great wit and laced with apt quotations from literature, with Latin phrases thrown in here and there. In all, the speech was an artistic unity, linking together academic, religious, and political elements, relating past to present, continuity to change, and international to national issues, all within one gestalt, a configuration which, with the help of the pomp and pageantry of the occasion, made a strong impact on the thousands of people present.

The first item in the speech was the extension of congratulations, first to all those receiving degrees and diplomas, then "to the chairman of the college council on having been appointed an officer of the most excellent order of the British Empire by Her Majesty the Queen," then to the same chairman and to the prime minister and to the president of the Methodist Conference in Sierra Leone—the three being also members of the Fourah Bay College Council—on receiving the honorary degree of doctor of civil law from the University of Sierra Leone.

The principal then dwelt at length on the uniqueness of the occasion. This was the last Durham congregation to be held in Sierra Leone, he noted, adding, "How I wish we could, like Tennyson, have said,"

> Old affiliation you must not die
> You come to us so readily
> You lived with us so steadily
> Old affiliation you shall not die.

"But we shall preserve a warm niche in our hearts for her and establish a communication link . . . to keep this college in live contact with the seven hills on which the great city of Durham and its cathedral, half church of God, half castle, supports the towers that have proved indomitable even to Scottish warriors." Affiliation with Durham had lasted for 90 years, during which time an impressive array of bishops and men of letters, who served not just in Sierra Leone but throughout West Africa, had graduated. The speaker surveyed the spectacular progress of the college as manifested in the increasing number of students and the diversification of subjects taught. Thus, for the first time, there were among the graduates two mathematicians, one of whom had obtained first class honours. He also mentioned the growing numbers of foreigners attending the college, among them twenty-six Americans interested in Black Studies.

The third part of the speech was an expression of thanks to the many institutions and associations who had helped the college in a variety of ways, including financial support in the form of grants and scholarships contributed by foreign businesses—British, Indian, and Lebanese. On behalf of the college, the principal sent greetings to its president, the archbishop of Canterbury, whose interest in it remained constant and warm. In conclusion, he requested the deputy visitor "to convey to Her Majesty, our Royal Visitor, our deep appreciation of her graciousness in accepting from this College a presentation copy of Sigmund W. Koelle's *Polyglotta Africana.*"

Thousands of bottles of soft drinks were distributed in the terraces, and the different items of procedure were interspersed with music by two military bands, who alternated in playing. That night, after the ceremony had ended, scores of joyous parties were held by the families of the graduates throughout the city.

In its strictly formal structure, the ceremony was almost a replica of similar ceremonies that are held at British or American universities. But there the similarity ends. Sierra Leone is a small country, Freetown is a small town; the difference in complexity is great, as the country is only slowly developing. The process of institutional differentiation had not proceeded far as yet. The ceremony was literally the talk of the town—indeed of the nation—for months, both before and after it was held. The proceedings were given great prominence on radio and television for days, and the speeches were serialized in the national papers. The ceremony was attended by almost the entire state elite, including the head of state, the prime minister and cabinet, permanent secretaries, representatives of every professional and public association in the country, and representatives of international organizations, including almost the whole of the diplomatic corps. It celebrated the hegemony of education and professionalism in the country. Politicians who had no academic titles were given honorary ones. Power was wedded to knowledge, and knowledge to power, on the highest level of state and of society. Knowledge is a universalistic value, and those who excel in it are the meritocracy, whose status is validated and supported in terms of a universally upheld ideology.

The Creole role in the ceremony was overwhelming. So was the degree of their involvement and concern with its symbolism and issues. Although less than 2 percent of the population, they accounted at the time for 64 percent of the academically trained professionals in the whole country (Harrell-Bond, 1975). For them, particularism and universalism were largely fused. In their families and social circles, education is not just an ideological value, but very much a way of life, into which children are inducted from an early age. Education structures their network of amity and pervades their entire culture. Formal educational instruction is only part of the process in the recruitment of Creole children to professionalism. A great part of the battle for education is achieved in the home, in the church, and in other communal institutions, which inculcate relevant values, norms, and discipline, and predispose the developing man or woman to high achievement.

Drama and the Leadership Process

In the series of ceremonies discussed in this chapter, I have indicated how a collectivity becomes aware of its current problems, deliberates them, and probes for solutions. In these activities, some members play more prominent roles than others and come to act as "leaders." Leadership arises in different spheres and on different levels of sociocultural life. Some leaders specialize in one sphere or on one level, while others straddle more than one sphere and range over more than one level. This can be seen in the roles of different individuals in the dramas of Creoledom during the past twenty-five years.

Some of the leaders can be described as "consciousness raisers." These are individuals who from time to time step out to talk in plain language and in public about the dangers threatening the collectivity, and propose formal practical steps to avert them. Thus, between 1947 and 1957 Dr. Bankole-Bright spoke bluntly about a gulf separating the Creoles from the provincials and advocated formal Creole independence in the former colony, or a strong measure of formal Creole power in the running of the country.

Again in 1970, the Creole Convention was led by a self-employed barrister who publicly spelled out the dangers facing the Creoles and proposed measures to avert them. Yet, although many Creoles may have sympathized with his views, the majority thought that *overt* formulations of this type were in the long run fraught with dangers to their power and interests, and were incompatible with their universalistic roles in the organization of the state. Such leaders have, therefore, had no great following, and have even been discredited publicly. But this does not mean that their message had no impact. An examination of the 1970 Creole Convention will highlight this issue.

The two meetings of the convention were attended by a small audience of about 200 men and women. The formal movement that the convention initiated eventually stalled, and, like similar movements in the past, soon died down. The majority of those who attended were retired men and women who were "die-hard" Creoles, and one of the two major issues raised in the convention was the danger of alienating houses and land to non-Creoles. This was an issue of particular significance to men and women of this age group. Many of them would already have asked their families that their estates not be divided up after their deaths. It was natural for them to uphold the sacredness of such a will and to enhance beliefs in the mystical powers of the dead. Old people have "finished with this world," as the Creoles put it, and feel strongly about the dead, whom they will soon join. When a member of their family is struck by affliction, they often trace the cause to the mystical activities of the dead. It is they who act as diviners and contact the dead through their dreams. Their beliefs and sentiments, and their concern for their property and the welfare of their children predisposed them to support the convention's call to keep property within the collectivity. Their individual concerns were also seen as the concerns of the collective and their beliefs and resolve were thereby strengthened. When through divination they attribute an affliction to the anger of the dead, they in effect act as leaders, translating a consciously advanced course of action in terms of non-rational mystical prescriptions. By proposing to hold an *awujoh*, or feast for the dead, and supervising it and playing an active part in it, such an individual in effect recreated, revived, strengthened, or kept alive the power of the dead in guiding action in conformity with the interests of the collective. Thus, to put it crudely, the chain of leadership passed from the formal leader of the convention to the elders who were present, to other elders not present, to the women who subsequently organized the feast, to the patrons who were under pressure to attend, and to ordinary Creoles generally. The causal link in this case went from the consciously and formally conceived political reality to the informal world of symbolic, non-rational beliefs and practices.

The second message of the convention was that the Creoles should develop their own businesses in order to absorb young Creole graduates who were not given jobs in government institutions. Here the link passed from one formal level to another. For many months after the convention, there were intensive discussions among Creole intellectuals, particularly economists and men with money, aimed at taking practical steps in developing Creole enterprise. It is, of course, not necessary to claim that a direct one-to-one causal connection existed between the convention and these discussions; it is obvious that the two developments were at one level or another interrelated, or that they were parts of the same reality. What is apparent is that there is mutual stimulation between politicians operating on the national level and business-minded individuals operating at grass-roots levels.

The leadership process also operates within the symbolic order itself at different levels. In the case of the ball discussed in chapter 1, the twelve members of the Moonlight Club perceived the necessity for the Creoles to stress and reemphasize their distinctiveness in the refinements of "culture." They conceived the cultural form this should take. Each of them decided who to approach as "candidates" for the ball and what techniques of persuasion to adopt in inducing them to participate. They displayed initiative and ability to organizing the event with all the complexities involved, such as hiring the hall, employing the band, arranging the catering, and fixing the program. In the process they contacted hundreds of men and women, and sought advice and help from many of them. No doubt they deliberated the various issues and distributed the tasks among themselves in accordance with their different experiences and competences. At the ball, three of them stood at the entrance, greeting the participants as they came in, while the other members took care of other tasks. Between them, throughout, they personified in their appearance and behavior the ideals of the club. On their part, many of the participants displayed "initiative" and "judgement" when they decided to go to the expense in time and money. They did not necessarily come in order to have a nice time. Indeed some of them were constrained to take part by various commitments and links. Many of them were patrons, "leaders" of "families," and felt it was their duty to their own relatives as well as to their friends to participate.

In the case of the Thanksgiving service, the stewards' union took the initiative in planning and organizing the event, in drawing up the list of patrons, in fixing the dramaturgical procedure, and especially in the choice of preacher. The preacher displayed great perception of the general mood in the choice of a theme and words that suited the occasion. The patrons felt duty-bound to sponsor the event, not only because of their personal sympathies towards the church, but also out of consideration for the feelings of their own followers.

Leadership in the conduct of family ceremonials may be difficult to appreciate, but is no less significant. The elders divining and officiating at the feasts for the dead, the chairman and other speakers at the wedding reception, the various patrons giving night parties, the women organizing the catering—these and many others are all in their ways, and their little arenas, leaders in their own right in the sense that they, more than others, took stock of a situation, recognized its problems, and provided practical solutions that were acceptable to the collectivity.

The patrons, generally the heads of the few hundred "families" that comprise the bulk of the Creoles, are "cross-order" leaders in the sense of being simultaneously officials and professionals and leading figures in religious, Masonic, and various cultural fields. Usually the higher their status and competence in the one area, the higher it is in the other. Many of them are at the same time national leaders, linking Creole and non-Creole publics by their sociocultural activities.

Take, as an example, Mr. James Davies (pseudonym), whom I know well and whose biography is public knowledge. He is the head of one of the leading educational institutions in the country. He has a high standing in the ritual hierarchy of the Masonic order, and is affiliated to several lodges. He is also one of the top religious leaders in the church hierarchy. He is politically active on the national level, and the leading patron of a number of overlapping families. He commands high respect in different circles on almost all levels. His multiple roles mean that he plays a crucial informal part in the sociocultural process, translating social issues into dramatic patterns.

An equally crucial mediating part, though of a different type, is played by the professor and head of the department of theology at the university, Principal of Fourah Bay College, author of many books and articles, and a canon in the Anglican cathedral. This man is also the patron of a large number of Creole men and women. He is one of the most humane, energetic people I have known anywhere. Throughout the day, and well into the night, he could be seen feverishly driving up and down Mount Aureol, where he lived on the university campus. He would put on his academic gown to give a lecture early in the morning; wear his ecclesiastical gown to go down to the cathedral to officiate at a wedding service; rush back to his office to receive the acting governor, a minister, or an important foreign visitor; return to town to attend a feast for the dead; go from there to participate in a christening party; and then on to one or another state-level ceremony. He is very much a national figure whose name is continuously in the public eye. His wife is the president of numerous societies, associations, and clubs, and is the patron of a large number of young men and women in her own right.

There are literally scores of Creole men and women of this calibre who are simultaneously eminent in different social and cultural fields, and whose activities form significant links in the chain of sociocultural change. In the analysis of the part played by leaders in the process of sociocultural causation, the question is often raised whether there are any basic psychological traits that characterize leaders in a system. During field study I collected detailed biographical notes about a number of the Creole leaders who were involved in the events discussed in this book. At the time, most of the men and women in the survey were forty or over. They had all been born and brought up during the colonial period, and had invariably been educated in one of the leading missionary schools. They spoke English well, and were Westernized in their style of life. In their youth, they had seen themselves as Englishmen, and their first ambition had been to go "home" to Britain, either to study, or on official duty, or on a visit. But on going "home" many had suffered a severe shock which proved to be traumatic, haunting their lives for years to come. They were treated as inferiors by white British society, which rejected their claims of identity, and were subjected to discrimination and humiliation in a variety of ways. At least one of the Creoles in my survey had a nervous breakdown as a result, and was confined for some time in an institution in Britain. When they fell back on their identity as Sierra Leoneans by returning to Freetown, they were once more caught up in the Creole-provincial cleavage. During the 1950s and the early 1960s their identity as Sierra Leoneans was threatened and at least temporarily rejected by the provincials.

Thus in 1970 they were caught in a basic contradiction. Their selfhood had been undermined by conflicting roles and identities. But, generally speaking, these subversive processes threatening the oneness of the self are continuously counterbalanced by symbolic action, in which the individual is always involved. By its very nature, symbolic action involves the totality of the self and not a segment of it. Selfhood is achieved through continual participation in patterns of symbolic activity. For the majority of people, these patterns are provided by the interest groups to which they are affiliated: lineage, tribe, caste, or "class." These interest groups always attempt to manipulate and structure the selves of their members to further their own ends. The self reacts to this in a variety of ways, including the creation of new symbolic patterns that are free from utilitarian interests. In time these new symbolic patterns are exploited by new or old interest groups, and the search for new patterns will be resumed. The process here is dialectical and cannot be analyzed in reductionist terms.

Many Creoles have experienced the crisis of identity outlined above and accordingly, respond to those leaders whose symbolic or ideological formulations help them to confront their own inner contradictions. Originality and creativity alone are not sufficient in characterizing a leader. A comparison between the biographies of two Creole women will demonstrate this. Both went through the traumatic experiences and suffered from the type of conflict discussed earlier. One became highly disillusioned, led a rather lonely life, and found her basic solution in art. She shunned Creole ceremonials and close interpersonal relationships with Creoles. Her artistic works were highly original and she had a number of successful exhibitions in Europe. But there was very little interest in her work among the Creoles themselves. She was regarded as odd, and some people even described her as a "witch." The other Creole woman had the same kind of background—education, journey to the West, and identity crisis—but on returning to Freetown immersed herself in a dense network of interpersonal relationships and participated actively as a prominent leader in Creole ceremonials, as well as in general, more universalistic affairs. She was less original in her thinking and in her creativity than the first woman, but was acclaimed in many circles as a leading personality. She organized ceremonies on different levels and took an active part in them. Both women were manipulators of symbols. The first was innovative and creative, but less successful as a leader; the second was more traditional, but more successful as leader.

Other paired comparisons of this kind can be made in order to demonstrate that originality and creativity are not in themselves sufficient to make a man or woman into a leader. Only those who provide solutions to current problems through interaction with the collectivity will be listened to and followed.

What this indicates is that leadership is a dialectical process, not a one-way activity. The leader is not fully created by the collectivity, and the collectivity is not the creation of leaders. There is, however, an element of original creativity involved in the leadership process. Transactionalism can certainly illuminate part of this process, but when carried to extremes it misses the other side of the dialectic and its formulations become mechanistic and unidimensional.

Dramaturgical Techniques

Nearly all leaders straddle both the symbolic and the power dimensions. But most of them differ in gravitation towards the one or the other. When a leader confines most of his activities to the symbolic order, he will be concerned principally with dramaturgical techniques, such as the production of a dramatic script; "staging" it; authenticating its action; objectifying its abstract concepts, values, and norms; inducing a state of ecstasy among the actors in an effort to create communion among them, and thereby inhibiting their differences and quarrels; enhancing the consciousness of the audience to enable it to receive an important message; transforming a collective obligation to a personal categorical imperative; and always trying to draw the totality of the selves of the participants into action in the interests of the collective.

Dress, music, poetry, dance, commensality, and rhetoric are all techniques that play a crucial part in the process of sociocultural causation. This is not to imply that these are not in themselves creative arts. A dress, a song, a poem can be an original artistic work in its own right, but when considered within the context of a drama, it is an aid used to enhance the dramatic effect, and can in that sense be regarded as a technique.

I have earlier discussed the limitedness of the repertoires of cultures. There are relatively few basic symbolic functions and basic symbolic forms. Cultures and sub-cultures, however, differ widely in the symbolic techniques they employ and in the different ways in which these techniques are combined, although even here the possibilities are not unlimited.

As in the production of a stage drama, the first and most widely employed technique of dramatization is dress. The effectiveness of this technique can be appreciated if, as Carlyle suggested (1954; see also Duncan, 1962:190–201; 1969:66–69) one imagines the removal of clothes from the people taking part in a ceremony such as the Fourah Bay College congregation described above. The whole affair would be reduced to utter chaos, and would lose its structure. It would be difficult to distinguish an academic from a diplomat, an army or police officer, a clergyman, and so on. It would be even more difficult to identify rank within each of these categories—to distinguish a bishop from an ordinary minister, a private soldier from a high-ranking commander, a graduate from a professor.

All cultures observe conventions of dress or personal appearance. Even in tropical societies, where little or no clothing is used, differentiations by sex, age, status, and rank are signified by such techniques as skin markings and decoration, the wearing of beads of different shapes and colors, the wearing of specific hairstyles, and so on (see Paulme, 1973).

Despite the hot climate, the Creoles have developed an elaborate dress lore. They are indeed one of the most dress-conscious groups to be found anywhere. It was no accident that in his speech, the principal of Fourah Bay College referred to the "multi-coloured array of learned men and women in scarlet and purple, in claret and gold and blue and white; some in cassimere others in velvet."

From very early on in their history in Sierra Leone, the Creoles adopted middle-class European-style dress in order to identify with the British rulers and distinguish themselves from the provincials (see Porter, 1963:101–3; Spitzer, 1974: 16–17; 19–20). This style has persisted, despite some serious dress reform movements, which have criticized the Creoles for aping European ways without establishing their own authentic identity, and have dwelt on its unsuitability for the climate of the country (see Spitzer, 1974:118–20; Fyfe, 1962:468). During the years leading to independence, there was a good deal of public discussion on the national radio and in the papers about the choice of a "national dress" for men, but nothing materialized. An article in the Sierra Leone *Daily Mail* (20 April 1956) attacked the emptiness of such discussion, and stated bitterly that the national costume of the Creole man would remain as ever: black suit, black shoes, and black tie, and that Creoles would continue to regard the provincial *agbada* as "jungle dress." The writer decried the custom of provincial men who, as soon as they came to Freetown, abandoned their tribal costume and adopted European dress. And indeed, it is still the case today that most of the provincial elite live in Freetown and wear Western-style clothes. For one thing, the country's independence did not involve a bitter conflict with the British, and there was therefore no urge among the nationalists to symbolize political differences in terms of dress. This left the Creoles free to continue dressing as before, and most men continue to wear full suits, many of them black, particularly to church service, in the lodges, and in other ceremonies. In 1970 men who were self-employed even wore bowler hats.

On the whole, men's dress is not widely varied, and social differentiation is often indicated by the addition of badges, special ties, gowns, and regalia. But with women the variety and sophistication are great. Their dress colours and designs are distinctive in their simplicity and subtlety, and this often differentiates them from provincial elite women, who tend to dress more colourfully and gaily in longer, so-called African-style clothes. Creole women who lead national women's organizations go out of their way on some rare occasions to wear this African-style dress in order to enhance their universalistic image. Otherwise, they have a most elaborate wardrobe, with more conventional colours and styles for different social occasions such as weddings, funerals, cocktail parties, and "elite evening parties." Within these conventions, there is a great deal of individual variation in design. Creole women do not buy ready-made dresses, but have them made to individual specifications by special dressmakers. There are many of these in Freetown, and they are constantly busy catering to individual tastes and producing new designs for different occasions. Often a woman will order a special new dress for every important social occasion.

Thus, while men uniformly tend to wear dark suits, the women display some degree of individualism in the choice of material, colour, and design. There are nevertheless occasions on which the women also display uniformity. In every church members of the sisterhood wear a special uniform dress with matching hat. At weddings and on a few other occasions, the women of a "family" and their close friends appear in *ashobi*, to display "family" solidarity. Creole children are trained from an early age in the conventions of dress. They have special clothes for Sunday church service, and wear uniforms in school.

Clothes help to define or to camouflage identity. A Creole woman in public employment told me that for two years after returning from her studies in Britain, she wore African-style dress in order to stop any comment to the effect that she had become British. She was ultra-sensitive, but her case indicates the significance attached to style of dress in the society. Stagers of ceremonies consistently manipulate clothing as a technique of signification.

Another dramaturgical technique is music, particularly in relation to Christian education and worship, which for nearly two centuries have punctuated Creole social life. As one Christian theologian has put it: "All true worship approaches towards ecstasy. Ecstasy means literally 'a standing out of oneself.'. . . And music is the very language of ecstasy, the true expression in sound of the man who is taken out of himself" (Dunlop, 1953:42–43). Here again, Creole children are systematically exposed to European music and are trained in choir singing. This is continued to adulthood, almost throughout life. Organ music is a well established, highly developed skill, and, as indicated in discussing ceremonies earlier on, there are a number of highly trained organists whose names recur in the programs of different types of celebrations.

Creole culture is, however, syncretic and rather dualistic, in that it combines European and African types of music. Reference has been made above to *Gumbe* music. Consisting of a deep rhythm, this follows a different tradition in the technique of inducing ecstasy. Often, such music evokes intensive dancing, which further enhances an ecstatic state, manifest particularly in "family" ceremonials, where as many as thirty to forty uniformly dressed women (sometimes joined by a few men) dance vigourously to achieve a high level of communion.

Producers of cultural performances also employ *commensality*, the act of eating and drinking together, as yet another dramaturgical technique for achieving communion. This is a univerally practised symbolic institution, a "language" in its own right, which creates, develops, and enhances communal relationships. It initiates communication between strangers, and transforms contractual and formal single-interest relationships into the multiplex relationships of amity. It helps in the demarcation of group identity and exclusiveness, and in the establishment of hierarchical commensal order between status groups. Indeed, in the Indian caste system, its symbolic significance in marking status hierarchy is greater than that of the pattern of marriage, which, though predominantly endogamous also allows hypergamy, i.e., the marriage of lower-caste women to higher-caste men. Commensality helps in cementing alliances and in the establishment of peace among potential or real enemies. It is also a symbolic technique used in the creation of communion between the living and the dead, and between men and gods.

These symbolic potentialities of commensality are exploited to the utmost in Creole ceremonials. Even in the Thanksgiving service and in some other church procedures, it is used symbolically in the administration of bread and wine to symbolize the communion of the worshippers with God and, indirectly, with one another. It plays a crucial symbolic role in the cult of the dead. An *awujoh*, a feast for the dead, involves lavish cooking for distribution among relatives and friends on a large scale, as well as the preparation and "serving" of a special food, *okara*, for the dead themselves. It is also common to see Creole men at any party murmuring a short invocation to the dead and pouring a libation of a few drops of alcohol before they begin drinking themselves. Food and drink are also left on a table in the house overnight so that the dead can help themselves. Communication with the dead is often achieved by means of the manipulation of halves of kola nuts. And, as indicated earlier, a wake is characterized by a great deal of eating and drinking of alcohol.

Again, as is the case among many peoples throughout West Africa, the Creoles use the kola nut extensively in the ceremonialization of various stages of betrothal, marriage, birth, and other occasions. On the wedding day alone, there is a libation for the dead in the morning, wine and bread to celebrate communion at midday, cake and drinks at the reception in the afternoon, and heavy eating and drinking of alcohol at night. Even in the organization of the Masonic order, the most important mechanism for transforming the lodge into a brotherhood is the prolonged period of drinking and eating together, following the formal rituals. Commensality is equally important in Rotary circles. On many of these occasions, the consumption of alcohol is pushed well beyond the symbolic function, often leading to deep intoxication and ecstasy.

Another dramaturgical technique extensively employed in Creole cultural performances is rhetoric. Here again, children are initiated very early on into the arts of public speaking, particularly in the frequent and extensive meetings of classes, societies, associations, and clubs connected with the churches. This involves not just the learning of skills of speech but the development of high degrees of poise and confidence. As is evident from the material presented earlier in this chapter, there is hardly any significant Creole ceremony without rhetoric: speeches at weddings, sermons in church services, addresses to the dead, the dramas of the Masonic lodges, and speaking at an extensive variety of public appearances on different levels of social organization. There are scores of widely known skilled public speakers on the national level, and a number of these specialize as masters of ceremonies on national occasions. At every party, ball, or public gathering, there are Creole masters of ceremonies whose names appear prominently on printed programs. The names of some of these are frequently mentioned on the radio or in the newspapers and magazines.

The organizers of ceremonies thus usually have at their disposal a number of dramaturgical techniques which can be combined in endless ways to deepen the impact of the drama on the participants, to enhance its current "meaning," and, generally, to mobilize the actors in the interests of the collectivity.

Sociocultural Dynamics

In this attempt to analyze the processes of sociocultural causation, a paradigm for the study of culture has been presented. In it, culture is seen in terms of symbolic dramatic performances that are frequently staged on various overt occasions, such as death, marriage, and graduation, but at the same time achieve covert organizational functions in the articulation of particularistic and universalistic interests. Culture responds to changes in interests, dispositions of power, and organization, and is therefore causally related to these in ways that can be apprehended and isolated by analysis. Cultural symbols have been analyzed in terms of symbolic functions, symbolic forms, and symbolic, or dramaturgical, techniques. These are shown to be dynamically interrelated in such a way that the same function, like the closure of a group to outsiders, can be achieved by different means, like affiliation within an exclusive ritual association or the development of a relatively closed network of amity. On the other hand, the same form, such as a cult of the dead, can contribute to the achievement of different functions, such as the creation of unity across class differences within an extended family, or the preservation of property within a whole collectivity. A change in form need not, therefore, indicate a change in function, and continuity of form need not indicate a continuity of function. Dramaturgical techniques may and usually do change from time to time, with no change in form or in function. Changes in function, in form, and in techniques thus follow different processes, even though they are intimately interrelated.

213

This interrelatedness is enhanced by the activities of different types of leaders, who are continuously "thrown up" in the course of interaction within the collectivity, and who operate in different fields, on different levels, with different degrees of consciousness and rationality.

In exploring the dynamic nature of these processes, a series of different types of symbolic dramatic performances, staged on different levels and on different occasions, have been discussed. I intentionally tried to avoid the exotic and the strange, and chose familiar, ordinary, day-to-day ceremonies, which may at times seem obvious and banal. But as Brecht pointed out, the most epic dramatic themes are embedded in what is usual and taken for granted.

Many of the performances may overtly seem of little relevance, in that their connections with political issues are neither direct nor clear-cut. This is because it is the very essence and force of the true drama that it poses mysteries that agitate the mind and the imagination. A drama which is clearly political in its message is "flat," or one-dimensional; its symbols are overtly converted into signs whose hold on the imagination, if any, is minimal. This was indeed Brecht's major criticism of the early Soviet propaganda theatre of the Stalin era, when actors ended up performing to empty seats. Brecht's theatre is said by some drama critics to be the Marxist theatre par excellence because it addresses itself to the creative imagination of the spectators and makes them think (see Esslin, 1959; 1976). Whatever political message the dramatist may have in mind is only covertly posed by the drama. The power of the Christian communion and its hold over the beliefs and sentiments of masses of people, as indicated in many of the performances discussed above, is essentially contained in its mystery, which is created by its basic bivocality. For one thing, the communicant is unclear whether the drama links him with God or with the congregation or with both. A Christian theologian (Dunlop, 1953:15) has said, "Where two or three are gathered together, there is He." It is only the analysis of the sociologists that establishes a link between the symbols of the drama and the relationships of power in society; in this sense, their work is essentially similar to that of the socially informed drama critic. What they try to do is establish a link between two very different realities, the one symbolic, governed by categorical imperatives, the other utilitarian, governed by hypothetical imperatives; the one timeless, rooted in the essence of the human condition, the other topical, related to ongoing social cleavages and alliances.

In this paradigm, culture emerges not as a logical system that can be studied in its own right, but as a syncretic body of symbolic patterns which is heterogeneous in its composition and is systematized only through interaction between individuals and groups. Creole culture consists of symbolic forms and symbolic techniques that are derived from different cultural "traditions" or "systems": Christian beliefs and practices in different denominations, cult of the dead, Masonic doctrines and rituals, ceremonials of kinship, friendship and godparenthood, patterns of decorum, different sources and forms of music and dance, and different languages in usage. As demonstrated above, the same ceremonial occasion, such as a wedding, is celebrated in terms of ideas and symbolic practices that are derived from different traditions. It is the very essence of the symbols of culture that they are ambiguous. Their meaning is charged in the course of social action, not through the working out of the logic of their own structure. Culture is elusively bivocal. It is like a rectangle, with two dimensions, one political and one existential. The dimensions can be varied in length. But if one is reduced to nil, the shape will cease to be a rectangle and the whole reality of culture will slip away.

Conclusion: 9
Universalism and Particularism
in Elite Organization

Dramaturgical Strategies: A Comparative Scheme
   Closure in Open Systems
   The Utilitarian in the Moral
   Sponsored Recruitment under Equality of Opportunity
   Small Scale Culture for Large Scale Organization
   Rational Ideology in Non-Rational Culture
Heuristic Pluralism

The discussion in the last part of the book gives only a glimpse of the ubiquity, intensity, variety, and dynamic nature of elite cultural performances, and of their continuous dialectic with changing economic and political interests and alignments. It is this cultural process that transforms a category of people, like the members of a profession or the officials of a state institution, into a concrete, corporate, interacting, cooperative, and cohesive group. Its symbols act to unite, camouflage or mystify a major contradiction underlying the development and organization of elite groups generally, a contradiction between their universalistic and particularistic tendencies, between the duties of their members to serve wider publics and their simultaneous endeavour to develop their own sectional interests.

A candidate for membership in such a group has to qualify in two distinct fields. First, in the long, arduous, and costly battle for formal education and professional training; second, in acquiring through continuous socialization the dramaturgical skills and idioms necessary for partaking in the group's dramas and general symbolic activities—its collective representations. This, of course, assumes that we are considering an elite in its "mature" phase of development; for it is conceivable that an elite will start its career as a category of disparate meritocrats, and later develop a culture of its own which will eventually transform it into a cohesive corporate group.

Formal education and professional training can be gained from schools and colleges, depending on fees and other material conditions. As Newman and others have claimed, however, cultural symbols cannot be learnt from books but only informally from the family, kin group, friends, peer groups, church congregations, and different social organizations. Sociologically, the educational process can be clearly observed, described, measured, and analyzed. But the second process, which is in many ways more crucial for membership in the inner circles of the elite, is subtle, vague, elusive, and mystifying. It occurs most frequently in exclusive gatherings and in face-to-face interaction with others, and is thus difficult to observe, document, and analyze. What is more, this process is closely interrelated with that of formal education, which is throughout permeated by its symbols and ideological orientations.

This is the main reason why studies of elites have been so few, so abstract, and so highly conjectural, and have often been concerned with the delineation of the elite as a category defined mechanically in terms of such criteria as education, income, and residence. There is extensive reference in the literature to "lifestyles," but on closer examination much of it turns out to be the description of quantifiable traits that indicate or express eliteness, without analysis of their instrumental function in elite organization. Analysis of this latter type demands the study of the structures and functioning of a series of dramatic performances that characterize elite culture.

In the present monograph, I have attempted to do this by developing a paradigm for the comparative study of elite cultures. In this paradigm, the culture of an elite is considered in its relation to corporate interests that are both particularistic and universalistic, with these two types of interests varying in their ratio in different elites, or at different phases in the career of the same elite.

These interests are developed and maintained by means of an organization which is complex in structure, being partly associative and partly communal. For example, an elite may include members of different professions, each of which may be organized in a formal association that caters to its own particular interests, but the links across the professional associations may be communal, like those of kinship, friendship, or ritual. On the one hand, even within essentially formal professional associations many communal relationships develop which substantially affect the functioning of the association as a whole; on the other, communal, cross-associational relationships may be partly formally organized, as in churches and religious denominations. In all these cases, the associational aspect is clearly visible, and its observation and study pose no methodological or analytical problems. It is the communal aspect that poses a challenge to the sociological imagination.

To deal with this latter aspect methodically and empirically, we can study it in its manifestations in symbolic or dramatic performances. For comparative purposes, these can be analyzed in terms of symbolic functions, symbolic forms, and symbolic techniques. A symbolic function, such as the achievement of communion between disparate individuals or groups, can be achieved by means of different symbolic forms, such as a church service, the celebration of the memory of an ancestor, or the staging of extensive ceremonials among overlapping groupings within the elite. Similarly, a symbolic form, such as a church service, can employ different techniques of signification, such as poetry, music, dancing, and commensality.

The symbolic process, involving functions, forms, and techniques, is geared by elite groups towards achieving solutions to basic organizational problems that are peculiar to the elite. I must hasten to point out, partly in reply to critics (see Firth, 1973:205–6; Turner, 1974) of similar statements that I have made in the past, that no reductionism of the symbolic in terms of the utilitarian is implied here. On the contrary, the assumption here is that the symbolic process is so basic to the human condition and so powerful in motivating action (see Cohen, 1974:48–64; 1977; 1979) that it is everywhere manipulated by collectivities of all sorts in their own interests. The result is that symbolic action is always bivocal, being both moral and utilitarian, steeped in the human psyche, yet greatly conditioned by the power order. This is why it is the very essence of symbols that they are ambiguous, and hence manipulable and mystifying. Nor is there an assumption here that the manipulation of the symbolic process is done consciously and rationally. A few leaders may at times do so, but for most of the time and most of the people the process is not consciously manipulated, as substantiated by the discussions of Creole ceremonials in this monograph.

Dramaturgical Strategies: A Comparative Scheme

Elite organizational problems are mostly related to the contradiction between their universalistic and particularistic activities, between the interests of the public which they serve and their own sectional interests. An elite performing universalistic tasks always seeks to protect itself, and/or is protected by others, in the name of the public. Clear cases are those of the major professions, like medicine and law, which form professional associations for the purpose. The associations are maintained in the public interest; at the same time they are used to develop and protect professional monopolies, maximal rewards, and favourable working conditions. Again, state rulers, popular and unpopular, are everywhere closely guarded and protected in the name of the public. In these and similar cases the issues are clear,

219

and the particularistic interests involved are precisely defined and articulated in terms of organizations that are formal and are thus public knowledge.

But in many other cases, elite organization is not given to formal, associative articulation. Thus an elite will have to (1) informally close its boundaries within a formally open system; (2) develop a network of moral relationships in order to fulfill utilitarian ends; (3) practice sponsored recruitment under the principle of equality of opportunity; (4) evolve small-scale, face-to-face, communal relationships in order to evolve a large-scale organization; (5) articulate a rational ideology in a non-rational cultural formation.

Elite culture can thus be seen as resolving, and in the process mystifying, these basic contradictions in elite organization. The process is partly ideological, partly dramaturgical; partly collective, partly individual, operating at different levels and at different paces, in complex chains of sociocultural links.

Closure in an Open System
For an organization to be effective, its membership, aims, and boundaries will have to be defined. But in a modern liberal type of society, formally based on egalitarian principles, an elite grouping ought not to exist and is therefore not publicly recognized as such. What is more, such a group will often camouflage or deny its own existence in public, and its members will adopt a low profile and attempt to fade into the general social landscape. At the same time, however, its members must know about one another, and should be able to recognize one another as co-members in order to coordinate their activities in the interests of the group and to avail themselves of the privileges of membership. In other words, they have to be visible to one another, but invisible as a group in public. This is why elites are sometimes described as being "conspiratorial."

This contradiction has been clearly demonstrated in the history of the Creoles over the last three decades or so. Previously, during most of the colonial period, they had gone out of their way to develop and even exaggerate their distinctiveness, segregating themselves sharply from the rest of the African population. But with the end of the colonial period, they went out of their way to deny that distinctiveness; indeed they did so at the very time when their solidarity and exclusiveness and their need for a corporate organization of their own had become more intense and pronounced than before.

To resolve this paradox, the elite develop a communal organization, defining their identity in symbolic and hence ambiguous terms, sometimes employing one symbolic form, like religion, as an articulating principle, but often utilizing a combination of different symbolic forms. Thus the Creoles mobilized the cult of the dead, overlapping kin group organizations, brotherhood within secret societies, decorum, and some other traits of what is generally known as lifestyle. In neighbouring Liberia, the dominant Americo-Liberians displayed a similar arrangement, though probably because of their overall economic and political domination, they have tended to put greater emphasis on kinship and endogamy. Thus Libenow (1969:136) states:

> Detailed knowledge of his own ties and the family ties of others is a *sine qua non* for the social and political survival of the individual. Birth and marriage are political events as much as they are social or economic ones and establish broader bonds than those among two or more individuals. . . . The self-conscious efforts of late to publicize "mixed" marriages only serve to emphasize the exceptional character of the act.

(See also Fraenkel, 1964.)

One of the ways in which the 40,000 or so wealthy families who form what has been called the upper class in twelve major cities in the United States achieve internal visibility and external anonymity is to be listed in the *Social Register* (see Mills, 1956; Baltzell, 1971; Domhoff, 1967; 1971). This is published by a private company owned by some members of this class, and is exclusive in the sense that, unlike *Who's Who*, it is not sold to the public, but is distributed internally among the families concerned on subscription bases. A family which aspires to be included in the *Register* will not only have to pass screening by the usually well-informed editors, but will also need written references from families already

221

registered which testify that the candidates do in fact belong to the right class, and are therefore eligible to be included. There are, of course, other, more communal indices of membership than the formality of the *Social Register*. Thus Domhoff (1967: 16) states:

> Underlying the American upper class are a set of social institutions which are its backbone—private schools, elite universities, the "right" fraternities and sororities, gentlemen's clubs, debutante balls, summer resorts, charitable and cultural organizations and such recreational activities as foxhunts, polo matches and yachting.

Similar institutions are also said to characterize the upper classes in Britain (see Lupton and Wilson, 1969; Sampson, 1962; Guttsman, 1963; 1969). Although there is much talk nowadays about "the decomposition" of the upper class in Britain, sociologists maintain that it continues to exist (see, for example, Giddens, 1972).

The Utilitarian in the Moral

Closure is most effectively attained through the operation of a network of amity which knits the members of the elite together. Such networks are developed to coordinate corporate action informally through mutual trust and cooperation. Like nearly all primary relationships, these are both moral and utilitarian, with each of the two elements dialectically acting on the other.

There are different types of relationships of amity, expressed in different symbolic forms and supported by different ideologies and dramaturgical techniques. Among the Creoles of Sierra Leone, different forms of amity relationships overlap considerably, and produce an overall network of dense, powerful interpersonal links. A major form is that of "cousinhood," which is created by extended bilateral kin groupings and made more intense and effective by a substantial degree of endogamy and by the ideology and elaborate symbolic patterns of action related to the dead. This network is further supported by church organizations and activities spanning the entire life cycle of the individual, from early childhood until death. "Poor" and wealthy, patron and client, the politically powerful and the less powerful, are drawn together across status boundaries within the group by these links, which make it possible to conduct various kinds of personal affairs. On a higher level of organization, this cousinhood network is closely knit together to deal with more fundamental and more general corporate issues through the membership of the patrons, i.e., the heads of the various "families," in the Masonic order, where an intense pattern of "brotherly" relationships is developed as a matter of principle. The overall outcome is a relatively small group of professional men and women who are linked and cross-linked by an exclusive network of multiplex relationships governed by a complex set of ritual and moral values and norms, which are in their turn continuously kept alive by extensive patterns of symbolic action. This network serves both the sectional and public utilitarian tasks of the corporate group.

In the Creoles' case, the reality of this network of amity is so well defined because it links a relatively small group who have lived in one small settlement all their lives. In more complex situations, such networks are more difficult to observe and delineate, and are often outlined by observers on the basis of conjecture and guesswork, particularly when one operates at the level of large-scale, complex societies like the United States or Britain. When a study is confined to a much smaller group and within one field of political or economic activity in such a society, the results can be relatively more informative and precise.

An insightful and interesting study of this kind has been carried out by two American political scientists on the organization and functioning of the British Treasury (Heclo and Wildavsky, 1974). Their major theme is that, contrary to general belief, the bulk of public money in Britain is dispensed through informal private dealings between a relatively small number of Treasury men. (The monograph is aptly titled *The Private Government of Public Money.*) Such dealings are made possible by the trust which characterizes interpersonal relationships—labeled "kinship" by the authors—between the Treasury men. Heclo and Wildavsky write (ibid. : xiv–15):

> The distinguishing feature of Treasury Men who deal with public spending is not their intellect or their ideas but their emotions. Their supreme skill lies in personal relations. . . . When we speak of family life in the Treasury or village life in Whitehall we are . . . speaking of people whose common kinship and culture separates them from outsiders . . . Life at the top in Britain may not be warm hearted chumminess, but it does demonstrate a coherence and continuity unknown in the United States. . . . Everyone who is anyone has got to have extensive personal contacts.

The book documents many features of the theme, though detailed description and analysis of the cultural life of the men involved are lacking.

A similar picture has been sketched for the operation of the City of London, the nerve centre of the British economy. Millions of pounds worth of business is conducted daily in the City without the use of written documents, on the basis of personal trust between a special breed (culturally speaking) of men, linked by relationships of amity of one form or another. (See Lupton and Wilson, 1959; Ferris, 1960; Sampson, 1962; Parry, 1969.) In another study (Cohen, 1969), a detailed account is given of the ways in which extensive business transactions are conducted on credit terms between men related by moral and ritual links within a large-scale network of Hausa trading communities that have for centuries conducted long-distance trade throughout West Africa.

In all these cases the persons involved are linked by relationships that are both moral and utilitarian, these two elements being closely related. In some cases, the utilitarian element came first, and with the help of the "psychological affinities" (see Mills, 1956:283) shared by the same men, the moral element soon developed. In other cases, the moral element was there from the start, and utilitarian interests were eventually built on it, modifying, strengthening, and restructuring it in the process. In some other cases, a corporation of interests may "employ" a whole group of men with a lifestyle different from its own to function as a system of communication. This may explain why the labour unions

Conclusion

in Britain, as represented by the Labour party, have been choosing as their MP's, not leaders from the unions or from a working-class background, but middle-class men and women (see Guttsman, 1974; Johnson, 1974). These are chosen not for their academic qualifications, although many of them are university graduates, but for their "mystique." Their lifestyle enables them to understand and communicate with officials in the bureaucracy and with the traditional "establishment" in Britain generally, who share the same culture and with whom they need continuous contact on behalf of their constituencies. When they are elected, they bring to the service of their political role their personal connections, their network of amity, old school ties, and friendships within the various exclusive gatherings of their status groups.

Sponsored Recruitment under Equality of Opportunity
Almost invariably, the elite in liberal societies zealously uphold the principle of equality of opportunity. Yet it is their own children who benefit most from it, ultimately achieving the same elite status as their parents, with the result that the collectivity becomes a corporation in the sense that it will survive the retirement or death of the present generation, and thus perpetuate itself.

Because of their relatively high income and connections with influential people in different fields, the elite are able to ensure good formal education for their children. Their material living conditions, the availability of space for study, comfort, the incentives, are all there to facilitate learning and development. And this is only part of the battle; the other part is more subtle and of greater significance for the corporation and sometimes for the system as a whole. Through socialization in the home, and then in extracurricular activities at exclusive schools, the children of the elite acquire interests, motives, skills, ideologies, and a world view that go hand in hand with the formal educational process. The achievement of higher education and of professionalism requires almost "unnatural" singlemindedness, which is enforced on or cultivated in the growing child,

225

who is subjected to continuous discipline by the family and by the school (referred to in this respect by Mills [1956] as a "surrogate" family). It also requires the motive, the impulse *to achieve*. In due course, the rising generation will through continuous socialization acquire all the traits, all the "psychological affinities" (ibid.: 283) that make up the exclusive culture, the mystique, of the group.

Many members of professional elites realize that their children are privileged. But they argue, or rather rationalize ideologically, that society needs the training and skills of professionals, and that they themselves are investing their resources and their efforts to achieve these. Society also needs their particular "mystique" for the prompt and efficient coordination of state services.

This seems to be the ideology behind Colonel Bingham and Cardinal Newman (see above, chapter 1). It is also that of the Creoles, who have for generations concentrated all their resources and efforts on professionalism, giving up farming and later business to evolve into a species of "literati" specializing in state service. They have not always been entirely self-recruiting. Like all elites, they do let outsiders in, despite their tendency to close their boundaries. Indeed, they have for long seen themselves as having a sacred mission to "civilize" and educate provincial children. It is well known that through their "ward system," they have brought up and educated many provincial men and women, missionizing them and giving them their own family names —in effect Creolizing them, and thus recruiting them to their ranks. Another process by which "outsiders" were taken in and Creolized has been through marriage. For a long time, non-Creole women were taken in marriage or as "outside wives" by Creole men, and came to identify themselves—and were identified by others—as Creole. I have recorded from observation many such cases, particularly of educated women from other African countries, who were at the time of research at different stages in their assimilation into the group. More recently, some provincial men have married Creole women, mostly while the couples were studying abroad, and have been admitted to Creole inner circles, though because of political factors and opportunities such men have in most cases been inhibited from identifying themselves with the Creoles.

Small-scale Culture for Large-scale Organization
The elite is held together as a corporate interest group principally by communal relationships. These are essentially of a personal, face-to-face nature, and are limited in their social range. This, according to Simmel (1959:90–93), is why aristocracies are small. For the members of the aristocracy should be "surveyable," and should know one another personally, in effect a "village at the top."

But elites in modern society are relatively large-scale national collectivities, and it is impossible for an individual to find enough time, energy, and resources to develop personal primary relationships with more than a few score people at a time. Moreover, the elite tend to be "spiralists" who are geographically as well as occupationally mobile. How, under these circumstances, can the network of amity be maintained and held together? More specifically, how can relationships of amity be established instantly, in a dynamic, mobile, essentially impersonal, multiplex society, with the "right kind" of person, i.e., with members of the same group?

Relationships of amity usually require time and exclusive channels to develop. In small-scale, preindustrial societies, people are strictly categorized by custom, and are told with whom they should have intimate primary relationships. Friends, kin, and enemies are all socially prescribed. As an aid in identification, these categories are often distinctly marked by name or emblem or even facial markings. They are also told from which group they can take a spouse and from which they cannot. In more complex, stratified systems, like that of traditional India, there is a more elaborate arrangement for classifying and ranking groups, whose boundaries and relations are regulated and sustained by a meticulous ideological and symbolic system.

But the members of an elite in modern, developing or developed liberal societies are interspersed within massive,

227

socially and culturally heterogeneous populations, particularly when there is pressure on them to "go invisible." It is this pressure which makes relevant the body of symbols and of symbolic patterns of action vaguely subsumed under the term lifestyle. The issue is well demonstrated by Mills (1956) in his discussion of the "power elite" in the United States. Having been brought up in similar educational, religious, and social institutions, the members of the elite acquire the same "psychological affinities," as he calls them. Each member "comes to incorporate into his own integrity, his own honor, his own conscience, the viewpoint, the expectations, the values of the others" (ibid.:283). All this makes it possible for them to say of one another: He is, of course, one of us. When two, hitherto unacquainted, members of such a group meet for the first time, a few minutes' conversation will be sufficient for them to recognize their common identity. Their "psychological affinities" will soon manifest themselves in linguistic nuances, manner of speech, dress, bodily movements, jokes, and ideas, as well as in gossip directed to the discovery of mutual friends and acquaintances. Soon they will feel that they have known one another all their lives, and a relationship of amity with its moral constraints—the collective representations of the group—is soon established. Most often, encounters of this type take place in institutionalized frameworks, like clubs, churches, lodges, colleges, and exclusive gatherings, where no great effort is needed for the preliminary explorations to ascertain status identity.

Although these are primary interpersonal relationships, and hence limited in scale, the culture that governs and regulates them is a corporate culture, which is continuously homogenized by a variety of mechanisms that make the relation between the parts and the whole a dialectical one. Personal and private though they are, relationships of amity become highly standardized in their forms, values, and norms. This is achieved through the operation of various mechanisms that continuously relate one section of the collectivity to another: multiple directorships, professional and occupational associations, overlapping cliques of friends, cousinhoods, brotherhoods, old school links, club memberships. These mechanisms link and cross-link the different parts of the elite and standardize their ideologies and style of behaviour. Thus the values, norms, and beliefs underlying relationships of amity are ultimately supported and upheld by the whole group, as the group's "collective representations."

Rational Ideology in Non-Rational Culture
An elite develops its organization by transforming rational, consciously thought-out organizational strategies into non-rational, self-mystifying symbolic forms.

The discussion in the last few pages may give the impression that elites are scheming groups conspiring to manufacture deception, manipulating the innermost feelings and sentiments of unsuspecting publics, and operating in accordance with a brazenly planned design—a grand conspiratorial ideology. There is no doubt that some individuals here and there may at one time or another think and act along such lines. But to assume that a whole collectivity consciously constructs and acts upon such an integrated ideological formation is to attribute superhuman traits to ordinary men and women and, more importantly, is to miss the whole point about the nature of ideology.

Nor is there a clear unified structure or system in the complex series of dramas and the frequent dramatic performances that are associated with ideology. Some of them are small in scale, like those developing and celebrating relationships between godparents and godchildren, between friend and friend, husband and wife. Others involve larger groupings, like family ceremonies, balls, church services. Yet others are events on the national level, like the university congregation described in the last chapter. The participants in these ceremonies often differ in sex, age, occupation, status, and educational qualifications. They also differ at any one time in rationality, consciousness, and systematic thinking about the nature and significance of the performances concerned; and the same kinds of difference can be found in the same person at different times. Moreover, various dramatic forms will have developed at different times in the history of the group, derived from different cultural traditions. People also differ in the strength of their convictions and beliefs at different times. There are thus no well-thought-out design, no clear intentions, no consistent logic, and no coherent body of ideas. Often, the contrary is nearer the truth—it is the symbolic performances that conjure up ideas and aspects of ideologies.

It is certainly important to record what different categories of individuals and groups believe, and to get an idea of the way they see their world. But anyone who has done research of this sort will know how complex, varied, and unreliable such accounts are, and how difficult it is to work out a clear, systematic *emic* (subjective) view of the world from them. People often express different ideas about the same subject at different times for a variety of reasons, depending on the mood and preoccupation of the hour. Thus, many Creoles—more particularly the intellectuals among them—genuinely believe that their claim of direct descent from the emancipated slaves has no historical validity, and demonstrate this by citing various kinship relationships—patrilateral, matrilateral, and affinal—with members of other ethnic groups in the country. But their way of life, the structure of their families and households, their speech, and their gatherings silently and largely unconsciously create and recreate their distinctiveness as Creoles.

The formation of an elite is a collective endeavour embodying the cumulative efforts, rational and non-rational, creative and routine, of all the men and women within the group. It is a construction which is continuously questioned, continuously modified, continuously created. As the collectivity confronts its problems and debates them, it throws up leaders of various types, who contribute to its strategies in different fields. But at any one time, the ability of a few individuals to change the collective culture is very limited. Organizational strategies become embedded in or expressed in terms of symbolic solutions to the perennial existential problems that confront the self (see Cohen, 1977). The same body of symbols thus develops to cater at one and the same time to both existential and organizational purposes. As the symbols acquire this bivocality of meaning, they become more potent, more constraining, more mystifying. In the process, the pragmatic is converted into the obligatory, both moral and ritual. The emerging cultural formation becomes a phenomenon sui generis, a new reality that exists in its own right and that cannot be reduced to, or explained away in terms of political relations or the structure of selfhood. Doubts about the validity of one meaning or another will not result in its abandonment or in substantially diminishing its constraining power. The underlying dialectic between the rational and the non-rational continues to maintain or modify it, but its performances retain their intrinsic irreducible value. The rational leaves its mark and fades away, but is eventually unconsciously achieved through the non-rational.

The elite are rational, busy men in the conduct of their formal duties, yet they devote much valuable time and substantial resources to non-rational dramatic performances, despite nagging doubts about the validity of the beliefs that go with them. This is because such performances are instrumentally crucial in the development and maintenance of their corporate organization as an elite, articulating those organizational functions that cannot be performed on formal, associational lines.

The success of these cultural strategies in achieving their organizational functions depends on the maintenance of their non-rational, self-mystifying nature. They are structured and shaped by the political process, but to be politically effective they must remain non-political. Once they are formally and consciously politicized, their symbols will be reduced to unidimensional signs, and thus lose their potency and efficiency in achieving their political ends. Thus, although the rational and non-rational are in a continuous dialectic in the formation of elite culture, at any one time the rational can be achieved only through the non-rational.

Heuristic Pluralism

The comparative study of elite groupings along these lines can in many ways become crucial for the future development of political anthropology—indeed of social anthropology generally—in that it will deepen our understanding of both culture and power and of the dynamic relations between them. But the concept "elite" must be clearly formulated and its study operationalized in terms of empirical criteria.

There is the danger that it may be interpreted ideologically as referring to the "chosen" ones, thus morally validating the commanding and often privileged positions of its members. This danger can be avoided by becoming consciously aware of it, and adopting a clear criterion for the status, such as the attainment of a university degree. As Giddens (1973:106) points out, when the term is stripped of some of the connotations with which it has sometimes been encumbered, it can be significant. This point is now so widely accepted that even some Marxian writers have been using the term. Mills (1956) made it central to his most important work, and more recently Miliband (1974) has used it in coining the term "state elite," which has been occasionally referred to in this monograph.

The main drawback in employing the term, however, is that it often connotes to people the notion that we are dealing here with individuals, or rather individualistic persons, such as certified meritocrats, who sociologically form only an aggregate or a category of persons. This is certainly the way the members of such elites would define themselves. This connotation is given indirect support in many sociological studies which, for lack of adequate data, describe an elite mainly in terms of criteria shared by individuals, such as income, academic qualifications, possessions, the hierarchical level of administrative positions they occupy, and so on. To discuss an elite in these terms alone is of little anthropological value, as it is no more than what Leach would call "butterfly collection," mere categorization and description. In the definition adopted from the start of this monograph, the concept refers not so much to the category of persons sharing such criteria, as to their patterns of interaction, cooperation, and coordination of corporate activities through communal relationships.

Some writers prefer to use the term "class" for all such groups, but for microsociological studies this is too wide in its connotations to be useful in analysis. There is also no consensus, even among Marxists, about its definition. It has often been used loosely in such phrases as "the middle classes," which, if one is dealing with a group of people who do not necessarily exercise any direct control over the means of production, can be irrelevant. A case in point is that of the middle-class Labour MP's in Britain, who represent the working classes and are employed in this capacity mainly because they "speak the same language" and share the culture or mystique of the personnel of the bureaucracy. Similarly, the Creoles of Sierra Leone have no direct control of the means of production and are not coterminous with any economically defined "class," although they can be said to be the agents of such a class as the traditional chiefs, or of international capitalism.

A closer term would be a "power group," but this would probably lead to vague and sometimes awkward formulations. One is therefore forced back to the concept "elite," which can be made to combine precise connotation with flexibility of denotation. It denotes a collectivity of people who occupy commanding positions in some sphere of social life, who do not overtly form a distinct group, but are nevertheless covertly a group, cooperating and coordinating their strategies of action informally.

In this sense the term will, in effect, denote a sociocultural group, which is analytically not very different from groupings described as "ethnic" or "religious." Indeed, we have seen in the case of the Creoles that there is a remarkable overlap between eliteness, ethnicity, religion, and cousinhood. It follows that elite studies are particularly instructive for social anthropologists, in that they enable them to probe deeper into the political potentialities of culture in complex society. For other social scientists, they highlight a dimension of power that has often eluded detailed and systematic analysis.

To operationalize the concept of such communal groups for social anthropological study, one is forced to adopt, *as a heuristic device* at least, a view of society as a nation-state consisting of a multiplicity of interest groups of all types, some of which are organized mainly informally through communal relationships.

Such a research strategy of isolating small areas of social life and subjecting them to intensive microsociological analysis, which has particularly characterized social anthropology, has been recently subjected to severe criticism by Marxian writers of one brand or another.

To begin with, Marxists argue that social anthropology, like all the other "bourgeois disciplines"—sociology, economics, political science, social psychology—compartmentalizes the study of social reality in separate domains, and thus prevents the student from apprehending the total structure of capitalism, imperialism, and neo-colonialism, and its exploitatory nature. Secondly, by focusing the study on small, concrete groups, the anthropologist in effect reifies these groups and presents them as given "in the nature of things," thereby implicitly validating the overarching system that brought them into being. This is supported by the functionalist, ahistorical approach, which further restricts the vision of students and prevents them from seeing how the system came to be what it is. As a result of all this, the anthropologist, in full consciousness or in false consciousness, wittingly or unwittingly, produces not objective, value-free studies as claimed, but an ideology which camouflages, mystifies, and justifies world capitalism. The implication of this critique is that there can be only one true science of society—historical materialism, which studies the total structure of world capitalism in all its past and present manifestations—economic, political, social, cultural, and psychological—for both theory and conscious political praxis.

This is not the place to discuss these fundamental issues in detail. There are certainly extensive studies that lend themselves to criticism along such lines. But a rapidly increasing number of social scientists are now aware of the pitfalls and the implications of their methodologies and analyses, and almost invariably the major textbooks in the different disciplines discuss both the potentialities and limitations of approaches and methods. In fact, the greatness of Marxism is manifest not so much in the writings of those who formally proclaim themselves to be Marxists, but in the penetration by Marxian ideas of current thinking in the social sciences generally. The very existence and expression of the Marxian critique within the social sciences in the West is itself part of this awareness. Perry Anderson (1976) —for many years the editor of the *New Left Review*— points out that Marxism, as a live critique of social thought and of social institutions exists today mainly in liberal societies; in the Soviet Union it was eradicated as early as 1924 when Lenin died.

There is no doubt that social scientists, including anthropologists, bring to their work their biases, ideologies, interests, and patterns of "false consciousness." The remedy, however, is not to abdicate from our intellectual endeavour and surrender our reason to the dictates of a monolithic ideology in the name of praxis, but in never-ending, constructive criticism directed at our formulations in classes, seminars, conferences, journals, papers, and books. The potentialities for such a permanent, institutionalized tradition of criticism already exist in many centers of sociocultural research. In these centers, the training of a social anthropologist involves continuous, rigorous criticism, often by students, teachers, and general readers who hail from different social, cultural, and ideological backgrounds.

The study of the total structure of world history must certainly be the goal of all social science; but if this study is not to be just the ideological doctrine of a monolithic political party, it should always unavoidably depend on the cumulative findings of numerous studies of various formations, aspects, and levels by different people with different experience, training, interests, and abilities. One can do *original* research in only a limited field at a time. Attempts at such research on a global, holistic scale by social scientists will only yield abstract generalizations that cannot be empirically substantiated. The statement by Diamond et al. (1976) that there are no methods that require special training in anthropology does not withstand close scrutiny. Historical research, the conduct of surveys, the study of international corporations, of demography, of law, of economics, of cultural performances, and many other fields all require knowledge of different sets of facts and the application of special techniques and concepts that can be learnt only after years of training and practice. This does not mean that social scientists, in whatever specialization, should not care about the total, global, holistic picture; indeed it is their duty to acquaint themselves with the outlines of that picture, relying on the latest findings of others working in other fields and on other levels. All true knowledge proceeds from the parts to the whole and from the whole to the parts.

The current tendency among some Marxists is to study a "social formation"—a unit defined in terms of both mode of production and the ideological institutions that are related to it. But the application of the concept is far from easy and clear-cut, and writers have been using it in a rather loose fashion, sometimes applying it to a small area of social life, sometimes to a whole complex nation-state, and sometimes even to the whole world (see O'Laughlin, 1975:367–68). A more pragmatic approach is to recognize the present nation-state as a meaningful context within which one can conduct an intensive study of smaller sociocultural units (see Wallerstein, 1960). This is particularly so inasmuch as even those societies that have a "socialist mode of production" today form separate nation-states, which are sometimes even in conflict with one another, as in the case of the Soviet Union and China, indicating that often national interests override class interests.

Pluralism of one type or another is a reality in all social systems. It is highly significant in this respect that communist parties in Western Europe have recently publicly announced the abandonment of the principle of the dictatorship of the proletariat, upholding the pluralistic nature of their societies.

However, pluralism can be adopted as a heuristic device, but not as a political ideology. The anthropologist who is interested in the study of an elite group may start with a rough outline of what is broadly known about the distribution of power in the nation-state in order to locate and delineate a manageable group of this type, in due course identifying its particularistic interests and universalistic functions, and its communal and associative organization. Concentration on analysis in depth of, for example, an exclusive school, a church, club, sorority, cousinhood, clique of friends, or a debutante ball, can yield a great deal of insight into the structure and functioning of what I have called power mystique. Eventually, the power mystique of one state elite can be compared with those of other states; and as there are only about 150 nation-states in the world today, such a cross-cultural comparison can in due course shed substantial light on the functions of a wide variety of symbolic forms. Comparisons on such a scale between nation-states have been attempted by political scientists (see, for example, Finer, 1970), but they have unavoidably been given only in outline, with emphasis on the formal organization of power. What is badly needed is a series of detailed ethnographic studies of small-scale elite groups or elite communal institutions.

Bibliography

ALTHUSSER, L. 1969. *For Marx*. Harmondsworth, Middlesex: Penguin Books.

———. 1970. *Reading Capital*. London: New Left Books.

———. 1971. "Ideology and Ideological State Apparatuses." In *Education: Structure and Society*, edited by B. R. Cosin, pp. 242–80. Harmondsworth, Middlesex: Penguin Books.

ANDERSON, P. 1976. *Considerations on Western Marxism*. London: New Left Books.

BALTZELL, E. D. 1971. *Philadelphia Gentlemen: The Making of a National Upper Class*. Chicago: Quadrangle Books.

BANTON, M. 1957. *West African City*. London: Oxford University Press.

BARROWS, W. 1976. *Grassroots Politics in an African State*. London: Holmes & Meier.

BART-WILLIAMS, P. J. 1970. *The Story of St. George's Cathedral*. Freetown: Government Printing Department.

BINNS, C. 1978. "The Development and Significance of the Soviet Festal and Ritual System." Paper presented to the annual conference of the National Association for Soviet and East European Studies, Cambridge, 8–10 April 1978.

BOTTOMORE, T. D., and RUBEL, M., eds. 1956. *Karl Marx: Selected Writings in Sociology and Social Philosophy*. London: Watts.

239

CARLYLE, T. 1954. *Sartor Resartus—On Heroes and Hero Worship*. London: Dutton.

CARTWRIGHT, J. R. 1968. "Shifting Forces in Sierra Leone," *Africa Report* 13, pp. 26–30.

———. 1970. *Politics in Sierra Leone 1947–1967*. Toronto: Toronto University Press.

CHALMERS' REPORT. 1899. Parts I & II. Parliamentary Papers.

CLAPHAM, C. 1976. *Liberia and Sierra Leone: An Essay in Comparative Politics*. Cambridge: Cambridge University Press.

COHEN, A. 1969. *Custom and Politics in Urban Africa*. Berkeley and Los Angeles: University of California Press.

———. 1971*a*. "The Politics of Ritual Secrecy." *Man*, 6, no. 3, pp. 427–48.

———. 1971*b*. "Cultural Strategies in the Organisation of Trading Diasporas." In *The Development of Indigenous Trade and Markets in West Africa*, edited by C. Meillassoux, pp. 261–81. London: Oxford University Press.

———. 1974. *Two-Dimensional Man*. Berkeley and Los Angeles: University of California Press.

———. 1977. "Symbolic Action and the Structure of the Self." In *Symbols and Sentiments*, edited by I. M. Lewis, pp. 117–28. London: Academic Press.

———. 1979. "Political Symbolism." *Annual Review of Anthropology (1978)* 7, pp. 87–113.

COHEN, E. G. 1971. "Recruitment to the Professional Class in Sierra Leone." Paper presented at the *Sierra Leone Symposium* held at the University of Western Ontario, London, Ontario, Canada.

———. 1973. "Recruitment to the Professional Class." Ph.D. thesis, University of Surrey.

———. 1979. "Women, Solidarity and the Preservation of Privilege." In *Women United, Women Divided*, edited by P. Caplan and J. Bujra, pp. 129–56. London: Tavistock Publications.

COX, Sir H. 1956. *The Sierra Leone Report of Commission of Inquiry into Disturbances in the Provinces. November 1955 – March 1956*. Freetown: Government Printer.

COX, T. S. 1976. *Civil-Military Relations in Sierra Leone*. Cambridge, Mass.: Harvard University Press.

D'AZAVEDO, W. L. 1973. "Mask Makers and Myth in Western Liberia." In *Primitive Art and Society*, edited by A. Forge. London: Oxford University Press.

DEWAR, J. 1966. *The Unlocked Secret: Freemasonry Examined*. London: William Kimber.

DIAMOND, S., SCHOLTE, B., and WOLF, D. 1976. "Anti-Kaplan: Defining the Marxist Tradition," *American Anthropologist* 77, no. 4, pp. 870–76.

DOMHOFF, G. W. 1967. *Who Rules America?* Englewood Cliffs, N. J.: Prentice-Hall.

———. 1971. *The Higher Circles: The Governing Class in America*. New York: Vintage Books.

DUNCAN, H. D. 1962. *Communication and Social Order*. London: Oxford University Press.

———. 1969. *Symbols and Social Theory*. New York: Oxford University Press.

DUNLOP, C. 1953. *Anglican Public Worship*. London: SCM Press.

DURKHEIM, E. 1933. *The Division of Labour in Society*. London: Macmillan.

EASMON, M. C. F. 1956. "Sierra Leone Doctors." *Sierra Leone Studies*, n.s., no. 6, pp. 81–96.

ESSLIN, M. 1959. *Brecht: A Choice of Evils*. London: Heinemann.

———. 1976. *An Anatomy of Drama*. London: Temple Smith.

EVANS-PRITCHARD, E. E. 1940. *The Nuer*. Oxford: Clarendon Press.

———. 1949. *The Sanusi of Cyrenaica*. Oxford: Clarendon Press.

———., and FORTES, M., eds. 1940. *African Political Systems*. London: Oxford University Press.

FASHOLE-LUKE, E. D. 1968. "Religion in Freetown." In *Freetown: A Symposium*, edited by C. Fyfe & E. Jones, pp. 127–42. Freetown: Sierra Leone University Press.

FERRIS, P. 1960. *The City*. Harmondsworth, Middlesex: Penguin Books.

FINER, S. E. 1970. *Comparative Government*. Harmondsworth, Middlesex: Penguin Books.

FIRTH, R. 1973. *Symbols: Public and Private*. Ithaca, N.Y. Cornell University Press.

FISHER, H. J. 1969. "Elections and Coups in Sierra Leone." 1967. *Journal of Modern African Studies* 7, pp. 611–36.

FORTES, M. 1940. See Evans-Pritchard.

FORTES, M. 1969. *Kinship and the Social Order*. Chicago: Aldine.

FRAENKEL, M. 1964. *Tribe and Class in Monrovia*. London: Oxford University Press.

FYFE, C. 1962. *A History of Sierra Leone*. London: Oxford University Press.

————. 1964. *Sierra Leone Inheritance*. London: Oxford University Press.

————. 1968. "The Foundation of Freetown." In *Freetown: A Symposium*, edited by C. Fyfe and E. Jones, pp. 1–8. Freetown: Sierra Leone University Press.

GIDDENS, A. 1972. "Elites." *New Society* 22 (November 16): 389–92.

————. 1973. *The Class Structure of the Advanced Societies*. London: Hutchinson.

————., and STANWORTH, P., eds. 1974. *Elites and Power in British Society*. London: Cambridge University Press.

GLUCKMAN, M. 1961. "Ethnographic Data in British Social Anthropology." *The Sociological Review*, n.s., 9, no. 1, pp. 5–17.

————., and DEVONS, E., eds. 1964. *Closed Systems and Open Minds*. Edinburgh: Oliver & Boyd.

GOULDNER, A. 1970. *The Coming Crisis of Western Sociology*. London: Heinemann.

GUTTSMAN, W. L. 1963. *The British Political Elite*. London: MacGibbon & Kee.

————., ed. 1969. *The English Ruling Class*. London: Weidenfeld & Nicolson.

————. 1974. "The British Political Elite and the Class Structure." In *Elites and Power in British Society*, edited by P. Stanworth and A. Giddens, pp. 22–44. London: Cambridge University Press.

HARLEY, G. W. 1941. "Notes on the Poro in Liberia." *Peabody Museum Papers* 19, no. 2.

————. 1950. "Masks as Agents of Social Control." *Peabody Museum Papers* 32, no. 2.

HARRELL-BOND, B. E. 1975. *Modern Marriage in Sierra Leone*. The Hague: Mouton.

————., and SKINNER, D. B. E. 1977. "Misunderstandings Arising from the Use of the Term 'Creole' in the Literature on Sierra Leone." *Africa* 47, no. 3, pp. 305–19.

HECLO, H., and WILDAVSKY, A. 1947. *The Private Government of Public Money*. London: Macmillan.

JOHNSON, R. W. 1974. "The Political Elite." *New Society* 24 (January 24): 188–91.

JOKO-SMART, H. M. 1969. "Inheritance to Property in Sierra Leone." *Sierra Leone Studies*, n.s., no. 24, pp. 2–25.

JONES, D. E. 1968. "Freetown: The Contemporary Cultural Scene." In *Freetown: A Symposium*, edited by C. Fyfe and E. Jones, pp. 99–211. Freetown: Sierra Leone University Press.

————. 1974. "Literary Amateurs Build Reputation Largely Through Non-fiction," *The Times* (London), supplement on Sierra Leone, 4 May 1974.

JORDAN, R. S. 1971. "The Place of the Creoles in the Bureaucracy of Sierra Leone with Special References to the Civil Service." Paper presented at the Sierra Leone Symposium held in 1971 at the University of Western Ontario, London, Ontario, Canada. Cited with the permission of the author.

KASFIR, N. 1977. *The Shrinking Political Arena*. Berkeley and Los Angeles: University of California Press.

KILSON, M. 1966. *Political Change in a West African State*. Cambridge, Mass.: Harvard University Press.

————. "Cleavage Management in African Politics." In *New States in the Modern World*, edited by Martin Kilson, pp. 75–88. Cambridge, Mass.: Harvard University Press.

KREUTZINGER, H. 1966. *The Eri Devils in Freetown, Sierra Leone*, Wien: Verlag Österreichische Ethnologische Gesellschaft Wien.

————. 1968. *The Picture of Krio Life: Freetown 1900–1920*. Wien: Verlag Österreichische Ethnologische Gesellschaft Wien.

LANE, C. 1979. "Ritual and Ceremony in Contemporary Soviet Society." *Sociological Review* 27, no. 2, 253–78.

LIBENOW, J. G. 1969. *Liberia: The Evolution of Privilege*. Ithaca, N.Y.: Cornell University Press.

LITTLE, K. 1948. "The Poro as an Arbiter of Culture," *African Studies* 7, no. 1, pp. 1–15.

————. 1951. *The Mende of Sierra Leone*. London: Routledge & Kegan Paul.

————. 1965. "The Political Function of the Poro." Part I. *Africa* 35, no. 4, pp. 349–65.

————. 1966. "The Political Function of the Poro." Part II. *Africa* 36, no. 1, pp. 62–72.

LUPTON, T., and WILSON, S. 1959. "Background and Connections of Top Decision-makers." *Manchester School* 28, no. 1 (January):30–51.

MACCORMACK, C. P. 1975. "Sande Women and Political Power in Sierra Leone." *The West African Journal of Sociology and Political Science* 1, no. 1, pp. 42–50.

MACIVER, R. M. 1947. *The Web of Government*. New York: Macmillan.

MARX, K. 1944. "Critical Notes on the Article 'The King of Prussia and Social Reform.'" In *Early Writings*, pp. 401–20.

Harmondsworth, Middlesex: Penguin Books, 1975. Translated by R. Livingstone and G. Benton.

———. 1956. In *Karl Marx: Selected Writings in Sociology and Social Philosophy*, edited by T. B. Bottomore & M. Rubel. London: Watts.

———., and ENGELS, F. 1970. *The German Ideology*. Edited and introduced by C. J. Arthur. (Written in 1846.)

MEISEL, J. H. 1962. *The Myth of the Ruling Class*. Ann Arbor: University of Michigan Press.

MICHELS, R. 1962. *Political Parties*. London: Collier-Macmillan.

MILLIBAND, R. 1969. *The State in Capitalist Society*. New ed. 1974. London: Quartet.

MILLS, C. W. 1956. *The Power Elite*. New York: Oxford University Press.

MOSCA, G. 1939. *The Ruling Class*. New York: McGraw-Hill.

NEWMAN, J. H. 1876. "Breeding and Education." In *The English Ruling Class*, edited by W. L. Guttsman, pp. 210–11. London: Weidenfeld & Nicolson, 1969.

O'LAUGHLIN, B. 1975. "Marxist Approaches in Anthropology." *Annual Review of Anthropology* 4, pp. 341–70

OLSON, G. W. 1969. *Church Growth in Sierra Leone*. Grand Rapids, Mich.: W. B. Eerdmans.

PARRY, G. 1969. *Political Elites*. London: Allen & Unwin.

PAULME, D. 1973. "Adornment and Nudity in Tropical Africa." In *Primitive Art and Society*, edited by A. Forge. London: Oxford University Press.

PETERSON, J. 1968. "The Sierra Leone Creole: A Reappraisal," in *Freetown: A Symposium*, edited by C. Fyfe and E. Jones, pp. 100–17. Freetown: Sierra Leone University Press.

———. 1969. *Province of Freedom*. London: Faber & Faber.

PORTER, A. 1963. *Creoldom: A Study of the Development of Freetown Society*. London: Oxford University Press.

PRATT, S. 1968. "The Government of Freetown." In *Freetown: A Symposium*, edited by C. Fyfe and E. Jones, pp. 154–65. Freetown: Sierra Leone University Press.

ROSE, R., 1966 ed. *Studies in British Politics*. London: Macmillan.

SAMPSON, A. 1962. *Anatomy of Britain*. New York: Harper & Row.

SAWYERR, H. 1965. "Graveside Libations in and near Freetown." *The Sierra Leone Bulletin of Religion* 7, no. 2, pp. 48–55.

SCOTT, D. J. R. 1960. "The Sierra Leone Election, May 1957." In *Five Elections in Africa*, edited by W. J. M. Mackenzie and K. Robinson, pp. 168–280. London: Oxford University Press.

SIERRA LEONE, GOVERNMENT OF. 1950. *Protectorate Assembly, Proceedings of the Seventh Meeting.* Freetown: Government Printing Department.

———. 1959. *Government Statement on Africanisation.* Freetown: Government Printing Department.

———. 1965. *1963 Population Census of Sierra Leone.* Vol. 2. *Social Characteristics.* Freetown: Central Statistics Office.

———. 1967. *Household Survey of the Western Province.* Freetown: Central Statistics Office.

———. 1968. *Household Survey of the Western Area: Final Report.* Freetown: Central Statistics Office.

———. 1969. *Report of the Percy Davies Committee into the Activities of the Freetown City Council from 1st January 1964 to 23rd March 1967 and the Government Statement Thereon.* Freetown: Government Printing Office.

———. 1970. *Report of the Commission of Inquiry into the Civil Service of Sierra Leone.* Freetown: Government Printing Office.

SIMMEL, G. 1950. *The Sociology of Georg Simmel.* Translated, edited and introduced by K. H. Wolff. New York: The Free Press.

SKINNER, D. See Harrell-Bond, 1977.

SPITZER, L. 1974. *The Creoles of Sierra Leone: Responses to Colonialism 1870–1945.* Madison: University of Wisconsin Press.

STANWORTH, P. See Giddens, 1974.

TOTH, L. 1969. "Some Aspects of the Pre-adolescent Freetown Pupils' Social Attitudes." *Journal of Education* (Sierra Leone) 4, no. 1, pp. 24–30.

TURNER, R. H. 1960. "Sponsored and Contest Mobility in the School System." *American Sociological Review* 25, no. 5., pp. 855–67.

TURNER, V. W. 1957. *Schism and Continuity in an African Society.* Manchester: Manchester University Press.

———. 1975. "Review of A. Cohen's *Two Dimensional Man.*" *Man* 10, no. 1, pp. 139–40.

URRY, J., and WAKEFORD, J., eds. 1973. *Power in Britain.* London: Heinemann Educational.

WAKEFORD, J. See Urry.

245

WALLERSTEIN, I. 1960. "Ethnicity and National Integration." *Cahiers d'Etudes Africaines* 3, no 1 (July): 129–38.

WEBER, M. 1947. *The Theory of Social and Economic Organization*. London: Collier-Macmillan.

WILDAVSKY, A. See Heclo.

WILLIAMS, R. 1976. *Key Words*. Glasgow: Fontana.

Author Index

247

Subject Index

THE POLITICS OF ELITE CULTURE

Bedouin, 127
Bingham, Colonel, 2, 4, 226
Bivocal symbolic forms, 151, 155, 214, 215, 219, 230
Blyden, E.W., III, xxi
Blyden, Edward Wilmot, 131
Bo, Sierra Leone, 92, 133, 134
Brahmins, 6
Brecht, Bertolt, 214
British: Creole identification with, 130, 131, 143, 147, 205; relations of, with Creoles, 142–143, 205. *See also* Colonial administration; Great Britain
British Treasury, 223–224
Brotherhood, 45, 124–125, 154, 155, 221, 223
Bundu initiation, 21
Bundu society, 100
Burden of elite culture, 33–37
Burials, 165, 171
Business, Creole activities in, 48–51, 58–59, 90, 141, 202

"Cannibalism," 100, 101
Capital of Sierra Leone, 92
Caste system, 6, 211
Central Myth, 10, 137
Ceremonials, Creole, 29, 30, 40; burden of, 33–36; costs of, 33–35; Creole identity influenced by, 37–38; in education, 188–200; in Freemasonry, 106–107, 119; group interests promoted by, 172–176; initiated by women, 80; kinship and family network maintained by, 67–75; "lodge talk" at, 123. *See also* Family ceremonials
Chiefly families, 133
Chiefs: paramount, 94, 121, 141; provincial, 98–100
Children: illegitimate, 63, 64, 82, 88, 189–191; procreation of, 178, 180; relation of, with parents, 64; socialization of, xx-xxi, 50–51, 57, 79, 84
Christenings, 63, 72; ceremony and education, 189–191
Christianity among the Creoles, 21–23, 37, 42, 69, 147, 152; and cult of the dead, 70–71, 165; cultural homogenization in, 31; and education, 57, 188–191; and marriage,

77, 82, 87; and sermons, 162–163
Churches, Creole, 21, 22, 31, 77; collection of donations for, 161–162; drama of services in, 158–164; hierarchy of authority of, 122; informal educational classes offered by, 191; male and female participation in, 32, 80; registration in and class dues for, 22, 159; social activities of, 22–23; wedding services in, 176, 177. *See also* Anglican church; Methodist church
Church Missionary Society, 191, 192, 196
Civil service, 108; challenges to Creole dominance in, 91, 93; Creole predominance in, 41–45, 114–115, 129, 136, 140, 146, 147; education for, 187; interpersonal relationships among Creoles in, 44–45; neutrality of, 135, 140; power exercised by Creoles in, 59; retirement age in, 49–50; senior posts in, held by Creoles, 43, 44, 59, 153
Class: awareness, 17; cleavage in Sierra Leone, 133; differentiation among the Creoles, 31, 69–70, 152; groups, xvii-xviii; as a term, 232–233
Clergy, 22, 162; "outside children" by, 63; status and income of, 47
Closure to outsiders, 37–38, 220–222
Clubs, 13; exclusive balls organized by, 23–25
Collectivity, and leadership, 207
Colonial administration, 48, 94, 114–115, 121, 142–143, 147, 152, 153, 154
Colonial period, 146, 152, 220–221
Combined Ratepayers' Association, 115
Commensality, 154, 211–212
Communal relationships, xvii, 7
Communion, Christian, 31–32, 161, 214; at wedding services, 178
Communion of Saints, 70–71
Communist societies, 8–9
Conflict theory, 5–9
Consensus theory, 5–9
Corporate organization among the Creoles, 94, 95–96, 125, 130, 147, 221

Compositor:	G & S Typesetters, Inc.
Printer:	Thomson-Shore, Inc.
Binder:	Thomson-Shore, Inc.
Text:	11/12 VIP Caledonia
Display:	VIP Caledonia
Cloth:	Holliston Roxite B53515
Paper:	50 lb. P & S Offset